ENGLISH MASQUES

HERBERT ARTHUR EVANS

ENGLISH MASQUES

EDITED AND
WITH AN
INTRODUCTION
BY
HERBERT ARTHUR EVANS

BOOKS FOR LIBRARIES PRESS
FREEPORT, NEW YORK

First Published 1897
Reprinted 1971

What masquing stuff is here?
—The Taming of the Shrew

INTERNATIONAL STANDARD BOOK NUMBER:
0-8369-5977-9

LIBRARY OF CONGRESS CATALOG CARD NUMBER:
71-169757

PRINTED IN THE UNITED STATES OF AMERICA
BY
NEW WORLD BOOK MANUFACTURING CO., INC.
HALLANDALE, FLORIDA 33009

PREFACE.

The debatable land which is occupied by the subject of the present volume has never been thoroughly explored by English writers. Our dramatic and musical historians, preoccupied as they were by questions of greater interest and weightier import, and tacitly subscribing to Bacon's dictum that "these things are but toyes to come among such serious observations", have been able to make but improvised and desultory excursions into its territories. Hence it is that the task of making a thorough exploration has been left to a German, and we are indebted to Dr. Oscar Alfred Soergel, of the University of Halle, for the first attempt at an adequate discussion of the Masque as a whole, in its origin, development, and decay. To his admirable little monograph, *Die Englischen Maskenspiele*, Halle, 1882, I desire to express my obligations.

In fixing the dates of the several performances I have consulted with advantage Mr. F. G. Fleay's valuable works on the stage. In the case of dates from January 1 to March 24, it should be noted that throughout the book the year is assumed to begin on January 1, and not on March 25.

The text of each masque is printed in full, but in the case of the *Masque at Lord Haddington's*

Marriage, the *Masque of Queens, Oberon,* and the *Masque of Augurs,* it has not been thought necessary to reproduce the whole of Jonson's learned annotations: the selections I have made from them are distinguished by his name.

This volume contains sixteen of the fifty printed masques still accessible; the reader who wishes for more will find the titles of the others in the list at the end of the Introduction.

HERBERT A. EVANS.

BEGBROKE, NEAR OXFORD,
August 14, 1897.

CONTENTS.

INTRODUCTION.

O F all the diversions to which Englishmen of
rank and wealth have devoted their idler hours
none has ever formed a closer alliance with literature than the subject of the present volume. The
masque in one form or another was long a favourite
amusement at the English Court; after a somewhat
chequered career of two centuries some faint fore-
shadowings of its literary glory are at length dis-
cernible under the last of the Tudors, but it did
not reach its full development, either in this respect
or in any other, till after the Stuarts came to the
throne. Although the outburst of splendour which
then signalized its maturity was largely due to
foreign influences, and although its very name was
of foreign origin, we shall see that it has every
claim to a pedigree indisputably English, and that
as a literary product it attained a distinction to
which its continental rivals could lay no claim. This
position it owed to the commanding genius of one
man. It was Jonson who first revealed to the age
the literary possibilities of the masque, and lesser
men were not slow to follow in the path which he
had marked out. Had it not been for Jonson, it is
hardly too much to say that the masque would to-
day be the exclusive property of the Court chronicler
and the antiquarian, and of no more significance

to literature than a tilting match or a Christmas
gambol.

We have to thank Sir Robert Spencer, the representative of a house to which lovers of literature
are still under obligations, for first enlisting the
talents of the great poet and playwright in a subject
apparently so trivial. In 1603 he was preparing to
entertain at Althorp, Queen Anne and her son
Prince Henry, who were about to pass through
Northamptonshire on their journey from Scotland
to London, and he commissioned Jonson to compose a little rustic drama for their reception.[1] So
successfully did the poet execute his task that from
that moment his position as purveyor-in-chief of
the Court amusements was assured. Among these
the place of honour was occupied by the Masque:
but the masque as understood by Jonson and his
contemporaries is distinguished in so many important details from the far less elaborate amusement
previously known by the same name, that it will be
convenient to avail ourselves, as far as practicable,
of a variation in the spelling of the word in order
to emphasize this difference, and to distinguish the
mask from the *masque*. Originally of Arabic origin,
the word came into English through the French
early in the sixteenth century, and according to the
English fashion of treating French words was uni-
formly spelt *mask* (or *maske*).[2]   But about the end

---

[1] This was the *Entertainment*, strictly so called, the nucleus of which
was a speech of welcome. It must be distinguished both from the
Masque, the nucleus of which was a dance, and from *Barriers*, the
nucleus of which was a sham tournament. Examples of each kind will
be found in Jonson's works.

[2] At this period the disguise for the face was known as a *visor*: see p.
xx, note 2.

of the century the French spelling, *masque*, began to come into vogue, an innovation adopted by Jonson; and hence it is that the majority of writers ever since have used the spelling *masque* in the sense of the entertainment, and *mask* in the sense of a visor.[1]

But the fact that the name did not exist in England before the sixteenth century is no proof of the non-existence of the thing denoted by it, and it would be a mistake to interpret too strictly a passage in which Edward Hall, the chronicler, records the introduction in the year 1513 of "a maske, a thing not sene afore in England"; we shall presently have to recur to this passage, and we shall then see that there is no reason to suppose that the performance in question was in all respects a novelty. The name no doubt was new, but there appears to have been also an important innovation in the thing, an innovation which henceforward became one of its established features, and which distinguishes it from the earlier stages of the same amusement. A brief review of these will explain our meaning.

Throughout its history the most essential and distinctive characteristic of the mask, to which all

---

[1] The earliest instance I have found of the spelling *masque* in the sense of entertainment is in the quarto of *Cynthia's Revels*, London, 1601, where the spelling is consistently *masque* and *masquer* throughout. In the sense of disguise or pretence it occurs in *The Masque of the League and the Spaniard discovered*, a translation from the French by Anthony Munday, 4to, London, 1592. Except in the case of such careful scholars as Jonson it is unsafe to argue from the printer's spelling to the author's, but in so far as it may be trusted, it will be found that Beaumont, Middleton, Carew, Shirley, and Davenant wrote *masque*; Daniel, Campion, Chapman, and Marston *maske*.

others, such as dialogue and singing, were but
subsidiary adjuncts, was the dance, and from an
early period a dance in masquerade was one of
the ordinary diversions of the European Courts,
the English among the rest. Such a masquerade
formed part of the *ludi domini regis* in 1348, when
Edward III. kept his Christmas at Guildford;
among the properties required on this occasion were
" eighty tunics of buckram of various colours, forty-
two visours of various similitudes; that is fourteen
of the faces of women, fourteen of the faces of men
with beards, fourteen of the heads of angels made
with silver ".[1] Sometimes the performers rode to
the Court on horseback, in order to entertain the
royal personages with dumb-shows and dancing:
thus in 1377 on the Sunday before Candlemas 130
citizens rode from Newgate to Kensington with
torches and music " for the disport of the yong
prince Richard, son to the blacke prince ",[2] and in
1401 when " the Emperor of Constantinople" visited
England, " the kyng helde his Christemasse at El-
tham, and men of London made a gret mummyng
to him of xii Aldermen and here sones, for whiche
they had gret thanke ".[3] These formal visitations
on horseback were known as *mummings*, a name
apparently equally applicable to the ordinary form
of the entertainment, which at this time, and much

---

[1] Collier, *Annals of the Stage* (1879), i. 22. A graphic illustration of
a masquerade of this kind will be found among Hans Burgmaier's wood-
cut illustrations to *Der Weiss Kunig*, i.e. the Emperor Maximilian I.

[2] Stow's *Survey of London*, quoted by Collier, i. 26. They played at
dice with the prince and danced with the royal party. The use of torches
is noteworthy: they remained an indispensable adjunct of the mask down
to the close of its history.   [3] Collier, *ibid.* from the Harleian MS. 565.

later, was commonly called a *disguising*.[1]   Indeed
this term did not altogether fall out of use for a
considerable time after the new designation *mask*
had been introduced: its disappearance was no
doubt gradual, but by 1622 at any rate it had
become antiquated, for in the *Masque of Augurs*,
produced in that year, Notch, the brewer's clerk,
explains to the groom of the Revels that, "disguise
was the old English word for a masque, sir, before
you were an implement belonging to the Revels".
These disguisings, as is clear from the accounts of
the expenses of the royal household still preserved,
were an important feature in the Christmas and
Shrovetide festivities of Henry VII. and Henry
VIII.; they followed the conclusion of an interlude
or other dramatic performance, and were conducted
according to certain strict rules, which may be seen
in a MS. of this period entitled *The Booke of all
manner of Orders concerning an Earle's house*.[2]   The
"disguisers", says this MS., were to be introduced
into the hall by torch-bearers, and on their entrance
the minstrels were to begin to play: if there were
women disguisers, they were to dance first, and

---

[1] In all probability the term *mumming* had special reference to the
dumb-show.   The following extract from a pamphlet entitled *Choice,
Chance and Change, or Conceits in their Colours*, 4to, London, 1606,
will show that it was long associated with masking, and also, as in the
instance of 1377, with dice-playing.   "[After supper] in comes . . . a
messenger from a maske, that delivered a speech: . . . ere the tale was
told with a drum and bagpipe came such a morice daunce, a maske I
would say ther; but they made fools merry and themselves sporte: . . .
who having daunced fel to dicing, being both maskers and mummers,
for though they cared not for their mony yet theire gaines would pay for
their vizards; and for theire clothes they were but borrowed of their
neighboures: but thus after they had masked and mummed, away they
went".   [2] Collier, i. 24.

then stand aside; then the men were to dance
"suche daunces as they be appointed", and stand
upon the other side. After this "the Morris to
come in incontinent as is apointed, yf any be
ordeynid. And when the saide Morris arrives in
the midist of the hall, than the said minstrallis to
play the daunces that is appointid for theim."
This done, "than the gentillmen to com unto the
women and make their obeisaunce, and every of
them to taike oon by thand, and daunce suche base
[slow and stately] daunces as is apointed theym;
and that doon, than to daunce such rounds as shall
be appointed them to daunce togeder by the maister
of the revills". From this description we see that,
although there is no hint of dialogue, or speech of
any kind, some of the fixed characteristics of the
later masque are already established. The disguisers, who would be gentlemen and ladies of the
Court, attended by their torch-bearers, answer to
the masquers; the morris-dancers, who would be
professionals, to the performers in the anti-masque,
and the order of the dances is the same in both;
first those of the men and women separately, and
secondly those of the men with the women, the
"base dances" corresponding to the slow measures,
the "rounds" to the lively galliards and corantos
which always followed the former.

So far the action in these performances appears
to have been confined almost entirely to dancing,
but it was only natural that, as time went on, the
dramatic tendencies inherent in them should find
a more definite expression, and that an attempt
should be made to enhance their attractions by the

introduction of some kind of stage machinery as well as of spoken words. For the former the artist had not far to seek: scenery of a primitive kind lay ready to his hand in the movable stages or scaffolds, on which the miracle-plays and moralities were represented. The word *Pageant*, which came finally to mean a spectacle or show, such as the Lord Mayor's, originally signified a scaffold of this kind, and it was only necessary to convert the pageant into a castle, a mountain, or a ship, and wheel it into the hall, in order to furnish a practicable scene for the disguising. Of such a scene we have an example on an elaborate scale in an account, to be found among the Harleian MSS., of "the banquets and disguisings used at the entertaynment in Westminster Hall [in the year 1501] of Katherine, wife to Prince Arthur, eldest sonne of King Henry VII."[1]. The first of three pageants moved into the hall on that occasion was a castle "right cunningly devised, sett upon certaine wheeles"; there were in this castle "disguised viij goodly and fresh ladyes looking out of the windowes of the same", while in the four corner turrets were four children who sang "most sweetly and harmoniously" as the castle moved up the hall. The second pageant was a ship from which descended

"two well beseene and goodly persons calling themselves Hope and Desire . . . in manner and forme as Ambassadors from Knights of the Mount of Love unto the ladyes within the Castle . . . making their meanes and entreates as wooers and breakers of the maters of love between the Knights and

[1] Quoted by Collier, i. 58, from the Harleian MS. 69, and previously printed in the Shakespeare Society's Papers for 1844, vol. i. p. 47.

the Ladyes : the said Ladyes gave their small answeare of utterly refuse, and knowledge of any such company, or that they were ever minded to the accomplishment of any such request, and plainely denyed their purpose and desire. The said two Embassadors, therwith taking great displeasure, shewed the said Ladyes that the Knights would for this unkind refusall make battayle and assault, so and in such wise to them and their Castle, that it should be grievous to abyde their power and malice. Incontinent came in the third Pageant in likeness of a great hill or mountaine, in whom there was inclosed viij goodly knights with their banners spredd and displayed, naming themselves the Knights of the Mount of Love."

On receiving the unfavourable report from their ambassadors, the knights

"therwith not being content, with much malice and courageous minde, went a little from the said Mount with their banners displayed, and hastely sped them to the rehearsed Castle, which they forthwith assaulted so and in such wise that the Ladyes, yielding themselves, descended from the Castle, and submitted themselves to the power, grace, and will of those noble Knights ".

The dancing then followed.

Such were the crude attempts at staging, which eventually developed into the elaborate scenery of the masque, while the dramatic element is represented by the parleyings between the ladies and the ambassadors, and the "sweet and harmonious" singing of the children. The next question to be decided is in what respects the mask differed from, or was an advance upon, a disguising, such as the one just described.

The passage in Hall's *Chronicle*, to which allusion has already been made, runs as follows:

"On the daie of the Epiphanie [1513] at night the king

with xi other were disguised after the manner of Italie, called a maske, a thing not sene afore in England: thei were appareled in garmentes long and brode, wrought all with golde, with visers and cappes of gold; and after the banket doen these Maskers came in with the six gentlemen disguised in silke, beryng staffe-torches, and desired the ladies to daunce: some were content, and some that knew the fashion of it refused, because it was a thing not commonly seen. And after thei daunced and commoned together, as the fashion of the maskes is, thei toke their leave and departed; and so did the Queene and all the ladies."[1]

From this time (1513) the word *mask* begins to be used in common with the older word *disguising*, and apparently in much the same sense;[2] it is not, in fact, till towards the close of the reign of Henry VIII. that the latter altogether disappears from the documents, and it may have held its own still longer in popular usage.[3] The king seems to have been particularly fond of amusements of the kind described by Hall; thus in 1527 the house of Cardinal Wolsey was honoured with one of these royal surprises, a minute description of which is given by Cavendish in his life of Wolsey, and which Shakespeare introduced into *Henry VIII.* Act i. Scene 4. In this instance the maskers were disguised as shepherds "in fine cloth of gold and fine crimson satin paned"; they wore visors, of course, and their hair and beards were of gold or silver wire or of black

[1] Quoted in Collier, i. 67. Hall's *Chronicle* was first published in 1548.

[2] In the *Liber Numerator Scaccarii* of Henry VIII., 1514, we find, "Johi Farlyon Custod. Vestuarum, sive apporatum omnium singulorum jocorum, larvatorum, vocat. Maskes, Revelles and Disguysings"; and in *The Kynges boke of payments,* 1519-20, occur the words "maskelyn" (masking) and "masculers" (maskers). Collier, i. 79.

[3] Compare the passage above quoted from the *Masque of Augurs,* p. xv.

silk, but apparently they did not find themselves altogether at their ease in this unwonted guise, for they did not challenge the ladies to dance till they had resumed their ordinary attire.

That there was an innovation of some kind in these performances is clear from the language of Hall, but modern writers have surely overstated the case, when they describe the mask as being in point of fact a novelty imported from Italy, or as an attenuated form of the Italian *mascherata*. This is hardly warranted by the expression "disguised after the manner of Italie", which need not after all mean more than that the Italian fashion was adopted in some details of costume or "make-up". There is nothing, in fact, in the Italian masquerades of this date [1] which is specially suggestive of the masks described by Hall and Cavendish. On the contrary, the reader will not fail to recognize in them the old native disguising, though with a modification "not sene afore in England". The difficulty is to decide in what this consisted: the fact that the performers wore visors can hardly be regarded as an innovation; [2] we have already seen that they were worn in the *ludi domini regis* as long ago as Edward III.'s time. Nor were the torch-bearers a novelty; what really constituted a new departure, as compared with the practice hitherto followed in the disguising, was the fact

[1] As described, for instance, by Mr. Symonds, *Shakspere's Predecessors*, p. 321 ff.

[2] It is a mistake to suppose that masks (entertainments) were so called because the performers wore masks (visors). The sense of "entertainment" was in fact the original meaning of the word in English, the sense of "visor" came later. See Skeat, *Etymological Dictionary*, s.v.

that the maskers "desired the ladies to daunce,
. . . and after thei daunced and commoned together, *as the fashion of the maskes is* thei toke
their leave ". In the disguising the dances had all
been executed by the disguised personages, the
dramatis personæ if we may so call them, and by
them only; the mask had this further peculiarity
that in one or two at least of the dances the spectators were invited to join with the performers.
This, as we shall see, was afterwards an established
practice in the masque, one of the regular dances
of which was always executed by the masquers
with partners of the opposite sex taken from the
audience. This, then, was probably what Hall
meant, if indeed he was not thinking more of the
name than the thing, when he called the mask "a
thing not sene afore in England". But it would
be quite superfluous to assume that this practice
was imported from Italy or anywhere else. It was,
in fact, nothing more than the combination of the
old-fashioned masquerade with the ordinary social
dance of everyday life, with all the attractions of a
surprise party superadded, and to an enterprising
and ingenious young monarch such as Henry VIII.
we may imagine that the expedient would be sufficiently obvious.

This, however, was a comparatively simple form
of the mask, and did not interfere with the more
complex form of the disguising, which continued
to develop under its new name. In the romantic
example of 1501 we have already witnessed the
introduction of a kind of movable scenery and of
speeches, or something like them—improvised by

the actors probably and not written beforehand,—
and though little improvement in the direction of
stage contrivances seems to have taken place before
the days of Inigo Jones, the use of spoken words
became more and more indispensable, and in the
Elizabethan mask not merely spoken words but
written speeches were the rule. Hanging as it did
upon the skirts of the regular drama, the mask in-
evitably took its colour from the prevalent dramatic
forms of the day. We have mentioned above that it
was a common custom for the disguising to follow
the performance of a morality or interlude, and it
was easy to make the combination still closer by
bringing on the mask in the middle of the performance instead of at the end. [1] The innate tediousness
of the morality was thereby relieved, and the freshness and life which it thus gained it repaid by imbu-
ing the mask with that allegorical character which
remained one of its permanent attributes, as well as
by handing on to it that long train of personified
virtues and vices which combined with the gods and
goddesses of classical mythology to form the staple
of its *dramatis personæ*. It must be admitted, however, that the student will not find that any considerable light is thrown upon the history of the mask
by a perusal of extant English interludes and moralities. The fact is, that although the performance of
masks is constantly recorded throughout the reigns
of Henry VIII. and Elizabeth, and also, but less frequently, during the reigns of Edward VI. and Mary,

[1] The title-page of the interlude of *The Nature of the Four Elements*
(1519), after giving directions for the shortening of the piece if desired,
provides that "also yf ye lyst ye may brynge in a dysgysinge".
Collier, ii. 237.

and although under Elizabeth they constituted a
stock feature of the royal progresses, and of the
Court festivities at Christmas and Shrovetide, yet
descriptions of them in any detail are extremely
scanty. This must be our excuse for printing at
full length the scheme of a mask drawn up for an
intended meeting between Elizabeth and Mary
Queen of Scots at Nottingham in 1562. The meeting, indeed, never took place, but the mask seems to
have been performed in a modified shape at Whitehall in 1572.[1] The scheme, as will be seen, may
serve to illustrate what has been said as to the connection of the mask and the morality, and may be
taken as a fair example of the general character of
Elizabethan mask at this date.

> "*Devices to be shewed before the Queenes Majestie, by
> waye of maskinge, at Nottingham castell, after the
> metinge of the Quene of Scotts.*[2]

"THE FIRSTE NIGHT.

"Firste a pryson to be made in the haule, the name
whereof is Extreme Oblyvion, and the Kepers name thereof,
Argus, otherwise called Circumspection : then a maske of
Ladyes to come in after this sorte.

"Firste Pallas, rydinge uppon an unycorne, havinge in
her hande a Standarde, in which is to be paynted ij Ladyes
hands, knitt one faste within thother, and over th' ands
written in letters of golde, *Fides*.

"Then ij Ladyes rydinge together, th' one uppon a golden
Lyon, with a crowne of gold on his heade: th' other uppon a
redd Lyon, with the like crowne of Gold; signifyinge ij Vertues,
that is to saye, the Lady on the golden Lyon is to be called
Prudentia, and the Ladye on the redd Lyon *Temperantia*.

"After this to followe vj or viij Ladyes maskers, bringinge

---

[1] Fleay, *History of the Stage*, 19.
[2] Printed by Collier, i. 176, ff. from the Lansdowne MS. 5.

in, captive, Discorde, and False Reporte, with ropes of gold about there necks. When theis have marched about the haule, then Pallas to declare before the Quenes Majestie in verse, that the goddes, understandinge the noble meteinge of those ij quenes, hathe willed her to declare unto them, that those ij vertues, *Prudentia* and *Temperantia*, have made greate and longe sute unto Jupiter, that it wold please hym to gyve unto them False Reporte and Discorde, to be punished as they thinke good; and that those Ladyes have nowe in there presence determyned to committ them faste bounde unto th' afforesayde pryson of Extreme Oblyvion, there to be kepte by th' afforesayde gaylor Argus, otherwise Circumspection, for ever; unto whome *Prudentia* shall delyver a locke where-uppon shalbe wrytten *In Eternum.* Then *Temperantia* shall likewise delyver unto Argus a key whose name shalbe *Nunquam*, signifyinge, that when False Report and Discorde are committed to the pryson of Extreme Oblyvion, and locked there everlastinglie, he should put in the key to lett them out *Nunquam*: and when he hathe so done, then the trompetts to blowe, and th' inglishe Ladies to take the nobilite of the straungers, and daunce.

"THE SECONDE NIGHT.

" First a Castell to be made in the haule, called the Courte of Plentye; then the maske after this sorte.

"Firste Peace, rydinge uppon a chariott drawen with an Oliphant, uppon whome shall ryde Fryndeshippe, and after them vj or viij Ladyes maskers; and when they have marched rounde aboute the haule, Fryndshippe shall declare before the quenes highnes in verse, that the goddes Pallas hath latelie made a declaracion before all the godds, howe worthilie the night precedent theis ij vertues, *Prudentia* and *Temperantia*, behaved them selves in judginge, and condempninge False Reporte and Discord to the prison of Extreme Oblyvion: and understandinge that those ij vertues do remaine in that Cowrte of Plentye, they have, by there mightie power, sent this vertu, Peace, there to dwell with those ij Ladyes, for ever. To this Castell perteyneth ij porters, th' one to *Prudentia*, called Ardent Desyer, and th' other porter to *Temperantia*, named

Perpetuitie; signifyinge that, by Ardent Desyer and Perpetuitie, perpetuall peace and tranquillitie maye be hadd and kept throughe the hole worlde. Then shall springe out of the Cowrt of Plentie conditts of all sorts of wynes, duringe which tyme th' inglish Lords shall maske with the Scottishe Ladyes.

"THE THYRDE NIGHT.

"Firste shall come in Disdaine rydinge uppon a wilde bore; with hym Prepencyd Malyce, in the similitude of a greate serpent. These ij shall drawe an orcharde havinge golden apples, in which orchard shall sitt vj, or viij, Ladyes maskers. Then Dysdaine shall declare before the quenes majestie in verse, that his Master Pluto, the greate god of hell, takith no little displeasure with Jupiter, the god of heaven, for that he, in the ij other nyghts precedent, hath firste by Pallas sent Discord and False Reporte, being ij of his chefe servants, unto *Prudentia* and *Temperantia*, to be punisshed at there pleasure; and not content with this, but hathe the laste night, sent unto those ij Ladyes his most mortall enymye, Peace, to be onlie betwene them ij imbraced: wherefore Jupiter shall well understande, that in dispite of his doings, he hath sent his chefeste Capitayne, Prepencyd Mallyce, and wyllithe ether Argus, otherwyse Circumspection, to delyver unto hym Discorde, and False Reporte, his saide Masters servants, or ells th' afforesaid ij porters, Ardent Dessyer, and Perpetuitie, to delyver hym there masters enymie, Peace, chuse them whether.

"Then shall come in Discretion; after hym Valyant Courage, otherwise Hercules, rydinge uppon a horse, whose name is Boldnes, Discretyon leadynge hym by the raynes of the brydell: after hym vj or viij Lords maskers. Then Discretion shall declare before the quenes highnes in verse, that Jupiter dothe well foresee the mischevous intent of Pluto, and therefore, to confounde his pollyces, hathe sente from heaven this vertu Valyant Courage, which shalbe suffycient to confounde all Plutos devices: neverthelesse thos ij dyvells, Dysdaine, and Prepencyd Malyce, are mervailous warryours; yea suche as unlesse theis vertues, *Prudentia* and *Temperantia*,

will of themselves by some signe or token conclude to im-
brace Peace, in such sorte as Jupiter hathe sent hym unto
them, it wilbe to harde for Valyant Courage to overcome
those vyces; but if they once speake but one worde, the battaill
is overcome as a trifle.   And therefore Jupiter hathe willed
Discretion, in the presence of those ij quenes, to repaier unto
the Cowrte of Plentie, and there firste to demande of *Prudentia*, how longe her pleasure is, of her honor, that Peace
shall dwell between her and *Temperantia?*   Then *Prudentia*
shall let downe unto Discretion, with a bande of golde, a
grandgarde of assure, whereuppon shalbe wrytten, in letters
of gold, *Ever.*   Then Discretion shall humblie demande of
Temperantia uppon her honor, when Peace shall departe
from *Prudentia*, and her grace?   Then *Temperantia* shall
lett downe unto Discretyon a girdell of assure, studded with
gold, and a sworde of stele, whereuppon shalbe written, *Never;*
which grandgarde, and sworde, Discretion shall bringe, and
laye at the fete of the ij quenes.   Then Discretion (after a
fewe words spoken) shall, before the quenes highnes, arme
Valyant Courage, otherwise Hercules, with the grandgard of
Ever, and gyrte hym with the sworde of *Never;* signifying
that those ij Ladies have professed that Peace shall ever dwell
with them, and never departe from them; and signifyinge also
that there Valyant Courage shalbe ever at defyance with Disdaine and Prepencyd Mallice, and never leave untill he have
overcome them.   And then shall valyant courage alone go
and fight with those ij; in the myddeste of which fight, Disdaine shall rune his wayes, and escape with life, but the
monster Prepencyd Mallyce shalbe slaine for ever: signifyinge
that some ungodlie men maye still disdaine the perpetuall
peace made betweene those ij vertues, but as for there prepencyd mallice, it is easye troden under theis Ladyes fete.
After this shall come out of the garden, the vi or viij Ladies
maskers with a songe, that shalbe made hereuppon, as full of
armony as maye be devised."[1]

---

[1] A very late example of the combination of the moral drama with the
masque will be found in *The World Tost at Tennis*, by Middleton and
Rowley, 1620.   This sets forth the triumph of Simplicity over Deceit in
the various departments of government, law, church, army, and navy.

It is not known who was the author of this scheme, but no doubt he was some poet of the day, who was commissioned to provide something suitable for the occasion. From the fact that the speeches delivered by Pallas, Friendship, Disdain, and Discretion are described as being in verse, we may infer that lines composed expressly for the purpose, and not merely impromptu utterances, are intended, and these, as well as the song "full of armony", seem to indicate that the mask had now outgrown the proportions of a mere dance in disguise. The services of the poet were in fact becoming indispensable: thus in 1572, or thereabouts, when Viscount Montacute was preparing to celebrate a double marriage in his family, some friends of his undertook to grace the festivities with a mask, and applied to George Gascoigne to furnish the "device". "There were eight gentlemen," says Gascoigne in his printed account of the performance,

"all of blood or alliaunce to the sayd Lord Mountacute, which had determined to present a Maske at the day appointed for the sayd marriages, and so far they had proceeded therein that they had alreadye bought furniture of Silkes, etc., and had caused their garmentes to bee cut of the Venetian fashion. Nowe then they began to imagine that, without some speciall demonstration, it would seeme somewhat obscure to have Venetians presented rather than other countrey men. Whereupon they entreated the Aucthour to devise some verses to be uttered by an Actor wherein might be some discourse convenient to render a good cause of the Venetians presence."

This he succeeded in doing in some 400 lines of (sufficiently tedious) fourteen-syllable verse. But, unattractive as Gascoigne's performance is from a literary stand-point, it is interesting as an early example of what became the established practice in the production of a mask. The great personages who planned the mask, and undertook the expenses of its presentation, called in the assistance of a poet, whose duty it was, in collaboration with the stage-artist, to supply the libretto and the *mise-en-scène*: as a rule the whole design of the piece was left to his invention, but sometimes, as in the present instance,[1] the presenters decided for themselves upon the particular character in which they wished to appear, and the poet had to arrange the plot accordingly. Again, in September 1589, a mask which the Queen sent to Scotland in honour of the marriage of James VI., is described as consisting of "six maskers, six torch-bearers, and of such persons as were to utter speeches". That there were four of these speech-makers may be inferred from the "foure heares [wigs] of silke and foure gar-landes of flowres" that are mentioned as required for their attire.[2]   Hence it is clear that by this time it had become the rule to introduce the maskers in a formal prologue, which not only interpreted the significance of the characters they represented, but also set forth the story accounting for their appear-ance.   Complimentary verses addressed to the Queen were also a stock feature of the Elizabethan mask, and if we may judge from the two groups of maskers, which Jonson brought upon the stage in the fifth act of his *Cynthia's Revels* (1600), but little advance in a dramatic direction had been effected

---

[1] Jonson's masques of *Blackness* and of *Beauty* are other instances.
[2] Collier i. 263, from the Lansdowne MS. 59.

by the end of the sixteenth century. In this play each group is introduced by a speech of the orthodox type, the first spoken by Cupid "like Anteros", the second by Mercury "as a Page". The dancing follows, and there is no dialogue; the lyric element is also absent.[1]

A new chapter opens with the accession of the house of Stuart to the English throne. The splendour and magnificence of the festivities during the forty years which followed are unequalled in the annals of the Court, and the *masque*, for we may henceforward adopt with advantage the Jonsonian spelling, was reinvigorated—we may almost say recreated—by a combination of literature and art unique in the history of either. This development was mainly due to the personal tastes of James and his queen. They shared all Elizabeth's passion for display, but they did not share those economical, not to say parsimonious, scruples which had restrained her from indulging it. While they were no less willing to avail themselves of the profuse hospitality of the nobility, their own entertainments at Whitehall were upon a scale far surpassing anything that the courtiers of the late Queen had ever witnessed.[2]

---

[1] At the end of the third edition of the *Arcadia*, 1598, was printed for the first time a short pastoral drama written by Sir Philip Sidney for the visit of Queen Elizabeth to the Earl of Leicester at Wanstead in 1578. It has neither title-page nor heading, but has been known as "The Lady of May" ever since it appeared under this title in the edition of Sidney's works published in 1725. The editor of this edition also took upon himself to describe the piece as "a masque"—a description to which it has no sort of claim; though it might with justice be termed an "entertainment" in the Jonsonian sense.

[2] Particulars of the enormous sums expended on masques may be seen in Collier, in Cunningham's *Revels at Court*, and in Nichols's *Pro-*

That they impoverished their exchequer and encumbered themselves with debt by the expenditure thus incurred is a fact with which we need not concern ourselves; at any rate they did not lavish their favours upon unworthy instruments. For the production of their masques they could command the services of some of the first writers of the most brilliant period of our dramatic history, while the greatest English architect of his day was engaged to provide the stage machinery and decoration.

Inigo Jones had studied in Italy, where he had doubtless witnessed some of those elaborate masquerades, which owed as much to the skill of the painter and the sculptor as to that of the playwright and the musician. From Italy this form of entertainment, like the opera, afterwards, passed into France, where it became famous as the *Ballet* or *Ballet d'action*; and in this shape also, although we have no direct evidence of the fact, it is not at all impossible that Jones may have made its acquaintance. Be this as it may, there was nothing in France which bore a closer resemblance to the English masque than the ballet, and it may therefore deserve a passing notice, especially when we bear in mind the intimate relations that prevailed between the two countries at this time.

The learned Jesuit Claude François Menestrier, who wrote in the latter part of the seventeenth century, describes the English masques as *ballets*,[1]

gresses of James I. It has been calculated that the average cost of the production of a masque was £1400, that is about £6000 of our present money.

[1] *Des ballets anciens et modernes selon les règles du Théâtre.* Paris, 1682.

and masques and ballets undoubtedly had this much in common, that both admitted of speeches, dancing, and singing, both employed elaborate stage apparatus and splendid costumes, and both were adapted to an allegorical setting; but there the resemblance ends. The ballet was longer and more formal; it was divided by the speeches into acts, and by the "entries" of the dancers into scenes; it was, in fact, a kind of dumb-show, the meaning of which was made intelligible to the spectators by the speeches and the songs. How far it affected the development of the masque can only be a matter of conjecture, but the elaboration of the dancing and of the spectacular effects may well have been due to its influence. Under Henry IV. and his two successors it was one of the favourite amusements of the French Court, but the earliest example that remains to us belongs to the reign of Henry III. This is the *Ballet comique de la royne*—so called because the queen (Louise of Lorraine) took part in it; it was written for the marriage of the queen's sister with the Duc de Joyeuse in 1581, and was printed at length in 1582. The story of Circe and her enchantments supplied the plot, and the principal dancers were the queen and her ladies. At the close of the performance the queen presented to the king, who was one of the audience, a gold medal bearing the figure of a dolphin, while her ladies made similar presents to the lords and gentlemen;[1] then they took out the princes to

---

[1] The making of presents was an occasional feature of the masque. See, for instance, Daniel's *Vision of the Twelve Goddesses,* and *Tethys' Festival.*

dance the "grand Bal",[1] and other dances followed. In order to enable the reader to judge for himself of the relation of the ballet to the masque we give in his own words Menestrier's description of two other examples.

The first is the *Ballet de la Cour du Soleil*, danced in 1628:

"La Nuit en fit l'ouverture, et à sa faveur des Ombres et des Follets firent une entrée assez plaisante sortant de divers endroits; mais la Nuit les avertissant de prendre garde que le Jour ne les surprît, ils se retirèrent dans leurs grottes, lors que l'Etoile matinière introduisit les visions du matin, les Songes guais [gais] qui sortirent par la porte d'yvoire. L'Etoile de Venus sortit de la mer pour annoncer la venue de la plus belle Aurore que l'on eut encore vue, et fit lever les Zephirs pour jetter des fleurs, les Rosées pour jetter des eaux parfumées et les influences les plus douces et les plus salutaires. L'Aurore les suivit, et étant descendue du Ciel elle fit paraître tout d'un coup le Palais du Soleil d'une Architecture Ionique; les sept Planètes et les douze Heures étoient dans des niches, d'où elles sortirent pour danser; les Muses dans d'autres niches firent les concerts; le Temps, l'Année, les Saisons, les Mois, et les Semaines firent la musique dans les loges de ce Palais."

The other is the *Ballet moral pour le jour de naissance du Cardinal de Savoye*, danced in 1634:

"Le sujet de ce ballet étoit la Verité ennemie des Apparences, et soutenue du Temps. Ce ballet commença par un chœur de faux bruits et de soupçons, qui précédent l'Apparence et les Mensonges. Ils étoient représentez par des personnes vêtues en coqs et en poules, qui chantoient un dialogue moitié Italien et moitié François, mêlé du chant des coqs et

[1] So called, says Menestrier, "parce que le nombre des danseurs y est toujours plus grand qu'en toutes les autres Entrées, et que l'on y fait un plus grand nombre de passages et de figures. Tous ceux qui ont dansé dans le Ballet se reunissent ordinairément pour cette Entrée." This taking out the princes also finds its parallel in the masque.

des poules. Après ĉe chant la scène s'étant ouverte on vid
[vit] sur un grand nuage accompagnè des vents l'Apparence
avec des ailes et une grande queue de paon vêtue de quantité
de miroirs, laquelle couvoit des œufs, d'où sortirent les Mensonges pernicieux, les Tromperies et les Fraudes, les Mensonges agréables, les Flatteries et les Intrigues, les Mensonges
bouffons, les Plaisanteries et les petits Contes. Le Temps
ayant chassé l'Apparence avec tous ces Mensonges fait ouvrir
le nid sur lequel l'Apparence couvoit; on y void [voit] une
grande Horloge à sable de laquelle le Temps fait sortir la
Verité et rappelant les Heures elles font avec elle le grand
Ballet."

Before proceeding further with the history of the
masque, it will be desirable to define[1] the meaning
of the word as precisely as possible, and this is all
the more necessary, since for the greater part of
the last three centuries there has not uncommonly
been considerable vagueness in its employment.[2]

[1] If the reader should feel any doubts as to the definition here given,
he is invited to test it by any one of the fifty extant examples enumerated
in the appendix to this Introduction.

[2] In 1637 Henry Lawes edited, without the author's name, what is
described on the title-page as "A Maske presented at Ludlow Castle
1634". It may be worth while to notice, however, that in his dedica-
tory epistle he calls it "This Poem"; and it is hardly necessary to
remark, that Comus, as it was afterwards called, is not a masque in the
true sense. A comparison with any one of Jonson's masques, for instance, makes this clear at a glance: there is no body of masquers, and
therefore no formal dances, while the musical element throughout is
entirely subordinate. Again, the identification of the three principal
actors with the actual children of the Earl of Bridgewater is too close to
admit of their assuming that allegorical or mythological character always
borne by the speakers in the main masque. Soergel well describes
how Jonson would have treated the subject: "Jonson would have represented the Lady as Virtue in the power of Comus: the latter would
have summoned his crew of monsters as an antimasque, in order to
display his magic art to Virtue. The Brothers with other young nobles
would have appeared as masquers representing the servants of Virtue,
and by their sudden entrance have put to flight Comus and his crew.
Then the dances of the masquers and the usual songs of a complimen-

The masque, then, is a combination, in variable proportions, of speech, dance, and song, but its essential and invariable feature is the presence of a group of dancers, varying in number, but commonly eight, twelve, or sixteen, called Masquers. These masquers never take any part in the speaking or in the singing: all they have to do is to make an imposing show and to dance. The dances are of two kinds— (1) stately figure dances performed by the masquers alone and carefully rehearsed beforehand, and commonly distinguished as the Entry, the Main, and the Going-out; (2) the Revels, livelier dances, such as galliards, corantos, and levaltos, danced by the masquers with partners of the opposite sex chosen from the audience. The Revels were regarded as *extras*, and are not numbered among the regular masque dances of the programme; they took place after the Main, and were doubtless often kept up for a considerable time. But the number of dances, as might be expected, is not a fixed one: sometimes, as in Campion's *Masque at Lord Hay's Marriage*, the Revels were preceded by a slower dance, "the measures",[1] also danced with partners, and sometimes, as in the *Masque of Queens*, a specially rehearsed dance by the masquers alone was interposed between the dance with partners and the Going-out or last dance.

---

tary nature would have brought the performance to a close." Not to mention other writers, we find even among Jonson's masques three to which the application of the word is not warranted by their contents, viz. *Christmas his Masque, A Masque of the Metamorphosed Gipsies,* and *The Masque of Owls.*

[1] The term *Measures* is also applied in a general sense to the slower dances of the masque in contradistinction to the *Revels.*

The masquers were dressed in gorgeous costumes, often minutely described by the writer of the masque, in accordance with the character they represented; and originally they also wore masks, but this unbecoming and unnecessary disguise was soon dispensed with.[1] The masquers being thus the central feature, and, as it were, the final cause of the masque, the writer's first object was to arrange his plot or "device" in such a way as to render their appearance on the scene as effective as possible. During the first part of the performance they were always concealed from view, and not till the proper moment arrived did they burst forth upon the eyes of the spectators in all their glory. Sometimes they issued from "a great concave shell", sometimes from "a microcosm or globe" or "a glorious bower"; sometimes they descended from the heavens on a cloud, sometimes from the zodiac or "the region of the moon"; rarely, as in the *Masque of Augurs*, they were merely "fetched out". They then danced their "Entry", and the main business of the masque began. The introductory part, however, gradually increased in importance, and from being a simple speech of the "Presenter", the sole design of which was to introduce the masquers, it became quite a little drama in itself. To this we must now direct our attention.

[1] It was still worn in 1604, as is evident from *The Vision of the Twelve Goddesses*. A later instance of its use is furnished by *The Masque of Flowers* (1614), at the conclusion of which "the Maskers uncovered their faces and came up to the State". On February 21st, 1618, John Chamberlain writes to Sir Dudley Carleton with reference to the Masque of Mountebanks: "On Thursday night the gentlemen of Gray's Inn came to court with their show, for I cannot call it a masque, seeing they were not disguised, nor had vizards".

In the earliest example of the Jacobæan masque that remains to us, Daniel's *Vision of the Twelve Goddesses* (1604), the opening displays but little advance upon the old conventional type. There is no real dialogue: Iris appears as Presenter, and after announcing that the goddesses, having quitted "their ancient delighting places of Greece and Asia", have vouchsafed to recreate themselves upon "this western mount of mighty Brittany", hands the reverend prophetess, Sibylla, a "prospective" or spy-glass, through which she reconnoitres the masquers at the other end of the hall, and describes them one by one in a long speech of rhymed stanzas. The masquers then make their entrance without further ado. Contrast with this the opening of Jonson's *Masque of Blackness*, presented just a twelvemonth later. The masquers are twelve Æthiopians, daughters of the river Niger, and an opening dialogue between Oceanus and Niger, in which the Moon under her surname of Æthiopia presently joins, explains how these damsels, dissatisfied with their dusky complexions, have made their way to Britain in order to beautify them in the beams of a sun,

"Whose beams shine day and night, and are of force
To blanch an Æthiop and revive a corse".

No formal description of the masquers is necessary, for the audience are sufficiently prepared for their appearance by the story thus set forth, and accordingly they at once dance their entry from "a great concave shell, like mother-of-pearl, curiously made to move on those waters and rise with the billow".

The difficulty of finding an adequate *motif* for the masque is thus solved by the invention of a fiction, the dramatic exposition of which fulfils all the requisite conditions, and set speeches, such as that of the Sibyl in Daniel's masque, are no longer necessary.[1]

It was not long, however, before a still further advance was made. The Court soon began to grow weary of the eternal procession of gods and goddesses, and allegorical personages paraded before their eyes with a regularity that had become monotonous. Nothing was more natural than that at a time when the public stage had achieved some of its most splendid successes by a due admixture of the grave and the gay, an attempt should be made to enhance the attractions of the masque by the introduction of a less serious element. The experiment was indeed justified by its success so long as this element was kept within due bounds, but its inherent tendency was dangerous and demoralizing, and it needed the high aims and severe restraint of a writer like Jonson to curb those extravagances which afterwards proved fatal to the masque as a work of high art, and reduced it well nigh to the level of a pantomime. This seductive novelty was the Antimasque[2], that is, as Jonson himself terms it, "a foil or false masque", and in its original intention it seems to have been destined

---

[1] Where the masquers each have an independent character of their own, as in Jonson's *Masque of Queens* and Daniel's *Tethys' Festival*, the characters are enumerated in a speech. See the speeches of " Heroic Virtue " in the former and of " Triton " in the latter instance.

[2] Misconceptions of the origin of the word on the part of some seventeenth-century writers (or their printers) have given us the spellings *antemasque* and *anticmasque.*

not merely to relieve the performance by the introduction of a humorous element, but to enhance the
effect which the masquers were to produce by the
very force of the contrast; if, in short, their own
appearance upon the scene would show what they
were, the antimasque would add to the effect by
showing what they were not, the exhibition of their
opposites would in fact throw their own magnificence
into greater relief. That some such design, more or
less conscious, existed, we may gather from Jonson's own words in his preparatory remarks to his
Masque of Queens: "her Majesty", he says, "had
commanded me to think on some dance or shew
that might precede hers and have the place of a
foil or false masque". Accordingly he produced
his twelve hags, "not unaptly sorting with the current and whole fall of the device", and the very
opposites of the twelve queens of the main masque.
In no other instance, however, is the contrast between the characters of the antimasque and those
of the main masque sustained with such tenacity of
purpose, or the balance so scrupulously adjusted.
Commonly, although the antithesis of opposite
characters is a device frequently employed,[1] the
contrast is less exact, and the antimasque is deemed
to answer its purpose, if it serves to relieve the for-
mality of the main masque, and (in the case of the
best writers) to accentuate its leading idea.

---

[1] Thus in *Love freed from Ignorance and Folly* we have the Follies *v.*
the Muses; in *Oberon* the Satyrs *v.* Oberon and his Knights; in *Mercury
vindicated from the Alchemists* the Monsters *v.* the Sons of Nature; in
The Golden Age restored the Evils *v.* the "Semi-gods"; and in *Love's
Triumph through Callipolis* the Depraved Lovers *v.* the Discreet
Lovers.

The development of the antimasque proceeded on similar lines to that of the masque itself. Its starting-point was a dance, in its nature resembling, and probably borrowed from, those comic performances of antics and tumblers already familiar at fairs and other popular entertainments. In most cases the dancers of the antimasque[1] like those of the main masque went through their performance in dumb-show, but in a few instances dialogue or songs were assigned to them. The *Masque of Queens* is the leading example of this; the dramatic force of the antimasque is such that it quite eclipses the main masque, which nothing but the magnificence of the spectacle and the skill of the dancers and the musicians can have rescued from producing the effect of an anticlimax. Another prominent instance is the *Masque of Oberon*, where the antimasque is danced by the Satyrs, who take a principal part both in the dialogue and the singing.[2] As we have just remarked, however, these cases are the exception; as a rule the interlocutors in the antimasque are distinct from the dancers, and this is the case in the earliest example we have, viz. Jonson's *Masque at Lord Haddington's marriage*[3] (1608). Here the antimasque consists of twelve boys representing "the Sports and pretty Lightnesses that

---

[1] The original application of the terms *masque* and *antimasque* was to the dances only, but they gradually became extended to include the dramatic growth which clustered round them.

[2] See also in this connection *The Irish Masque, Christmas his Masque,* a species of antimasque without a main masque, and *For the Honour of Wales,* an antimasque written for a second performance of *Pleasure reconciled to Virtue.* In all these the dancers of the antimasque have parts assigned them.

[3] Called by Gifford *The Hue and Cry after Cupid.*

accompany Love"; they are introduced by Cupid
in a speech of half a dozen lines, and fall into their
"subtle capricious dance" without further ceremony.
So too in *Love freed from Ignorance and Folly*
(1610), the Sphinx similarly introduces the "Follies
which were twelve She-Fools". Here we have the
antimasque in its simplest form; its presenters,
Cupid and the Sphinx respectively, are each persons of the main masque, the thread of which is
but slightly interrupted—interrupted only, in fact,
by the introduction of a comic or lively dance. But
it soon assumed larger proportions, and its encroach-
ments became more and more serious. Indeed so
popular did the antimasque become that the audience were not content with one only, but demanded
at least two. The masques written by Chapman
and Beaumont for the marriage of the Princess
Elizabeth in 1613 have each two antimasques,
and after this date one becomes the exception. A
further innovation on this occasion was made by
Beaumont: hitherto the characters had been all of
the same kind, Witches, Satyrs, Follies for instance;
Beaumont's antimasques, however, are "not of one
kind or livery, because that had been so much in
use heretofore", and his first is composed of Nymphs,
Hyades, Cupids, and Statues; while his second is
"a May dance, or rural dance, consisting likewise
not of any suited persons, but of a confusion or
commixture of all such persons as are natural and
proper for country sports". Jonson, whose ideal
was a lofty one, and who, as we shall see directly,
regarded these pantomimic tendencies with contempt, held out against the new fashion for several

years, and did not admit any "commixture" into
his antimasques till *Neptune's Triumph* (1624), and
then only to ridicule it. His self-respect as an
artist demanded something higher than this: a
dance, one or more than one, there must be, but it
is upon the dramatic setting of the dance that he
will stake his reputation. Chapman[1] in his masque
of 1613 had introduced his antimasque of Baboons
by a lively dialogue between the God of Riches
and "a Man of Wit"; and, adopting perhaps the
hint thus given, we find that Jonson has prefixed
to his *Love Restored* (1614), where curiously enough
no antimasque is danced, to *Mercury Vindicated
from the Alchemists* (1615), to *The Vision of Delight*
(1617), and to *Pleasure reconciled to Virtue* (1618),
a dramatic introduction consisting of humorous
dialogue,—a happy device which in *News from
the New World discovered in the Moon* (1621), *The
Masque of Augurs* (1622), and subsequent masques,
rises to the level of the fine low-comedy style of
Bartholomew Fair.

We have said that Jonson's ideal was a lofty one:
the moral purpose with which his best comedies
are instinct he attempted to introduce also into the
masque. More emphatically than any contemporary writer he held that it should be a vehicle not
only for amusement but also for instruction,—a
theory that was not likely to find a wide acceptance
with his patrons. King James and his eldest son
were among the few exceptions, and of them he is

---

[1] In 1619 Jonson told Drummond "That next himself, only Fletcher
[a mistake of Drummond's for Beaumont?] and Chapman could make a
Mask".

probably thinking when, in the short preface to his *Hymenæi* (1606), he describes "the most royal princes and greatest persons" as "curious after the most high and hearty inventions . . . and those grounded upon antiquity and solid learnings; which though their voice be taught to sound to present occasions, their sense or doth or should always lay hold on more removed mysteries". Again, in the preface to the Masque of Queens (1609), he tells us he has observed "that rule of the best artist to suffer no object of delight to pass without his mixture of profit and example"; and even as late as 1631, when the best days of the masque were over, in his prologue to *Love's Triumph through Callipolis*, he writes, "All representations, especially those of this nature in court, public spectacles, either have been, or ought to be, the mirrors of man's life, whose ends, for the excellence of their exhibitors (as being the donatives of great princes to their people), ought always to carry a mixture of profit with them no less than delight". Accordingly, in the *Masque of Queens* we are shown the discomfiture of "Ignorance, Suspicion, Credulity, etc.", in the persons of the twelve hags, by Heroic Virtue, and in *The Golden Age Restored* (1616), the Evils of the Iron Age, Avarice, Fraud, Slander, etc., are turned into statues at the sight of the shield of Pallas, the harbinger of Astræa and the Golden Age. But Jonson was too shrewd an observer of human nature to have had any great faith in the efficacy of a bare antithesis between virtue and vice, however elevated and poetical the language of the setting. As a satirist he had long ago made his mark, and the dreaded instrument lay ready to his hand: if Folly could not be made to blush, she might at least be made to wince, and he determined to make the antimasque the scourge. This expedient, too, solved a further difficulty: he was able to cater for the increasing demand for the humorous without compromising his own position. Already in 1614 in *Love Restored* he had ridiculed the Puritans under the character of Plutus, and in 1615 the Alchemists in *Mercury Vindicated*;[1] but from the masques of the next few years satire in any real sense is absent. We have already spoken of *The Golden Age Restored*, and in the antimasques of *The Vision of Delight* (1617), and *Pleasure reconciled to Virtue* (1618), the production of ludicrous effect seems to be the chief end to be attained. In *News from the New World discovered in the Moon* (1621), and in the best masques which follow it, satire again becomes the leading purpose of the antimasque. In this masque the newsmongers of the day are attacked, in *Time Vindicated to himself and to his Honours* George Wither, the author of "Abuses stript and whipt", is satirized under the name of Chronomastix, and in *The Fortunate Isles* the absurdities of the Rosicrucians are exposed. In the *Masque of Augurs* the antimasque itself does not escape: to the question, "What has all this to do with our mask?" Vangoose, "a rare artist and a projector of masques", replies, "O, sir, all de better vor an antick-mask, de more absurd it be, and vrom de purpose, it be ever all de better. If it go from de nature of de ting, it is de more

---

[1] He had previously done this effectively in *The Alchemist*, 1610.

art; for dere is art, and dere is nature, yow sall see."

By the masque writers who succeeded Jonson these precepts of Vangoose are only too faithfully carried out. The greater the absurdity of the anti-masques, and the more numerous they are, the better; "How many antimasques have they?" asks Fancy in Shirley's *Triumph of Peace* (1634), "of what nature? For these are fancies that take most; your dull and phlegmatic inventions are exploded; give me a nimble antimasque."[1] Even Jonson him-self, in his latter days, found it necessary to con-form to the prevailing fashion. In *Love's Triumph through Callipolis* (1631), written for a monarch less learned and less critical than the patron of his former masques, the admirable low-comedy intro-duction is abandoned, and is replaced by the brief, though still manly, prologue, to which we have already referred, while in *Chloridia*, a Queen's masque produced a month later, the antimasque is for the first time broken up into eight several "entries"—a device which, responding as it did to the increasing demand for pantomime, proved eminently successful, and continued to increase in popularity till at last in Davenant's *Salmacida Spolia* (1640) we have an antimasque consisting of no less than twenty.

The colossal learning displayed by Jonson in his masques has often been the subject of remark. In the words of Dryden, "He invades authors like a

---

[1] Middleton in his *Inner Temple Masque* (1619) has an amusing intro-duction ridiculing the belief in lucky and unlucky days; two antimasques follow, one of Candlemas Day, Shrove Tuesday, &c., and one of Good days, Bad days, and Indifferent days.

monarch, and what would be theft in other poets is
only victory in him". The elaborate notes appended
to some of the masques of which he himself super-
intended the printing, are evidence of the extraordinary extent of his reading. His *Hymenæi*,
written for the ill-omened marriage of the Earl of
Essex in 1606, shows his familiarity with all the
minutiæ of the Roman marriage ceremonial, while
from his Masque of Queens it is evident that at
one time or other he had ransacked the whole of
the literature of the black art, ancient and medi-
æval; as he says in his letter to Prince Henry prefixed to this masque, "Though it hath proved a
work of some difficulty to me to retrieve the particular authorities (according to your gracious command, and a desire born out of judgment) to those
things which I writ out of fulness and memory of
my former readings; yet now I have overcome it,
the reward that meets me is double to one act;
which is, that thereby your excellent understanding
will not only justify me to your own knowledge,
but decline the stiffness of other's original ignorance already armed to censure"—and a mass of
learned annotations is the result. It must be
admitted that allusions, which required so much
explanation to render them intelligible to the
reader, must have been quite lost upon the
majority of the spectators, and we are therefore
not surprised to find writers, whose scholarship was
of a less robust order, affecting, in "the stiffness
of their original ignorance", to despise such re-
condite accomplishments. "Whosoever strives",
says Daniel,

"to shew most wit about these Puntillos of Dreames and shews, are sure sick of a disease they cannot hide, and would fain have the world to think them very deeply learned in all mysteries whatsoever. . . . And let us labour to shew never so much skill or art, our weaknesses and ignorance will be seen, whatsoever covering we cast over it."[1]

And again,

"For these figures of mine, if they come not drawn in all proportions to the life of antiquity (from whose tyranny I see no reason why we may not emancipate our inventions, and be as free as they to use our own images), yet I know them such as were proper to the business, and discharged those parts for which they served with as good correspondency as our appointed limitations would permit".[2]

But to no one did the lofty pretensions of Jonson give greater umbrage than to his chief collaborator. Inigo Jones claimed for the artist who was responsible for the spectacular part of the masque a position of equal if not superior dignity to the poet who furnished the words, and to this claim Jonson sturdily refused to submit.[3] He was determined that, so far as in him lay, literature should not be degraded to the position of a mere adjunct to stage carpentry and scene-painting, and as long as King James lived he held his ground. In his earlier masques he was quite ready to accord a courteous acknowledgment to the services of his colleague: at the end of his *Hymenæi* he writes:—

[1] *Vision of the Twelve Goddesses.*   [2] *Tethys' Festival.*

[3] Other writers were more complacent; thus Daniel says, "In these things, wherein the only life consists in shew, the art and invention of the architect gives the greatest grace, and is of most importance; ours the least part, and of least note in the time of the performance thereof, and therefore have I intersected the description of the artificial part, which only speaks M. Inigo Jones". *Tethys' Festival.* Compare what Davenant says of Jones in the preface to *Salmacida Spolia.*

" The design and act of all which, together with the device of their habits, belong properly to the merit and reputation of Master Inigo Jones, whom I take modest occasion in this fit place to remember, lest his own worth might accuse me of an ignorant neglect from my silence".[1]

But differences more or less pronounced broke out between them, and it seems that for several years they ceased to work together. At any rate we have no evidence that they were both engaged in the production of any masque between *The Masque of Oberon* (1611) and *Time Vindicated* (1623), and that their relations during this period were the reverse of friendly is apparent from what Jonson told Drummond in 1619, " He said to Prince Charles of Inigo Jones, that when he wanted words to express the greatest villain in the world he would call him an Inigo " (*iniquo*). " Jones having accused him for naming him behind his back a fool, he denied it; but, says he, I said he was an arrant knave and I avouch it."[2] In 1631 the quarrel burst forth again, and this time with more disastrous consequences. The *casus belli* was paltry enough: the printed copies of the Twelfth Night and Shrovetide Masques of this year, viz. *Love's Triumph* and *Chloridia*, were ascribed on their title-pages to " The Inventors, Ben Jonson; Inigo Jones", and the latter, indignant at finding his name second instead of first, exerted his influence in high quarters so effectually that Jonson was not employed again upon the Court masques. Next year, to quote a contemporary letter:—

---

[1] 4to, 1606. It is significant that this passage is withdrawn from the folio of 1616. [2] *Conversations with William Drummond*, xvii.

"The inventor or poet . . . was Mr. Aurelian Townshend, sometime steward to the lord treasurer Salisbury; Ben Jonson being for this time discarded by reason of the predominant power of his antagonist, Inigo Jones, who this time twelve-month was angry with him for putting his own name before his in the title-page."[1]

Jonson retaliated in his fierce *Expostulation with Inigo Jones*, in the course of which the following rugged and uncompromising lines very plainly set forth his view of the masque as it became when his rival had his own way with it:

> "O shows, shows, mighty shows!
> The eloquence of masques! what need of prose,
> Or verse or prose t' express immortal you?
> You are the spectacles of state, 't is true,
> Court-hieroglyphics, and all arts afford,
> In the mere perspective of an inch-board;
> You ask no more than certain politic eyes,
> Eyes, that can pierce into the mysteries
> Of many colours, read them, and reveal
> Mythology, there printed on slit deal.
> Or to make boards to speak! there is a task!
> Painting and carpentry are the soul of masque.
> Pack with your peddling poetry to the stage,
> This is the money-got, mechanic age."

Townsend, Carew, Shirley and Davenant were henceforward the poets commissioned to write the Court masques. Two specimens have been printed in the present volume, and the reader will therefore be able to judge for himself as to the justice of Jonson's strictures.

We have already had occasion to remark that the seasons for the performance of Court masques were

[1] Mr. Pory to Sir Thomas Puckering, Bart., Jan. 12, 1632, printed in Gifford's Jonson ed. 1875, vol. i. p. cxxxii.

Christmas and Shrovetide.[1] The place was the Banqueting-house at Whitehall. This consisted of a large hall, with rooms beneath it used as government offices, and had been rebuilt in an improved style by James in 1607. On January 12th, 1619, it was burnt to the ground, and the building which still exists, and of which Inigo Jones was the architect, was erected in its place. The following extract from a contemporary letter is not without interest to us:—

" The unhappy accident that chanced at Whitehall last week by fire, you cannot but have heard of; but haply not the matter how,—which was this. A joiner was appointed to mend some things that were out of order in the device of the Masque [the Twelfth-night masque, 1619, perhaps by Sir John Maynard, but not now extant], which the king meant to have repeated on Shrovetide, who, having kindled a fire upon a false hearth to heat his glue-pot, the force thereof pierced soon, it seems, the single brick, and, in a short time that he absented himself upon some occasion, fastened upon the basis, which was of dry deal board underneath, which suddenly conceiving flame, gave fire to the device of the masque, all of oiled paper and dry fir, and so in a moment dispersed itself among the rest of that combustible matter, that it was past any man's approach almost before it was discovered. Two hours began and ended that woful sight."[2]

In the case of the Tudor masks it does not appear that the performance was confined to a stage at one end of the hall, and even in the Hampton Court

[1] The only masques represented at Whitehall at any other time were *Tethys' Festival*, June 5, 1610, in honour of the creation of the King's eldest son, Henry, Prince of Wales, and *The Masque of Augurs*, the Twelfth-night masque of 1622, which was repeated on May 6, in honour of the new Spanish ambassador, Don Carlos de Coloma.

[2] Mr. Lorkin to Sir Thomas Puckering, January 19, 1619, *apud* Nichols, iii. 523. The Shrovetide performance in question took place "in the Hall at Whitehall", *i.e.* the ordinary hall of the palace. *Ibid.* 527.

masque of 1604 the mountain from which the goddesses descended was erected at the lower end of
the hall, and the Temple of Peace at the upper.
But afterwards the lower, or minstrels' gallery, end
was occupied by the stage, while at the opposite end
on the dais was "the state", that is a canopy with
seats beneath it for the king and queen. Along
both sides of the hall ran scaffolding containing
seats for the accommodation of the courtiers and
others who had been lucky enough to gain admit-
tance. These would naturally be persons of rank
and position, but room was also found for a few
spectators of the middle class, and the privilege
was eagerly competed for by the citizens and their
wives. An amusing illustration of this will be
found in *Love Restored*, where Robin Goodfellow
gives a most graphic account of the many shifts
he had been put to in order to gain admission.
Many of the masques themselves contain elaborate
descriptions of the scenery, and therefore it is unnecessary to recapitulate them here. The machinery
employed for changing the scenes was brought to
a state of great perfection by Inigo Jones in the
Carolan masque; previously this purpose had ordi-
narily been effected by the fall of a "travers" or
curtain. In some cases, as in Campion's *Lords'
Masque*, when the lower part of the scene had to
be discovered before the upper, two traverses were
arranged one above the other, the upper one not
being withdrawn till it was time for the denizens
of the sky to appear. In Campion's masque of
December 26th, 1613, sometimes called the *Squires'
Masque*, the Proscenium consisted of "an arch

triumphal passing beautiful ", but commonly it was
a frieze resting on two pillars, and bearing the
name of the masque. At a lower level in front of
the stage, and communicating with it by steps, was
a platform for the dances, or at any rate "a parti-
tion for the dancing place".[1] It is possible that
only the set dances took place on this, and that the
" Revels" were danced in the body of the hall.

It would be no matter for astonishment if to
the majority of modern readers the masque were
simply known as a promising hunting-ground for
some of the most graceful lyrics of the seventeenth
century. A closer examination will show that
these lyrics are not merely graceful and charming
in themselves, but also strictly germane to the
business in hand. Although a second anti-masque
is sometimes introduced either after the "main"
dance or the Revels, the dramatic action of the
piece has served its purpose when it has led up
to the masquers, and it finds its climax in their
appearance. Something further is therefore required to fill up the necessary intervals between the
dances, while the dancers are resting, and this is
the function of the songs. It will be seen that
these songs are for the most part addressed to the
masquers, rehearsing their noble qualities, calling
upon them to take rest, or "exciting" them to
fresh efforts, while the concluding song warns them
of the approach of morning and summons them
away.[2] It must not be supposed, however, that the

[1] Shirley's *Triumph of Peace.* Campion's *Masque at Lord Hay's
marriage.*

[2] Compliments to royalty, and in the case of marriage masques, good
wishes to the bride and bridegroom are also common themes in the songs.

disposition and management of the lyric portion of
the masque proceed on any uniform rule. While it
is so contrived as to serve the purpose just indicated,
the utmost variety prevails in the details: sometimes the masque opens with a song; sometimes,
as in *Oberon* and *The Golden Age*, the lyrical element is predominant throughout,[1] while in *Lovers
Made Men* we have a foretaste of the opera of a
hundred years later, for "the whole masque was
sung after the Italian manner, *stylo recitativo*".

The performers in the anti-masque were profes-
sional actors engaged for the purpose: the masquers,
as already noticed, were personages of rank and
distinction. King James himself, who was not
remarkable for his personal graces, and who was
verging upon forty when he succeeded to the
English throne, was never ambitious of taking an
active part in these performances, but other members of the royal family delighted to do so. Queen
Anne, her sons Henry and Charles—the latter,
both before and after he became king, and Queen
Henrietta Maria, all appeared as masquers at various
times. Unfortunately no complete cast of the
speakers,—to be distinguished, it must not be forgotten, from the masquers,—in any masque survives,
but in all probability they were the ladies and
gentlemen of the Court.[2] The music, both vocal

[1] Compare also in this respect—*Love freed from Ignorance and Folly,
The Vision of Delight*, and *Pleasure reconciled to Virtue*.

[2] In the *Masque of Beauty* we are expressly told that the part of
Thamesis "was personated by master Thomas Giles, who made the
dances", and from a letter of Mr. John Pory to Sir Robert Cotton dated
January, 1606 (Nichols, ii. 33), it appears that Jonson himself acted the
part of Hymen in *Hymenæi*. Pory's words are, "Ben Jonson turned
the globe of earth, standing behind the altar".

and instrumental, was performed by the Court musicians,[1] assisted by the choir boys of the Chapel Royal, and sometimes also by those of St. Paul's. In the case of masques presented by the four Inns of Court, whether in their own halls or at Court, the masquers were of course members of the Society. All the four Inns combined for the presentation of the magnificent *Triumph of Peace* in 1634, and when they were associated in pairs, as was the case in 1613 for the presentation of the masques at the Princess Elizabeth's marriage, the Middle Temple combined with Lincoln's Inn, and the Inner Temple with Gray's Inn. An example of a masque presented by the members of one Inn alone is *The Masque of Flowers*, performed at the Earl of Somerset's marriage in 1614 by the gentlemen of Gray's Inn, and to the same society belongs *The Masque of Mountebanks*, performed in 1618. Entertainments of this kind were strictly in accordance with precedent, for many of the students belonged to some of the oldest and wealthiest families throughout the length and breadth of the country, and Christmas festivities on a costly scale had long been a tradition amongst them. An elaborate account of the festivities at Gray's Inn in 1595 under the authority of an elected potentate, called the Prince of Purpool, was printed in 1688

---

[1] These were a permanent body in the pay of the sovereign. In 1571 Elizabeth had 18 trumpeters, 7 violins, 6 flutes, 6 sackbuts and 10 musicians, *i.e.* singers or "musicians for the voice" (Treasurer of the Chamber's accounts in Collier, i. 193). In 1606 New-Year's gifts to James I. were presented by 26 musicians, each "one payre of perfumed playne gloves" (Nichols, i. 598), and in 1617 payment was made to 22 musicians (*Ibid.* 599).

under the title *Gesta Grayorum*.[1] They include
"a very stately mask", in which His Highness took
a prominent part, and his royal state was kept up
with much ceremony during the whole time the
holidays lasted. Masques of a less ambitious character than those in London were also performed
occasionally at the country-seats of the nobility.
Many, probably most, of these have not been preserved, but examples still extant are Marston's
*Lord and Lady Huntingdon's Entertainment of the
Countess of Derby* at Ashby-de-la-Zouch in 1607,
Campion's *Entertainment to the Queen at Cavers-
ham House* in 1613, and Cockayne's *Masque at
Bretby*, Derbyshire, in 1640. In the two former
instances the masque is an indoor sequel to an out-
door entertainment.

With the outbreak of the civil war the history
of the Masque comes to an end; but though dead
itself the traces of it remained. In the altered
conditions of the public stage after the Restoration
its influence is palpable at once: to the Whitehall
pageants of the previous generation may be ascribed
the movable scenes, the women actors, and, above
all, the development of the spectacular, at the
expense of the dramatic, element, which distinguished
the two Patent Houses from the pre-restoration
stage. Quite early in the century the experiment
had been tried of introducing a kind of miniature
masque into a stage-play, and when it was found
that this hit the popular taste the practice became

---

[1] Reprinted by Nichols, *Progresses of Queen Elizabeth*, vol. iii.,
together with *Gesta Grayorum*, part ii. (from a MS.), which contains
The Masque of Mountebanks.

more and more frequent.[1] Then when the theatres
were re-opened after the Puritan rule was over the
demand for scenic display burst forth with renewed
vigour, and operatic additions were resorted to in
order to make even the plays of Shakespeare attrac-
tive to a popular audience. We cannot therefore be
surprised that no serious effort was made to revive
the masque after the Restoration.[2] Its attractions
had been transferred to the theatre, and at the theatre
the king was now a constant attendant. Court performances were therefore no longer necessary, and
as for dancing, frequent balls, whether masked or
otherwise, helped the Whitehall of Charles the
Second to forget the more formal and stately performances of a bygone age.

In the preceding pages we have attempted to
sketch the history of a literary and artistic pheno-
menon unique in its kind. We have seen how from
a rude and inarticulate infancy it reached a short-
lived but splendid maturity, and we have indicated
the causes of its decline. Little more remains to be
said. Although it is on its literary side that the
masque is chiefly interesting to us at the present
day, yet we must not forget that its connection with

[1] Fletcher's *Women Pleased* and Shirley's *Cardinal* may be taken as
examples: the "vision" in the fourth act of *The Tempest* with its dance
of Reapers and Nymphs may also be compared. Soergel analyses one
or two of these "Dramenmasken", and well illustrates the purpose they
serve in relation to the plot of the play.

[2] In 1675 the daughters of the Duke of York and many of the young
nobility appeared in *Calisto*, a so-called masque by John Crowne. The
piece is in fact a five-act pastoral play, interspersed with "entries" of
Winds, Gipsies, Africans, &c., and preceded by a masque-like prologue,
in which "the Princesses and other Ladies danced several sarabands
with castanets. A minuet was also danced by his Grace the Duke of
Monmouth."

literature at all is only incidental, and that to bring
it to the test of a severe critical standard would be
as futile as it would be unfair.   Shortcomings were
inevitable and to be expected; the wonder is that
in spite of its limitations so much was achieved.
If the measure of dramatic success was considerable,
the capabilities of the alliance between poetry and
the sister arts have never been more happily exem-
plified.   The songs were worthy of the music, and
the music worthy of the songs, while the dances
were some of the most highly-finished performances
of the days when dancing was still a fine art and
had not yet forfeited its title to be called the poetry
of motion.

It is of course impossible that a bare printed
version of one of these complex entertainments can
ever fully conjure up for the imagination the magnificence of the actual spectacle; much of "the
glory of all these solemnities" has necessarily
"perished like a blaze and gone out in the
beholders' eyes":[1] but the reader who makes due
allowance for this drawback, and who bears in mind
the fact that the masque was written not to be read
but to be acted, may still feel the spell of its original
fascination.   Nor will he be disappointed if in the
majority of examples he fails to detect any deeper
purpose than the simple enjoyment of the moment.
With Jonson it is true—and to Jonson belong very
nearly half of the whole number of examples
remaining to us[2]—a lesson of some kind, seriously

---

[1] Jonson, Preface to *Hymenæi.*

[2] Of the fifty extant masques enumerated in the Appendix it will be
seen that Jonson contributes twenty-two, Campion and Davenant four

or humorously conveyed, is the rule. It was, as we have already seen, his ambition to "lay hold on more removed mysteries", and to combine instruction with amusement, but even he failed to act up to his standard consistently, and sometimes, as in *Oberon*, is content to give us a *tour de force* of pure lyrical enjoyment, or an unadulterated combination of the absurd and the picturesque, as in *The Vision of Delight*. Other writers are less anxious to instruct than to please. To say nothing of the Carolan writers, Campion—who, for the beauty of his lyrics, and, in spite of his rhymed decasyllables, often reminding us irresistibly of a modern burlesque, must be ranked next to Jonson as a masque-writer—with his love of transformation scenes, and his superb musical effects,[1] Beaumont, with his stately blank verse and beautiful imagery, and Chapman, with his humorous "induction" and poetic aspirations—all fall short of the Jonsonian ideal, and fail in a greater or less degree "to carry a mixture of profit with them no less than delight". But inferior as these writers are to the great master of their art, their defects need not blind us to their merits; in them, too, one great charm which the masque has for us moderns is sufficiently manifest. It is the expression of the exuberant light-heartedness of an age which had not yet paused to inquire whether it was right or wise to make enjoyment an end in itself. We feel that there is inherent in the

each, Daniel and Townsend two each, and the rest only one apiece, while five are anonymous.

[1] Campion was himself a skilled musician, and the musical reader should turn to his *Masque at Lord Hay's marriage*, an example perhaps unsurpassed for the richness and variety of its musical combinations.

masque a freshness, an *abandon*, a total absence of
self-consciousness, which must have been stifled in
the cynical atmosphere of the court of the Restoration. The world was still young, but the great
Puritan wave swept over the land, carrying away
with it things evil and good, and the masque disap-
peared for ever.

APPENDIX.

APPENDIX.

CHRONOLOGICAL LIST OF MASQUES EXTANT IN PRINT. 1604-1640.

Date of Production.	Author.	Masque.		Date and Particulars of Publication.
1604	Daniel	The Vision of the twelve goddesses	1604 4to	Edward Allde. London.
1605	Jonson	The masque of Blackness	[1608] 4to	The characters of two royall Masques. Imprinted at London for Thomas Thorp.
1606	Jonson	Hymenæi	1606 4to	Hymenæi: or the solemnities of Masque and Barriers. At London. Printed by Valentine Sims for Thomas Thorp.
1607	Campion	Masque in honour of the Lord Hay and his bride	1607 4to	London. Imprinted by John Windet for John Brown.
1607	Marston	Lord and Lady Huntingdon's entertainment of the countess of Derby	1801 8vo	Printed in the fifth volume of Todd's Milton.
1608	Jonson	The masque of Beauty	[1608] 4to	With the masque of Blackness as above.
1608	Jonson	Masque at the marriage of Viscount Haddington	[1608] 4to	No date, place, or printer's name.
1609	Jonson	The masque of Queens	1609 4to	London. Printed by Nicholas Okes.
1610	Daniel	Tethys' festival, or the Queen's wake	1610 4to	Printed, with the order of the creation of Prince Henry Prince of Wales, &c., for John Budge.
1611	Jonson	Oberon, the Fairy Prince	1616 fol.	London. Printed by W. Stansby, in The Workes of Benjamin Jonson.

[1611]	Jonson	Love freed from Ignorance and Folly	1616	fol.	London. Printed by W. Stansby, in The Workes of Benjamin Jonson.
[1611]	Anon.	The masque of the Twelve Months	1848	8vo	Printed, with Cunningham's Life of Inigo Jones, for the Shakespeare Society.
1613	Campion	The Lords' masque	1613	4to	London. Printed, with the Entertaiment at Caversham House, for John Budge.
1613	Chapman	The masque of the Middle Temple and Lincoln's Inn	[1613]	4to	Printed by F. K. for George Norton, London.
1613	Beaumont	The masque of the Inner Temple and Gray's Inn	[1613]	4to	Imprinted by F. K. for George Norton, London.
1613	Campion	Entertainment to the Queen at Caversham House	1613	4to	With the Lords' masque as above.
[1613]	Jonson	Love restored	1616	fol.	London. Printed by W. Stansby, in The Workes of Benjamin Jonson.
1613	Campion	Masque at the marriage of the Earl of Somerset	1614	4to	London. Printed by E. A. for Laurence Lisle.
1613	Jonson	The Irish Masque	1616	fol.	London. Printed by W. Stansby, in The Workes of Benjamin Jonson.
1614	Anon.	The masque of Flowers	1614	4to	London. Printed by N. O. for Robert Wilson,
[1615]	Jonson	Mercury vindicated from the Alchemists	1616	fol.	London. Printed by W. Stansby, in The Workes of Benjamin Jonson.
1616	Jonson	The Golden Age restored	1616	fol.	London. Printed by W. Stansby, in The Workes of Benjamin Jonson.
1617	Jonson	The Vision of Delight	1640	fol.	Printed in the second volume of The Workes of Benjamin Jonson.
[1617]	Browne	Inner Temple masque	1772	8vo	Printed in the third volume of The Works of William Browne
1617	Jonson	Lovers made Men	1617	4to	No place or printer's name.
1617	White	Cupid's Banishment	1828	4to	Printed in the third volume of Nichols's Progresses of James I.
1618	Anon.	The masque of Mountebanks	1805	4to	Printed in the third volume of Nichols's Progresses of Queen Elizabeth.

CHRONOLOGICAL LIST OF MASQUES—*Continued.*

Date of Production.	Author	Masque.		Date and Particulars of Publication.
1618	Jonson	Pleasure reconciled to Virtue	1640 fol.	Printed in the second volume of The Workes of Benjamin Jonson.
1619	Middleton	The Inner Temple masque, or masque of Heroes	1619 4to	London. Printed for John Browne.
1621	Jonson	News from the new World discovered in the Moon	1640 fol.	Printed in the second volume of The Workes of Benjamin Jonson.
1622	Jonson	The masque of Augurs	[1622] 4to	No date, place, or printer's name.
1623	Jonson	Time vindicated to himself and to his Honours	1640 fol.	Printed in the second volume of The Workes of Benjamin Jonson.
[1623]	Jonson	Pan's Anniversary, or the Shepherds' Holiday	1640 fol.	Printed in the second volume of The Workes of Benjamin Jonson.
1624	Jonson	Neptune's Triumph for the return of Albion	[1624] 4to	No date, place, or printer's name.
[1625]	Jonson	The Fortunate Isles and their Union	[1624] 4to	No date, place, or printer's name.
1631	Jonson	Love's Triumph through Callipolis.	1631 4to	Printed by I. N. for T. Walkley, London.
1631	Jonson	Chloridia: Rites to Chloris and her Nymphs	[1631] 4to	Printed for T. Walkley, London.
1632	Townsend	Albion's Triumph	1632 4to	London. Printed by A. Mathewes for Robert Allet.
1632	Townsend	Tempe restored	1632 4to	London. Printed by A. M. for Robert Allet and George Baker.
1634	Shirley	The Triumph of Peace	1634 4to	London. Printed by John Norton for William Cooke.

1634	Carew	Coelum Britannicum	4to	London.	Printed for Thomas Walkley.
1635	Davenant	The Temple of Love	4to	London.	Printed for Thomas Walkley.
1636	Davenant	The Triumphs of the Prince d'Amour	4to	London.	Printed for Richard Meighen.
1636	Kynaston	Corona Minervæ	4to	London.	Printed for William Sheares.
1636	Anon.	The King and Queen's Entertainment at Richmond	4to	Oxford	Printed by Leonard Lichfield.
1638	Davenant	Britannia Triumphans	4to	London.	Printed by John Haviland for Thomas Walkley.
1638	Anon.	Luminalia, or the Festival of Light	4to	London.	Printed by John Haviland for Thomas Walkley.
1638	Nabbes	A Presentation intended for the Prince's Birthday	4to	London.	Printed [with other poems] by J. D. for Charles Greene.
1658	Cockayne	Masque at Bretby	8vo		Printed in A Chain of Golden Poems by W.G., and are to be sold by Isaac Pridmore.
1640	Davenant	Salmacida Spolia	4to	London.	Printed by T. H. for Thomas Walkley.

** The above is intended to be a complete list of all the Masques, properly so called, from 1604 to 1640, which are still accessible in print. The date in the fourth column is of course that of first printing. Reprints will be found in the collected works of the several authors, whose works have been published collectively.

ENGLISH MASQUES.

I.

SAMUEL DANIEL.
(1562–1619.)

THE VISION OF THE TWELVE GODDESSES,

PRESENTED IN A MASK THE EIGHTH OF JANUARY [1604]
AT HAMPTON COURT, BY THE QUEEN'S MOST
EXCELLENT MAJESTY, AND HER LADIES.

[Owing to the prevalence of the plague in London, the king kept the
first Christmas after his accession at Hampton Court. Sir Thomas
Edmonds, who was with the Court, writes to the Earl of Shrewsbury,
Dec. 23, 1603: "Both the K.' and Q.' Majesties have an humor to
have some Masks this Christmas time; and therefore, for that purpose,
both the younge Lordes and chief Gentlemen of one *parte*, and the
Queene and her Ladyes of the other *parte*, doe severallie undertake
the accomplishing and furnishing thereof; and because theer is use of
invention therein, speciall choice is made of Mr Sanford to dyrect the
order and course of the Ladyes". If this means that the lords and
gentlemen were preparing a separate masque of their own, it has not
been preserved. The present masque, although it has little to recommend
it from a literary point of view, is animated by a genuine spirit of patriot-
ism, and is besides interesting as the earliest complete example which
has come down to us. For the arrangement of the scenery, see Introduction, p. l.]

TO THE RIGHT HONOURABLE THE LADY LUCY,
COUNTESS OF BEDFORD.
Madam.

IN respect of the unmannerly presumption of an indiscreet
printer,[1] who without warrant hath divulged the late show

[1] Edward Allde, 1604.—This letter is prefixed to the authorized edition
which Daniel himself published in the same year, and which was printed

at Court, presented the eighth of January, by the Queen's Majesty and her Ladies, and the same very disorderly set forth: I thought it not amiss, seeing it would otherwise pass abroad, to the prejudice both of the Mask and the invention, to describe the whole form thereof in all points as it was then performed, and as the world well knows very worthily performed, by a most magnificent Queen, whose heroical spirit and bounty only gave it so fair an execution as it had. Seeing also that these ornaments and delights of peace are, in their season, as fit to entertain the world, and deserve to be made memorable as well as the graver actions,—both of them concurring to the decking and furnishing of glory, and Majesty, as the necessary complements requisite for State and Greatness.

And therefore first I will deliver the intent and scope of the project: which was only to present the figure of those blessings, with the wish of their increase and continuance, which this mighty Kingdom now enjoys by the benefit of his most gracious Majesty, by whom we have this glory of peace, with the accession of so great state and power. And to express the same, there were devised twelve Goddesses, under whose images former times have represented the several gifts of heaven, and erected temples, altars, and figures unto them, as unto divine powers, in the shape and name of women. As unto *Juno* the Goddess of empire and *regnorum praesidi*, they attributed that blessing of power: to *Pallas*, wisdom and defence: to *Venus*, love and amity: to *Vesta*, religion: to *Diana*, the gift of chastity: to *Proserpina*, riches: to *Macaria*, felicity: to *Concordia*, the union of hearts: *Astraea*, justice: *Flora*, the beauties of the earth: *Ceres*, plenty: to *Tethys*, power by sea.

in 12mo by T. C. for Simon Waterson. Allde's pirated edition is referred to by the Earl of Worcester writing to the Earl of Shrewsbury, Feb. 2, 1604: "Whereas youer Lo. saythe youe wear never perticulerly advertised of the Maske, I have been at 6d charge wth youe to send youe the booke, wch wyll inform youe better then I can, having noted the names of the Ladyes applyed to eche Goddes; and for the other, I would lykewyse have sent youe the ballet, yf I could have got yt for the money; but these bookes, as I heare, are all cawled in, and in truth I wyll not take uppon mee to set that downe wchj wyser then myself doe not understand".

And though these images have oftentimes divers significations, yet it being not our purpose to represent them with all those curious and superfluous observations, we took them only to serve as hieroglyphics for our present intention, according to some one property that fitted our occasion, without observing other their mystical interpretations, wherein the authors themselves are so irregular and confused,—as the best mythologers, who will make somewhat to seem any thing, are so unfaithful to themselves,—as they have left us no certain way at all, but a tract of confusion to take our course at adventure. And therefore owing no homage to their intricate observations, we were left at liberty to take no other knowledge of them, than fitted our present purpose, nor were tied by any laws of heraldry to range them otherwise in their precedences, than they fell out to stand with the nature of the matter in hand. And in these cases it may well seem *ingenerosum sapere solum ex commentariis quasi maiorum inventa industriae nostrae viam praecluserint, quasi in nobis effoeta sit vis naturae, nihil ex se parere*, or that there can be nothing done authentical, unless we observe all the strict rules of the book.

And therefore we took their aptest representations that lay best and easiest for us. And first presented the hieroglyphic of empire and dominion, as the ground and ma``ᵗᵗᵉʳ`` whereon this glory of state is built; then those blessings, and beauties that preserve and adorn it: as armed policy, love, religion, chastity, wealth, happiness, concord, justice, flourishing seasons, plenty, and lastly power by sea, as to imbound and circle the greatness of dominion by land.

And to this purpose were these Goddesses thus presented in their proper and several attires, bringing in their hands the particular figures of their power which they gave to the Temple of Peace, erected upon four pillars, representing the four Virtues that supported a globe of the earth.

I

Juno in a sky-colour mantle embroidered with gold, and figured with peacocks' feathers, wearing a crown of gold on her head, presents a sceptre.

2

Pallas (which was the person her Majesty chose to represent) was attired in a blue mantle, with a silver embroidery of all weapons and engines of war, with a helmet-dressing on her head, and presents a lance and target.

3

Venus, in a mantle of dove-colour, and silver, embroidered with doves, presented (instead of her *cestus*[1]) the girdle of amity,—a scarf of divers colours.

4

Vesta, in a white mantle embroidered with gold-flames, with a dressing like a nun, presented a burning lamp in one hand, and a book in the other.

5

Diana, in a green mantle embroidered with silver half-moons, and a croissant of pearl on her head, presents a bow and a quiver.

6

Proserpina, in a black mantle embroidered with gold-flames, with a crown of gold on her head, presented a mine of gold-ore.

7

Macaria, the Goddess of felicity, in a mantle of purple and silver, embroidered with the figures of Plenty and Wisdom (which concur to the making of true happiness), presents a *caduceum*[2] with the figure of abundance.

8

Concordia, in a party-coloured mantle of crimson and white (the colours of *England* and *Scotland* joined) embroidered with silver hands-in-hand, with a dressing likewise of party-coloured roses, a branch whereof in a wreath or knot she presented.

---

[1] Girdle: the word was specially used of the girdle of Venus.
[2] A herald's staff.

9

Astraea, in a mantle crimson, with a silver embroidery, figuring the sword and balance as the characters of justice which she presented.

10

Flora, in a mantle of divers colours, embroidered with all sorts of flowers, presents a pot of flowers.

11

Ceres, in straw colour and silver embroidery, with ears of corn, and a dressing of the same, presents a sickle.

12

Tethys, in a mantle of sea-green, with a silver embroidery of waves, and a dressing of reeds, presents a trident.

Now for the introducing this show: it was devised that the *Night* represented in a black vesture set with stars, should arise from below, and come towards the upper end of the Hall: there to waken her son *Somnus*, sleeping in his cave, as the proem to the Vision. Which figures when they are thus presented in human bodies,—as all virtues, vices, passions, knowledges, and whatsoever abstracts else in imagination are, which we would make visible,—we produce them using human actions; and even sleep itself (which might seem improperly to exercise waking motions) hath been often showed us in that manner, with speech and gesture. As for example:

> *Excussit tandem sibi se; cubitoque levatus*
> *Quid veniat (cognovit enim) scitatur.*

> *Intanto sopravenne, e gli occhi chiuse*
> *A i signori, ed a i sergenti il pigro Sonno.*

And in another place:

> *Il Sonno viene, e sparso il corpo stanco*
> *Col ramo intimo nel liquor di Lethe.*

So there, *Sleep* is brought in as a body, using speech and motion: and it was no more improper in this form to make

him walk, and stand, or speak, than it is to give voice or
passion to dead men, ghosts, trees, and stones: and therefore in such matters of shows, these like characters (in what
form soever they be drawn) serve us but to read the intention
of what we would represent: as in this project of ours, *Night*
and *Sleep* were to produce a Vision, an effect proper to their
power, and fit to shadow our purpose; for that these apparitions and shows are but as imaginations and dreams that
portend our affections, and dreams are never in all points
agreeing right with waking actions: and therefore were they
aptest to shadow whatsoever error might be herein presented.
And therefore was *Sleep* (as he is described by *Philostratus
in Amphirai imagine*) apparelled in a white thin vesture cast
over a black, to signify both the day and the night, with
wings of the same colour, a garland of poppy on his head;
and instead of his ivory and transparent horn, he was showed
bearing a black wand in the left hand, and a white in the
other, to effect either confused or significant dreams, according to that invocation of *Statius*,

> ——*Nec te totas infundere pennas*
> *Luminibus compello meis, hoc turba precatur,*
> *Laetior extremo me tange cacumine virgae.*

And also agreeing to that of *Sil. Ital.*,

> ——*Tangens Lethea tempora virga.*

And in this action did he here use his white wand, as to
infuse significant visions to entertain the spectators, and so
made them seem to see there a Temple, with a *Sibylla*
therein attending upon the sacrifices; which done, *Iris* (the
messenger of *Juno*) descends from the top of a Mountain
raised at the lower end of the Hall, and marching up to the
Temple of Peace, gives notice to the *Sibylla* of the coming
of the Goddesses, and withal delivers her a prospective[1],
wherein she might behold the figures of their Deities, and
thereby describe them; to the end that at their descending,
there might be no stay or hindrance of their motion, which
was to be carried without any interruption to the action of

---

[1] Spy-glass.

other entertainments that were to depend one of another
during the whole show: and that the eyes of the spectators
might not beguile their ears, as in such cases it ever happens,
whiles pomp and splendour of the sight takes up all the intention without regard what is spoken, and therefore was it
thought fit their descriptions should be delivered by the
Sibylla.

Which as soon as she had ended, the three *Graces* in silver
robes with white torches, appeared on the top of the Mountain, descending hand in hand before the Goddesses; who
likewise followed three and three, as in a number dedicated
unto sanctity and an incorporeal nature, whereas the *dual,
hieroglyphicè pro immundis accipitur.* And between every
rank of Goddesses, marched three Torch-bearers in the like
several colours, their heads and robes all decked with stars;
and in their descending, the cornets sitting in the concaves
of the Mountain, and seen but to their breasts, in the habit
of *Satyrs,* sounded a stately march, which continued until
the Goddesses were approached just before the Temple, and
then ceased, when the consort music (placed in the *cupola*
thereof, out of sight) began: whereunto the three *Graces*
retiring themselves aside, sang; whiles the Goddesses one
after another with solemn pace ascended up into the Temple,
and delivering their presents to the *Sibylla* (as it were but in
passing by) returned down into the midst of the Hall, preparing themselves to their dance; which (as soon as the
Graces had ended their Song) they began to the music of the
viols and lutes placed on one side of the Hall.

Which dance being performed with great majesty and art,
consisting of divers strains framed unto motions circular,
square, triangular, with other proportions exceeding rare and
full of variety; the Goddesses made a pause, casting themselves into a circle, whilst the *Graces* again sang to the music
of the Temple, and prepared to take out the Lords to dance.
With whom after they had performed certain measures[1],
galliards[2], and corantos[3], *Iris* again comes and gives notice

[1] Slow, stately dances.
[2] A lively dance with a hopping step.
[3] Another lively dance with a gliding step, also called a *courant.*

of their pleasure to depart: whose speech ended, they drew themselves again into another short dance with some few pleasant changes, still retiring them toward the foot of the Mountain, which they ascended in that same manner as they came down, whilst the cornets taking their notes from the ceasing of the music below, sounded another delightful march.

And thus, Madam, have I briefly delivered both the reason and manner of this Mask; as well to satisfy the desire of those who could not well note the carriage of these passages, by reason (as I said) the present pomp and splendour entertained them otherwise (as that which is most regardful in these shows); wherein (by the unpartial opinion of all the beholders, strangers and others) it was not inferior to the best that ever was presented in Christendom: as also to give up my account hereof unto your Honour, whereby I might clear the reckoning of any imputation that might be laid upon your judgment, for preferring such a one to her Majesty in this employment, as could give no reason for what was done.

And for the captious censurers, I regard not what they can say, who commonly can do little else but say; and if their deep judgments ever serve them to produce any thing, they must stand on the same stage of censure with other men, and peradventure perform no such great wonders as they would make us believe: and I comfort my self in this, that in Court I know not any under him who acts the greatest parts, that is not obnoxious to envy and a sinister interpretation. And whosoever strives to show most wit about these punctilios of dreams and shows, are sure sick of a disease they cannot hide, and would fain have the world to think them very deeply learned in all mysteries whatsoever. And peradventure they think themselves so, which if they do, they are in a far worse case than they imagine; *Non potest non indoctus esse qui se doctum credit.* And let us labour to show never so much skill or art, our weaknesses and ignorance will be seen, whatsoever covering we cast over it. And yet in these matters of shows (though they be that which most entertain the world) there needs no such exact sufficiency in this kind; for, *Ludit istis animus, non proficit.* And therefore, Madam, I will no longer

idly hold you therein, but refer you to the speeches, and so to
your better delights, as one who must ever acknowledge myself especially bound unto your Honour.   SAM. DANIEL.

The *Night* represented, in a black vesture set with stars, comes
and wakens her son *Somnus* (sleeping in his cave) with this speech.

A WAKE, dark *Sleep*, rouse thee from out this cave:
   Thy mother *Night* that bred thee in her womb
   And fed thee first with silence and with ease,
Doth here thy shadowing operations crave:
   And therefore wake, my son, awake and come;
     Strike with thy horny wand the spirits of these
     That here expect some pleasing novelties,
And make their slumber to beget strange sights,
   Strange visions and unusual properties
Unseen of later ages, ancient rites
   Of gifts divine, wrapt up in mysteries.
Make this to seem a Temple in their sight,
   Whose main support, holy Religion frame;
And *Wisdom, Courage, Temperance* and *Right*
   Make seem the pillars that sustain the same.
Shadow some *Sibyl* to attend the rites,
   And to describe the Powers that shall resort,
With th' interpretation of the benefits
   They bring in clouds, and what they do import.
Yet make them to portend the true desire
   Of those that wish them waking, real things:
Whilst I will hov'ring, here aloof retire
   And cover all things with my sable wings.

Somnus.

Dear mother *Night*, I your commandement
   Obey, and dreams t' interpret dreams will make,

As waking curiosity is wont;
  Though better dream asleep, than dream awake.
And this white horny wand shall work the deed,
  Whose power doth figures of the light present;
When[1] from this sable *radius*[2] doth proceed
  Nought but confused shows, to no intent.
Be this a Temple; there *Sibylla* stand,
Preparing reverent rites with holy hand.
And so, bright visions, go, and entertain
All round about, whilst I 'll to sleep again.

Iris, the messenger of the Goddesses descending from the Mount, where they were assembled (decked like the rainbow), spake as followeth.

I the daughter of Wonder (now made the messenger of Power) am here descended, to signify the coming of a celestial presence of Goddesses, determined to visit this fair Temple of Peace, which holy hands and devout desires have dedicated to unity and concord. And leaving to show themselves any more in *Samos, Ida, Paphos,* their ancient delighting places of *Greece,* and *Asia,* made now the seats of barbarism and spoil, vouchsafe to recreate themselves upon this *Western Mount of mighty Brittany,* the land of civil music and of rest; and are pleased to appear in the self-same figures, wherein antiquity hath formerly clothed them, and as they have been cast in the imagination of piety, who hath given mortal shapes to the gifts and effects of an eternal power; for that those beautiful characters of sense were easier to be read than their mystical *ideas,* dispersed in that wide, and incomprehensible volume of Nature.

And well have mortal men apparelled all the *Graces,* all the *Blessings,* all *Virtues* with that shape wherein

---

[1] Whereas.   [2] Wand.

themselves are much delighted, and which work the best motions, and best represent the beauty of heavenly Powers.

And therefore reverend Prophetess, that here attendest upon the devotions of this Place, prepare thy self for those rites that appertain to thy function, and the honour of such Deities; and to the end thou mayest have a fore-notion what Powers, and who they are that come, take here this prospective, and herein note and tell what thou seest: for well mayest thou there observe their shadows, but their presence will bereave thee of all, save admira-tion and amazement, for who can look upon such Powers and speak? And so I leave thee.

Sibylla, decked as a nun in black upon white, having received this message, and the prospective, useth these words.

What have I seen? where am I? or do I see all? or am I anywhere? was this *Iris*, (the messenger of *Juno*) or else but a phantasm or imagination? will the divine Goddesses vouchsafe to visit this poor Temple? Shall I be blest to entertain so great Powers? it can be but a dream: yet so great Powers have blest as humble roofs, and use, out of no other respect than their own graceful-ness, to shine where they will. But what prospective is this? or what shall I herein see? Oh, admirable Powers! what sights are these?

Juno.

First here imperial *Juno* in her chair,
　　With sceptre of command for kingdoms large,
Descends all clad in colours of the air,
　　Crown'd with bright stars, to signify her charge.

Pallas.

Next war-like *Pallas* in her helmet drest,
   With lance of winning, target of defence,
In whom both wit and courage are expressed,
   To get with glory, hold with providence.

Venus.

Then lovely *Venus* in bright majesty
   Appears with mild aspect, in dove-like hue:
With th' all combining scarf of amity,
   T' engird strange nations with affections true.

Vesta.

Next holy *Vesta* with her flames of zeal
   Presents herself, clad in white purity,
Whose book the soul's sweet comfort doth reveal
   By the ever-burning lamp of piety.

Diana.

Then chaste *Diana*, in her robes of green,
   With weapons of the wood herself addrests[1]
To bless the forests, where her power is seen,
   In peace with all the world, but savage beasts.

Proserpina.

Next rich *Proserpina*, with flames of gold,
   Whose state although within the earth, yet she
Comes from above, and in her hand doth hold
   The mine of wealth with cheerful majesty.

Macaria.

Then all in purple Robes, rich *Happiness*
   Next her appears, bearing in either hand

---

[1] Addresses, prepares; formed as if the word came from a verb *ad-rest*, for the sake of the rhyme.

Th' Ensigns both of wealth and wits,[1] t' express
    That by them both her majesty doth stand.

Concordia.

Next all in party-coloured robes appears,
    In white and crimson, graceful *Concord* drest
With knots of union, and in hand she bears
    The happy joined roses of our rest.

Astraea.

Clear-eyed *Astraea*, next, with reverend brow
    Clad in celestial hue, which best she likes,
Comes with her balance, and her sword to show
    That first her judgment weighs before it strikes.

Flora.

Then cheerful *Flora*, all adorn'd with flowers,
    Who clothes the earth with beauty and delight
In thousand sundry suits, whilst shining hours
    Will scarce afford a darkness to the night.

Ceres.

Next plenteous *Ceres* in her harvest weed,
    Crown'd with th' increase of what she gave to keep
To gratitude and faith: in whom we read,
    Who sows on virtue shall with glory reap.

Tethys.

Lastly comes *Tethys*, *Albion's* fairest love,
    Whom she in faithful arms doth deign t' embrace
And brings the trident of her power, t' approve
    The kind respect she hath to do him grace.

    Thus have I read their shadows, but behold!
    In glory where they come as Iris *told.*

[1] Viz. the figure of abundance and the caduceum.

The *Graces* march before the *Goddesses*, descending down the
Mountain with loud music, and coming up to the upper end, stay
and sing this song, whilst the *Goddesses* go up to the Temple with
presents, and from thence march down the Hall.

Gratia sunt dantium, reddentium, et promerentium.

1

Desert, Reward, and Gratitude,
   The *Graces* of society,
Do here with hand in hand conclude
   The blessed chain of amity:
      For we deserve, we give, we thank:
      Thanks, Gifts, Deserts, thus join in rank.

2

We yield the splendent rays of light
   Unto these blessings that descend:
The grace whereof with more delight
   The well disposing doth commend;
      Whilst Gratitude, Rewards, Deserts,
      Please, win, draw on, and couple hearts.

3

For worth and power and due respect,
   Deserves, bestows, returns with grace
The meed, reward, the kind effect,[1]
   That give the world a cheerful face,
      And turning in this course of right,
      Make virtue move with true delight.

[1] Worth deserves the meed, power bestows reward, due respect returns
with grace the kind effect.

The Song being ended, and the *Maskers* in the midst of the Hall, disposing themselves to their dance: *Sibylla* having placed their several presents on the altar, uttereth these words.

O Powers of powers, grant to our vows we pray,
　That these fair blessings which we now erect
In figures left us here, in substance may
　Be those great props of glory and respect.
Let kingdoms large, let armed policy,
　Mild love, true zeal, right shooting at the white
Of brave designs: let wealth, felicity,
　　Justice, and concord, pleasure, plenty, might
　　　And power by sea, with grace proportionate,
　　　Make glorious both the Sovereign and his State.

After this the *Maskers* danced their own measures, which being ended, and they are ready to take out the Lords, the three *Graces* sang.

　　Whiles worth with honour make their choice
　　　For measured motions ordered right,
　　Now let us likewise give a voice
　　　Unto the touch of our delight.

　　For comforts lock'd up without sound
　　　Are th' unborn children of the thought:
　　Like unto treasures never found
　　　That buried low are left forgot.

　　Where words our glory do not show,
　　　There like brave actions without fame,
　　It seems as plants not set to grow,
　　　Or as a tomb without a name.

The *Maskers* having ended their dancing with the Lords, *Iris* gives warning of their departure.

Iris.

As I was the joyful messenger to notify the coming, so am I now the same of the departure of these divine

Powers. Who having clothed themselves with these appearances, do now return back again to the spheres of their own being from whence they came. But yet, of my self, this much I must reveal,—though against the warrant of a messenger, who I know had better to fail in obedience than in presumption,—that these Deities by the motion of the all-directing *Pallas*, the glorious Patroness of this mighty Monarchy, descending in the majesty of their invisible essence upon yonder Mountain, found there the best, (and most worthily the best) of LADIES disporting with her choicest attendants, whose forms they presently undertook, as delighting to be in the best-built-temples of beauty and honour; and in them vouchsafed to appear in this manner, being otherwise no objects for mortal eyes. And no doubt, but that in respect of the persons under whose beautiful coverings they have thus presented themselves, these Deities will be pleased, the rather at their invocation, (knowing all their desires to be such) as evermore to grace this glorious Monarchy with the real effects of these blessings represented.

After this, they fell to a short departing dance, and so ascended the Mountain in the same order as they came down.

BEN JONSON.

(1572–1637.)

THE DESCRIPTION OF THE MASQUE WITH THE NUPTIAL
SONGS, AT THE LORD VISCOUNT HADDINGTON'S
MARRIAGE AT COURT [WHITEHALL], ON THE SHROVE-
TUESDAY [FEBRUARY 9] AT NIGHT, 1608.

[In his masque written for the ill-starred marriage of the Earl of
Essex in 1606, Jonson had shown how the subject could be dignified by
the sustained use of classical imagery and allusions. Here he is less
severe, and the result is the most graceful wedding-masque ever produced.
In both masques the marriage is kept prominently in view throughout,
and in this respect they may be contrasted with the treatment of the
same theme by other writers in Nos. VI., VII., and VIII. The bridegroom, Sir John Ramsey, afterwards Viscount Haddington and Earl of
Holderness, had been chiefly instrumental in rescuing the king from the
treasonable attempt of John Ruthven, third Earl of Gowrie, and his
brother Alexander, in 1600. The bride was Elizabeth, daughter of
Robert Ratcliffe, fifth Earl of Sussex. Gifford called this masque "The
Hue and Cry after Cupid".]

THE worthy custom of honouring worthy marriages with
these noble solemnities hath of late years advanced
itself frequently with us; to the reputation no less of our
Court than Nobles: expressing besides (through the diffi-
culties of expense and travail, with the cheerfulness of under-
taking) a most real affection in the personaters to those for
whose sake they would sustain these persons. It behoves
then us, that are trusted with a part of their honour in these
celebrations, to do nothing in them beneath the dignity of
either. With this preposed part of judgment I adventure to
give that abroad which in my first conception I intended
honourably fit: and though it hath laboured since under
censure, I—that know truth to be always of one stature, and
so like a rule, as who bends it the least way must needs do
an injury to the right—cannot but smile at their tyrannous

ignorance that will offer to slight me (in these things being an artificer) and give themselves a peremptory licence to judge, who have never touched so much as to the bark, or utter shell of any knowledge. But their daring dwell with them. They have found a place to pour out their follies; and I a seat to sleep out the passage.

The scene to this Masque was a high, steep, red cliff, advancing itself into the clouds, figuring the place, from whence (as I have been, not fabulously, informed) the honourable family of the Radcliffs first took their name, *a clivo rubro*, and is to be written with that orthography; as I have observed out of M. Camden, in his mention of the Earls of Sussex. This cliff was also a note of height, greatness, and antiquity. Before which, on the two sides, were erected two pilasters, charged with spoils and trophies of Love and his Mother, consecrate to marriage: amongst which were old and young persons figured, bound with roses; the wedding garments, rocks[1] and spindles, hearts transfixed with arrows, others flaming, virgins' girdles, gyrlonds, and worlds of such like; all wrought round and bold: and over head two personages, Triumph and Victory, in flying postures, and twice so big as the life, in place of the arch, and holding a gyrlond of myrtle for the key. All which, with the pillars, seemed to be of burnished gold, and embossed out of the metal. Beyond the cliff was seen nothing but clouds, thick and obscure; till on the sudden, with a solemn music, a bright sky breaking forth, there were discovered first two doves, then two swans with silver geers, drawing forth a triumphant chariot; in which Venus sat, crowned with her star, and beneath her the three Graces, or Charites, Aglaia, Thalia, Euphrosyne, all attired according to their antique figures. These, from their chariot, alighted on the top of the cliff, and descending by certain abrupt and winding passages, Venus having left her star only flaming in her seat, came to the earth, the Graces throwing gyrlonds all the way, and began to speak.

Venus. It is no common cause, ye will conceive, My lovely Graces, makes your goddess leave

---

[1] Distaffs.

Her state in heaven to-night to visit earth.
Love late is fled away, my eldest birth,
Cupid, whom I did joy to call my son;
And, whom long absent, Venus is undone.
Spy, if you can, his footsteps on this green;
For here, as I am told, he late hath been,
With divers of his brethren,[1] lending light
From their best flames, to gild a glorious night;
Which I not grudge at, being done for her,
Whose honours to mine own I still prefer.
But he not yet returning, I'm in fear
Some gentle Grace or innocent Beauty here
Be taken with him: or he hath surprised
A second Psyche, and lives here disguised.
Find ye no track of his strayed feet?

1 *Grace.*   Not I.

2 *Grace.* Nor I.

3 *Grace.*   Nor I.

Venus.   Stay, nymphs, we then will try
A nearer way.   Look all these ladies' eyes,
And see if there he not concealed lies;
Or in their bosoms, 'twixt their swelling breasts;
The wag affects to make himself such nests:
Perchance he hath got some simple heart to hide
His subtle shape in; I will have him cried,
And all his virtues told! that, when they know
What spright he is, she soon may let him go
That guards him now; and think herself right blest,
To be so timely rid of such a guest.
Begin, soft Graces, and proclaim reward
To her that brings him in.   Speak to be heard.

---

1 In the *Masque of Beauty*, performed on the 10th of January previous,
"a multitude of Cupids" had appeared as torch-bearers.

1 *Grace.* Beauties, have ye seen this toy[1]
Called Love, a little boy,
Almost naked, wanton, blind;
Cruel now, and then as kind?
If he be amongst ye, say!
He is Venus' runaway.

2 *Grace.* She that will but now discover
Where the winged wag doth hover,
Shall to-night receive a kiss,
How or where herself would wish:
But who brings him to his mother,
Shall have that kiss, and another.

3 *Grace.* He hath of marks about him plenty:
You shall know him among twenty.
All his body is a fire,
And his breath a flame entire,
That being shot, like lightning, in,
Wounds the heart, but not the skin.

1 *Grace.* At his sight, the sun hath turned,
Neptune in the waters burned;
Hell hath felt a greater heat;
Jove himself forsook his seat:
From the centre to the sky,
Are his trophies reared high.

2 *Grace.* Wings he hath, which though ye clip,
He will leap from lip to lip,
Over liver, lights, and heart,
But not stay in any part;
And if chance his arrow misses,
He will shoot himself in kisses.

---

[1] This beautiful lyric is imitated from the first Idyl of Moschus.

3 *Grace.* He doth bear a golden bow,
   And a quiver, hanging low,
   Full of arrows, that outbrave
   Dian's shafts; where, if he have
   Any head more sharp than other,
   With that first he strikes his mother.

1 *Grace.* Still the fairest are his fuel.
   When his days are to be cruel,
   Lovers' hearts are all his food;
   And his baths their warmest blood:
   Nought but wounds his hands doth season,
   And he hates none like to Reason.

2 *Grace.* Trust him not; his words, though sweet,
   Seldom with his heart do meet.
   All his practice is deceit;
   Every gift it is a bait;
   Not a kiss but poison bears;
   And most treason in his tears.

3 *Grace.* Idle minutes are his reign;
   Then the straggler makes his gain
   By presenting maids with toys,
   And would have ye think them joys:
   'T is the ambition of the elf,
   To have all childish as himself.

1 *Grace.* If by these ye please to know him,
   Beauties, be not nice, but show him.

2 *Grace.* Though ye had a will to hide him,
   Now, we hope, ye'll not abide him.

3 *Grace.* Since ye hear his falser play;
   And that he's Venus' runaway.

At this, from behind the trophies, CUPID discovered himself, and
came forth armed; attended with twelve boys, most antickly attired,
that represented the Sports, and pretty Lightnesses that accompany
Love, under the titles of *Joci* and *Risus;* and are said to wait on
Venus, as she is Praefect of Marriage.

Cupid.   Come, my little jocund Sports,
        Come away; the time now sorts
        With your pastime: this same night
        Is Cupid's day.   Advance your light.
        With your revel fill the room,
        That our triumphs be not dumb.

Wherewith they fell into a subtle capricious dance, to as odd a music,
each of them bearing two torches, and nodding with their antic faces,
with other variety of ridiculous gesture, which gave much occasion of
mirth and delight to the spectators. The dance ended, *Cupid* went
forward.

Cupid.   Well done, anticks! now my bow,
        And my quiver bear to show,
        That these beauties here may know
        By what arms this feat was done,
        That hath so much honour won
        Unto Venus and her son.

At which, his mother apprehended him: and circling him in with
the *Graces,* began to demand.

  Venus. What feat, what honour is it that you boast,
My little straggler? I had given you lost,
With all your games, here.
    Cupid.   Mother!
    Venus.   Yes, sir, she.
What might your glorious cause of triumph be?
Have you shot Minerva[1] or the Thespian dames?

[1] She urges these as miracles, because Pallas and the Muses are most
contrary to Cupid.—JONSON.

Heat aged Ops again[1] with youthful flames?
Or have you made the colder Moon to visit
Once more a sheep-cote?   Say, what conquest is it
Can make you hope such a renown to win?
Is there a second Hercules brought to spin?
Or, for some new disguise, leaves Jove his thunder?

    Cupid. Nor that, nor those, and yet no less a won-
        der[2]——   [*He espies* Hymen.
Which to tell, I may not stay:
Hymen's presence bids away;   [*Slips from her.*
'T is already at his night,
He can give you farther light.
You, my Sports, may here abide,
Till I call to light the Bride.

Enter Hymen.

    Hymen. Venus, is this a time to quit your car?
To stoop to earth, to leave alone your star
Without your influence, and on such a night,[3]
Which should be crowned with your most cheering sight
As you were ignorant of what were done
By Cupid's hand, your all-triumphing Son?
Look on this state[4]; and if you yet not know

---

[1] Rhea, the mother of the gods, whom Lucian makes to have fallen franticly in love by Cupid's means with Atys.   So of the moon with Endymion, Hercules, &c.—JONSON.

[2] Here Hymen, the god of marriage, entered; and was so induced here as you have him described in my *Hymenaei.*—JONSON.   "In a saffron-coloured robe, his under vestures white, his socks yellow, a yellow veil of silk on his left arm, his head crowned with roses and marjoram, in his right hand a torch of pine-tree."

[3] When she is *nuptiis praefecta*, with Juno, Suadela, Diana, and Jupiter himself.—JONSON.

[4] A canopy with raised seats beneath it for the king and queen.   The word is of constant occurrence.

What crown there shines, whose sceptre here doth grow[1];
Think on thy loved Aeneas[2], and what name
Maro, the golden trumpet of his fame,
Gave him, read thou in this.   A prince that draws
By example more than others do by laws:
That is so just to his great act and thought,
To do, not what kings may, but what kings ought.
Who, out of piety, unto peace is vowed,
To spare his subjects, yet to quell the proud;
And dares esteem it the first fortitude,
To have his passions, foes at home, subdued.
That was reserved until the Parcae spun
Their whitest wool; and then his thread begun,
Which thread, when treason would have burst,[3] a soul,
To-day renowned and added to my roll,
Opposed: and by that act to his name did bring
The honour to be saver of his king.
This king, whose worth, if gods for virtue love,
Should Venus with the same affections move,
As her Aeneas; and no less endear
Her love to his safety, than when she did cheer
After a tempest long-afflicted Troy
Upon the Libyan shore; and brought them joy.

    Venus. I love, and know his virtues, and do boast
Mine own renown, when I renown him most.
My Cupid's absence I forgive and praise,
That me to such a present grace could raise.

---

[1] Adulation of royal personages was a duty which no writer of these compositions could venture to shirk: the reader may find it pall sometimes, but he must remember that no doctrine of a parliamentary title had as yet given a shock to the divinity that doth hedge a king.

[2] Aeneas, the son of Venus, Virgil makes throughout the most exquisite pattern of piety, justice, prudence, and all other princely virtues, with whom (in way of that excellence) I confer my sovereign, applying in his description his own word usurped of that poet, *Parcere subiectis, et debellare superbos.*—JONSON.

[3] In that monstrous conspiracy of E[arl] Gowry.—JONSON.

His champion shall hereafter be my care:
But speak his bride, and what her virtues are.

Hymen. She is a noble virgin, styled The Maid
Of the Red-cliff, and hath her dowry weighed
No less in virtue, blood, and form, than gold;
Thence, where my pillars reared you may behold,
Filled with love's trophies, doth she take her name.
Those pillars did uxorious Vulcan frame,
Against this day, and underneath that hill,
He and his Cyclopes are forging still
Some strange and curious piece, to adorn the night,
And give these graced nuptials greater light.

Here *Vulcan* presented himself, as over-hearing *Hymen*, attired in
a cassock girt to him, with bare arms, his hair and beard rough; his
hat of blue, and ending in a cone; in his hand a hammer and tongs,
as coming from the forge.

Vulcan. Which I have done; the best of all my life:
And have my end if it but please my wife,
And she commend it to the laboured worth.
Cleave, solid rock! and bring the wonder forth.

At which, with a loud and full music, the Cliff parted in the midst,
and discovered an illustrious concave, filled with an ample and
glistering light, in which an artificial sphere was made of silver,
eighteen foot in the diameter, that turned perpetually: the *coluri*
were heightened with gold; so were the arctic and antarctic circles,
the tropics, the equinoctial, the meridian and horizon; only the
zodiac was of pure gold; in which the masquers, under the characters
of the twelve signs, were placed, answering them in number; whose
offices, with the whole frame as it turned, *Vulcan* went forward to
describe.

It is a sphere I have formed round and even,
In due proportion to the sphere of heaven,
With all his lines and circles; that compose
The perfect'st form, and aptly do disclose

G

The heaven of marriage: which I title it:
Within whose zodiac I have made to sit,
In order of the signs, twelve sacred powers,
That are presiding at all nuptial hours:

The first, in Aries' place, respecteth pride
Of youth and beauty; graces in the bride.

In Taurus, he loves strength and manliness;
The virtues which the bridegroom should profess.

In Gemini, that noble power is shown
That twins their hearts, and doth of two make one.

In Cancer, he that bids the wife give way
With backward yielding to her husband's sway.

In Leo, he that doth instil the heat
Into the man: which from the following seat

Is tempered so, as he that looks from thence
Sees yet they keep a Virgin innocence.

In Libra's room, rules he that doth supply
All happy beds with sweet equality.

The Scorpion's place he fills, that makes the jars
And stings in wedlock; little strifes and wars:

Which he in th' Archer's throne doth soon remove,
By making with his shafts new wounds of love.

And those the follower with more heat inspires,
As in the Goat the sun renews his fires.

In wet Aquarius' stead, reigns he that showers
Fertility upon the genial bowers.

Last, in the Fishes' place, sits he doth say,
In married joys all should be dumb as they.

And this hath Vulcan for his Venus done,
To grace the chaster triumph of her son.

Venus. And for this gift will I to heaven return,
And vow for ever that my lamp shall burn
With pure and chastest fire; or never shine
But when it mixeth with thy sphere and mine.

Here *Venus* returned to her chariot with the *Graces*; while *Vulcan*, calling out the priests of *Hymen*, who were the musicians, was interrupted by *Pyracmon*.[1]

Vulcan. Sing then, ye priests.

Pyracmon. Stay, Vulcan, shall not these
Come forth and dance?

Vulcan. Yes, my Pyracmon, please
The eyes of these spectators with our art.[2]

Pyracmon. Come here then, Brontes, bear a Cyclop's part,
And Steropes, both with your sledges stand,
And strike a time unto them as they land;
And as they forwards come, still guide their paces,
In musical and sweet proportioned graces;
While I upon the work and frame attend,
And Hymen's priests forth, at their seasons, send
To chaunt their hymns; and make this square admire
Our great artificer, the god of fire

---

[1] One of the Cyclops, of whom, with the other two, Brontes and Steropes, see Virg. *Aeneid.*

    Ferrum exercebant vasto Cyclopes in antro,
    Brontesque, Steropesque et nudus membra Pyracmon, &c.—JONSON.

[2] As when Hom. *Iliad.* Σ, makes Thetis for her son Achilles to visit Vulcan's house, he feigns that Vulcan had made twenty tripods or stools, with golden wheels, to move of themselves miraculously, and go out and return fitly. To which the invention of our dance alludes, and is in the poet a most elegant place, and worthy the tenth reading.—JONSON.

Here the musicians, attired in yellow, with wreaths of marjoram, and veils like *Hymen's* priests, sung the first staff of the following Epithalamion: which, because it was sung in pieces between the dances, shewed to be so many several songs, but was made to be read an entire poem. After the song they came forth (descending in an oblique motion) from the Zodiac, and danced their first dance; then music interposed (but varied with voices, only keeping the same chorus), they danced their second dance. So after, their third and fourth dances, which were all full of elegancy and curious device. The two latter were made by M. Tho. Giles, the two first by Master Hie. Herne: who, in the persons of the two Cyclopes, beat a time to them with their hammers. The tunes were M. Alphonso Ferra-bosco's.[1] The device and act of the scene M. Ynigo Jones his, with addition of the trophies. For the invention of the whole and the verses, *Assertor qui dicat esse meos, imponet plagiario pudorem.*

The attire of the masquers throughout was most graceful and noble; partaking of the best both ancient and later figure. The colours carnation and silver, enriched both with embroidery and lace. The dressing of their heads, feathers and jewels; and so excellently ordered to the rest of the habit, as all would suffer under any description of the shew. Their performance of all, so magnificent and illustrious, that nothing can add to the seal of it, but the subscription of their names:

THE DUKE OF LENOX,	LORD HAY,
EARL OF ARUNDELL,	LORD SANKRE,
EARL OF PEMBROKE,	SIR RO. RICHE,
EARL OF MONTGOMERY,	SIR JO. KENNETHIE,
LORD D'AUBIGNY,	[MR. OF MAR],[2]
LORD OF WALDEN,	M. ERSKINE.

[1] Alfonso Ferrabosco was the representative of a musical Italian family settled in England; he died in 1628. His father (fl. 1544-1587), and his son, who died in 1661, were also named Alfonso.

[2] This name, completing the number of twelve masquers, is omitted by Jonson. It occurs in a list of the masquers given in a contemporary letter quoted by Gifford. The Master of Mar would of course be an Erskine, and his omission may be due to his having been confused with the Master Erskine, called young Erskine in the letter, who concludes the list.

EPITHALAMION.

Up, youths and virgins, up, and praise
The god whose nights outshine his days;
   Hymen, whose hallowed rites
Could never boast of brighter lights;
   Whose bands pass liberty.
Two of your troop, that with the morn were free,
   Are now waged to his war.
     And what they are,
   If you 'll perfection see,
     Yourselves must be.
Shine, Hesperus, shine forth, thou wished star!

   What joy or honours can compare
   With holy nuptials, when they are
     Made out of equal parts
   Of years, of states, of hands, of hearts!
     When in the happy choice
The spouse and spoused have the foremost voice!
     Such, glad of Hymen's war,
       Live what they are,
    And long perfection see:
       And such ours be.
Shine, Hesperus, shine forth, thou wished star!

   The solemn state of this one night
   Were fit to last an age's light;
     But there are rites behind
Have less of state, but more of kind:
     Love's wealthy crop of kisses,
And fruitful harvest of his mother's blisses.
     Sound then to Hymen's war:
       That what these are,
    Who will perfection see,
       May haste to be.
Shine, Hesperus, shine forth, thou wished star!

Love's commonwealth consists of toys;
His council are those antic boys,
   Games, Laughter, Sports, Delights,
That triumph with him on these nights;
   To whom we must give way,
For now their reign begins, and lasts till day.
   They sweeten Hymen's war,
     And in that jar,
   Make all that married be
     Perfection see.
Shine, Hesperus, shine forth, thou wished star!

   Why stays the bridegroom to invade
Her that would be a matron made?
   Good-night, whilst yet we may
Good-night to you a virgin say:
   To-morrow rise the same
Your mother is, and use a nobler name.
   Speed well in Hymen's war,
     That, what you are,
   By your perfection we
     And all may see.
Shine, Hesperus, shine forth, thou wished star!

   To-night is Venus' vigil kept.
This night no bridegroom ever slept;
   And if the fair bride do,
The married say, 't is his fault too.
   Wake then, and let your lights
Wake too; for they 'll tell nothing of your nights.
   But that in Hymen's war
     You perfect are.
   And such perfection we
     Do pray should be.
Shine, Hesperus, shine forth, thou wished star!

That ere the rosy-fingered morn
Behold nine moons, there may be born
   A babe, t' uphold the fame
Of Ratcliffe's blood and Ramsey's name:
   That may, in his great seed,
Wear the long honours of his father's deed.
   Such fruits of Hymen's war
     Most perfect are;
   And all perfection we
     Wish you should see.
Shine, Hesperus, shine forth, thou wished star!

III.

BEN JONSON.

(1572–1637.)

THE MASQUE OF QUEENS.

CELEBRATED FROM THE HOUSE OF FAME, BY THE QUEEN
OF GREAT BRITAIN, WITH HER LADIES, AT
WHITEHALL, FEB. 2, 1609.

[In the course of this masterpiece the reader will be reminded both of Macbeth's Weird Sisters and of Prospero's invocation. This will not, however, cause him any searchings of heart, and he will not feel called upon to enter the lists, with Gifford, against the Shakespearian commentators, not doubting but that two great poets may handle similar themes without any design either of pillaging or of travestying one another. This was the third masque of Jonson's in which Queen Anne appeared as the chief masquer.]

To the glory of our own, and grief of other nations, my Lord HENRY, Prince of Great Britain, &c.

SIR,

When it hath been my happiness (as would it were more frequent) but to see your face, and, as passing by, to consider you, I have with as much joy as I am now far from flattery in professing it, called to mind that doctrine of some great inquisitors in *Nature*, who hold every royal and *heroic* form to partake and draw much to it of the heavenly virtue. For whether it be that a divine soul being to come into a body, first chooseth a palace for itself; or being come, doth make it so; or that *Nature* be ambitious to have her work equal, I know not; but what is lawful for me to understand and speak, that I dare; which is, that both your *virtue* and your *form* did deserve your *fortune*. The one claimed that you should be born a *prince*, the other makes that you do become it. And when *Necessity*, excellent lord, the mother of the *Fates*, hath so provided that your *form* should not more insinuate you to the eyes of men, than your *virtue* to their minds: it comes near a wonder to think how sweetly that habit flows in you, and with so hourly testimonies which to all posterity might hold the dignity of examples. Amongst the rest, your favour to letters, and these gentler studies that go under the title of *Humanity*, is not the least honour of your wreath. For if once the worthy professors of these learnings shall come (as heretofore they were) to be the care of *princes*, the crowns their *sovereigns* wear will not more adorn their temples, nor their stamps live longer in their medals, than in such subjects' labours. *Poetry*, my lord, is not born with every man, nor every day: and in her general right it is now my minute to thank your *Highness*, who not only do honour her with your care, but are curious to examine her with your eye, and enquire into her beauties and strengths. Where, though it hath proved a work of some difficulty to me to retrieve the particular *authorities* (according to your gracious command, and a desire born out of judgment) to those things which I writ out of fulness and memory of my former readings: yet now I have overcome it, the reward that meets me is double to one act; which is, that thereby your excellent understanding will not only justify me to your own knowledge, but decline the stiffness of others' original ignorance, already armed to censure. For which singular bounty, if my *fate*, most excellent *Prince* and *only Delicacy* of *mankind*, shall reserve me to the age of your actions, whether in the camp or the council-chamber, that I may write at nights the deeds of your days[1]; I will then labour to bring forth some work as worthy of your fame, as my ambition therein is of your pardon.

By the most true admirer of your *Highness's* virtues,
And most hearty celebrater of them,

BEN JONSON.

It increasing now to the third time of my being used in these services to her majesty's personal presentations, with the ladies whom

---

[1] This aspiration was not realized: Prince Henry died on November 6, 1612.

she pleaseth to honour; it was my first and special regard to see that the nobility of the invention should be answerable to the dignity of their persons. For which reason I chose the argument to be *A celebration of honourable and true Fame, bred out of Virtue*; observing that rule of the best artist,[1] to suffer no object of delight to pass without his mixture of profit and example. And because Her Majesty (best knowing that a principal part of life in these spectacles lay in their variety) had commanded me to think on some dance, or shew, that might precede hers, and have the place of a foil, or false masque: I was careful to decline,[2] not only from others, but mine own steps in that kind, since the last year[3] I had an antimasque of boys; and therefore now devised that twelve women, in the habit of hags or witches, sustaining the persons of Ignorance, Suspicion, Credulity, &c., the opposites to good Fame, should fill that part, not as a masque, but a spectacle of strangeness, producing multiplicity of gesture, and not unaptly sorting with the current and whole fall of the device.

His majesty then being set, and the whole company in full expectation, the part of the Scene which first presented itself was an ugly Hell; which flaming beneath, smoked unto the top of the roof. And in respect all evils are morally said to come from hell; as also from that observation of Torrentius upon Horace his *Canidia, quae tot instructa venenis, ex Orci faucibus profecta videri possit*: these witches, with a kind of hollow and infernal music, came forth from thence. First one, then two, and three, and more, till their number increased to eleven, all differently attired; some with rats on their head, some on their shoulders; others with ointment-pots at their girdles; all with spindles, timbrels, rattles, or other venefical instruments, making a confused noise, with strange gestures. The device of their attire was Master Jones his, with the invention and architecture of the whole scene and machine. Only I prescribed them their properties of vipers, snakes, bones, herbs, roots, and other ensigns of their magic, out of the authority of ancient and late writers, wherein the faults are mine if there be any found; and for that cause I confess them.

These eleven WITCHES beginning to dance (which is an usual ceremony at their convents or meetings, where sometimes also they

[1] Hor. *in Art. Poetic.*—JONSON.

       Omne tulit punctum qui miscuit utile dulci,
       Lectorem delectando pariterque monendo.

[2] Afraid of declining.

[3] In the masque at my Lord Haddington's wedding.—JONSON.

are vizarded and masqued), on the sudden one of them missed their
chief, and interrupted the rest with this speech:—

> Sisters, stay, we want our Dame;
> Call upon her by her name,
> And the charm we use to say;
> That she quickly anoint, and come away.

1 *Charm.*

> "Dame, dame! the watch is set:
> Quickly come, we all are met.—
> From the lakes, and from the fens,
> From the rocks, and from the dens,
> From the woods, and from the caves,
> From the churchyards, from the graves,
> From the dungeon, from the tree
> That they die on, here are we!"

> > Comes she not yet?
> > Strike another heat.

2 *Charm.*

> "The weather is fair, the wind is good,
> Up, dame, on your horse of wood:[1]
> Or else tuck up your grey frock,
> And saddle your goat,[2] or your green cock,[3]
> And make his bridle a bottom of thrid,
> To roll up how many miles you have rid.

---

[1] Delrio, *Disq. Mag.* lib. 2, quaest. 6, has a story out of Triezius of this horse of wood: but that which our witches call so, is sometimes a broomstaff, sometimes a reed, sometimes a distaff.—JONSON.

[2] The goat is the Devil himself, upon whom they ride often to their solemnity, as appears by their confessions in Rem[igius] and Bodin. His majesty also remembers the story of the devil's appearance to those of *Calicut* in that form, *Daemonol.* lib. 2, cap. 3.—JONSON.

[3] Of the green cock we have no other ground (to confess ingenuously) than a vulgar fable of a witch, that with a cock of that colour and a bottom of blue thread, would transport herself through the air; and so escaped (at the time of her being brought to execution) from the hand of justice. It was a tale when I went to school.—JONSON.

Quickly come away;
For we all stay."

          Nor yet! nay then,
          We 'll try her agen.

3 *Charm.*

"The owl is abroad, the bat, and the toad,
    And so is the cat-a-mountain,
The ant and the mole sit both in a hole,
    And frog peeps out o' the fountain;
The dogs they do bay, and the timbrels play,
The spindle[1] is now a turning;
    The moon it is red, and the stars are fled,
    But all the sky is a burning:
The ditch is made, and our nails the spade,
With pictures full of wax and of wool;
Their livers I stick with needles quick;
There lacks but the blood, to make up the flood.
    Quickly, dame, then bring your part in,
    Spur, spur upon little Martin[2],
Merrily, merrily, make him sail,
A worm in his mouth, and a thorn in 's tail,
Fire above and fire below,
With a whip i' your hand to make him go."

          O, now she 's come!
          Let all be dumb.

At this the DAME[3] entered to them, naked-armed, barefooted, her
frock tucked, her hair knotted, and folded with vipers; in her hand

---

[1] All this is but a periphrasis of the night, in their charm, and their
applying themselves to it with their instruments, whereof the spindle in
antiquity was the chief: and was of special act to the troubling of the
moon.—JONSON.

[2] Their little Martin is he that calls them to their conventicles, which
is done in a human voice, but coming forth, they find him in the shape
of a great buck goat, upon whom they ride to their meetings, Delr. *Disq.
Mag.* quaest. 16, lib. 2.—JONSON.

[3] This Dame I make to bear the person of Ate, or Mischief (for so I
interpret it), out of Homer's description of her.—JONSON.

a torch made of a dead man's arm, lighted, girded with a snake. To whom they all did reverence, and she spake, uttering, by way of question, the end wherefore they came. Which if it had been done either before or otherwise, had not been so natural. For to have made themselves their own decipherers, and each one to have told upon their entrance *what they were and whither they would,* had been a most piteous hearing, and utterly unworthy any quality of a poem : wherein a writer should always trust somewhat to the capacity of the spectator, especially at these spectacles: where men, beside inquiring eyes, are understood to bring quick ears, and not those sluggish ones of porters and mechanics, that must be bored through at every act with narrations.

> *Dame.* Well done, my Hags! And come we fraught
> with spite,
> To overthrow the glory of this night?
> Holds our great purpose?
>
> *Hag.*   Yes.
>
> *Dame.*   But wants there none
> Of our just number?
>
> *Hags.*   Call us one by one,
> And then our dame shall see.
>
> *Dame.*   First then advance[1]
> My drowsy servant, stupid Ignorance,
> Known by thy scaly vesture; and bring on
> Thy fearful sister, wild Suspicion,
>   [*As she names them they come forward.*

---

[1] In the chaining of these vices, I make as if one link produced another, and the Dame were born out of them all, so as they might say to her, *Sola tenes scelerum quicquid possedimus omnes.* Nor will it appear much violenced, if their series be considered, when the opposition to all virtue begins out of Ignorance, that Ignorance begets Suspicion (for Knowledge is ever open and charitable): that Suspicion, Credulity, as it is a vice; for being a virtue, and free, it is opposite to it : but such as are jealous of themselves, do easily credit anything of others whom they hate. Out of this Credulity springs Falsehood, which begets Murmur: and that Murmur presently grows Malice, which begets Impudence: and that Impudence, Slander: that Slander, Execration: Execration, Bitterness: Bitterness, Fury: and Fury, Mischief.—JONSON.

Whose eyes do never sleep; let her knit hands
With quick Credulity, that next her stands,
Who hath but one ear, and that always ope;
Two-faced Falsehood follow in the rope;
And lead on Murmur, with the cheeks deep hung;
She, Malice, whetting of her forked tongue;
And Malice, Impudence, whose forehead's lost;
Let Impudence lead Slander on, to boast
Her oblique look; and to her subtle side,
Thou, black-mouthed Execration, stand applied;
Draw to thee Bitterness, whose pores sweat gall;
She, flame-eyed Rage; Rage, Mischief.

Hags.   Here we are all.

Dame. Join now our hearts, we faithful opposites[1]
To Fame and Glory.   Let not these bright nights
Of honour blaze, thus to offend our eyes;
Shew ourselves truly envious, and let rise
Our wonted rages: do what may beseem
Such names and natures; Virtue else will deem
Our powers decreased, and think us banished earth,
No less than heaven.   All her antique birth,
As Justice, Faith, she will restore; and, bold
Upon our sloth, retrieve her age of gold.
We must not let our native manners thus
Corrupt with ease.   Ill lives not but in us.
I hate to see these fruits of a soft peace,
And curse the piety gives it such increase.
Let us disturb it then, and blast the light;
Mix hell with heaven, and make nature fight

---

[1] Here again by way of irritation [incitement] I make the Dame pursue the purpose of their coming, and discover their natures more largely: which had been nothing if not done as doing another thing, but *moratio circa vilem patulumque orbem*; than which the poet cannot know a greater vice, he being that kind of artificer to whose work is required so much exactness, as indifferency is not tolerable.—JONSON.

Within herself; loose the whole hinge of things;
And cause the ends run back into their springs.

Hags. What our Dame bids us do,
We are ready for.

Dame. Then fall to.
But first relate me what you have sought,
Where you have been, and what you have brought.

1 *Hag.* I have been all day looking after[1]
A raven feeding upon a quarter;
And soon as she turned her beak to the south,
I snatched this morsel out of her mouth.

2 *Hag.* I have been gathering wolves' hairs,
The mad dog's foam, and the adder's ears;
The spurging[2] of a dead-man's eyes,
And all since the evening star did rise.

3 *Hag.* I last night lay all alone
O' the ground, to hear the mandrake[3] groan;

---

[1] For the gathering pieces of dead flesh, Cornel. Agrip. *de occult. Philosoph.* lib. 3, cap. 42, and lib. 4, cap. ult., observes that the use was to call up ghosts and spirits with a fumigation made of that (and bones of carcasses), which I make my witch here, not to cut herself, but to watch the raven; as if that piece were sweeter which the wolf had bitten, or the raven had picked, and more effectuous: and to do it at her turning to the south, as with the prediction of a storm. Which though they be but minutes in ceremony, being observed, make the act more dark and full of horror.—JONSON.

[2] Frothy decomposition. The word was properly applied to the frothing of beer in the process of fermentation.

[3] Pliny, writing of the mandrake, *Nat. Hist.* l. 25, c. 13, and of the digging it up, hath this ceremony, *Cavent effossuri contrarium ventum, et tribus circulis ante gladio circumscribunt, postea fodiunt ad occasum spectantes.* But we have later tradition, that the forcing of it up is so fatally dangerous, as the groan kills; and therefore they do it with dogs, which I think but borrowed from Josephus's report of the root Baaeras, lib. 7 *de Bel. Judaic.* Howsoever, it being so principal an ingredient in their magic, it was fit she should boast to be the plucker up of it herself. And that the cock did crow, alludes to a prime circumstance in their work: for they all confess, that nothing is so cross or baleful to them in their nights as that the cock should crow before they have done. Which makes that their little masters or martinets, whom I have men-

And plucked him up, though he grew full low;
And as I had done the Cock did crow.

4 *Hag.* And I ha' been choosing out this skull
From charnel-houses that were full;
From private grots and public pits;
And frighted a sexton out of his wits.

5 *Hag.* Under a cradle I did creep
By day; and when the child was asleep
At night I sucked the breath; and rose,
And plucked the nodding nurse by the nose.

6 *Hag.* I had a dagger: what did I with that?
Killed an infant to have his fat.
A piper it got, at a church-ale,
I bade him again blow wind i' the tail.

7 *Hag.* A murderer yonder was hung in chains,
The sun and the wind had shrunk his veins;
I bit off a sinew; I clipped his hair,
I brought off his rags that danced i' the air.

8 *Hag.* The scrich-owl's eggs and the feathers black,
The blood of the frog and the bone in his back,
I have been getting; and made of his skin
A purset to keep Sir Cranion[1] in.

---

tioned before, use this form in dismissing their conventions: *Eia, facessite propere hinc omnes, nam iam galli canere incipiunt.* Which I interpret to be, because that bird is the messenger of light, and so, contrary to their acts of darkness.—JONSON.

[1] Her "fly" or familiar spirit. In *Bartholomew Fair* (Act i. Sc. 1) Squire Cokes is described as the possessor of "Sir Cranion-legs" *i.e.* spindle-shanks, "Sir Cranion" being a name for the insect we call a crane-fly or daddy-long-legs. In *The Alchemist* Dapper has his *fly* given him in a purse:

> Here is your fly in a purse about your neck, cousin;
> Wear it, and feed it about this day sev'n night
> On your right wrist.—Act v. Sc. 2.

9 *Hag.* And I ha' been plucking plants among,
Hemlock, henbane, adder's-tongue,
Night-shade, moon-wort, libbard's-bane;[1]
And twice by the dogs was like to be ta'en.

10 *Hag.* I from the jaws of a gardener's[2] bitch
Did snatch these bones, and then leaped the ditch:
Yet went I back to the house again,
Killed the black cat, and here's the brain.

11 *Hag.* I went to the toad breeds under the wall,
I charmed him out, and he came at my call;
I scratched out the eyes of the owl before,
I tore the bat's wing: what would you have more?

Dame. Yes, I have brought, to help our vows,
Horned poppy, cypress boughs,
The fig-tree wild that grows on tombs,
And juice that from the larch-tree comes,
The basilick's blood and the viper's skin:
And now our orgies let's begin.

Here the *Dame* put herself in the midst of them, and began her following Invocation: wherein she took occasion to boast all the power attributed to witches by the ancients, of which every poet (or the most) do give some: Homer to Circe, in the *Odyss.*; Theocritus to Simatha, in *Pharmaceutria*; Virgil to Alphesibaeus, in his *Eclogue*; Ovid to Dipsas, in *Amor.*, to Medea and Circe, in *Metamorph.*; Tibullus to Saga; Horace to Canidia, Sagana, Veia, Folia; Seneca to Medea, and the nurse in *Herc. Oete.*; Petr. Arbiter to

---

[1] *Cicuta, hyoscyamus, ophioglosson, solanum, martagon, doronicum, aconitum,* are the common venefical ingredients remembered by Paracelsus, Porta, Agrippa, and others: which I make her to have gathered, as about a castle, church, or some vast building (kept by dogs) among ruins and wild heaps.—JONSON.

[2] Gardener's, as imagining such persons to keep mastiffs for the defence of their grounds, whither this hag might also go for simples: where, meeting with the bones, and not content with them, she would yet do a domestic hurt in getting the cat's brains: which is another special ingredient; and of so much more efficacy by how much blacker the cat is.—JONSON.

his Saga, in *Frag.*; and Claudian to Megaera, lib. 1 *in Rufinum*; who takes the habit of a witch, as they do, and supplies that historical part in the poem, beside her moral person of a Fury; confirming the same drift in ours.

You fiends and furies (if yet any be
Worse than ourselves), you that have quaked to see
These[1] knots untied and shrunk, when we have charmed:
You that to arm us have yourselves disarmed,
And to our powers resigned your whips and brands
When we went forth, the scourge of men and lands:
You that have seen me ride when Hecate
Durst not take chariot; when the boisterous sea
Without a breath of wind hath knocked the sky;
And that hath thundered, Jove not knowing why;
When we have set the elements at wars,
Made midnight see the sun, and day the stars;
When the winged lightning in the course hath stayed;
And swiftest rivers have run back, afraid
To see the corn remove, the groves to range,
Whole places alter, and the seasons change;
When the pale moon, at the first voice down fell
Poisoned, and durst not stay the second spell:
You, that have oft been conscious of these sights;
And thou[2], three-formed star, that on these nights
Art only powerful, to whose triple name
Thus we incline, once, twice, and thrice the same;
If now with rites profane and foul enough
We do invoke thee; darken all this roof
With present fogs: exhale earth's rot'nest vapours,
And strike a blindness through these blazing tapers.

[1] The untying of their knots [of hair] is, when they are going to some fatal business.—JONSON.

[2] Hecate, who is called Trivia, and Triformis, of whom Virgil, *Aeneid.* lib. 4, *Tergeminamque Hecaten, tria virginis ora Dianae.* She was believed to govern witchcraft; and is remembered in all their invocations. —JONSON.

Come, let a murmuring Charm resound,
The whilst we bury all i' the ground.
But first, see every foot be bare;
And every knee.

Hag. Yes, Dame, they are

4 *Charm.*
"Deep,[1] O deep we lay thee to sleep;
We leave thee drink by, if thou chance to be dry;
Both milk and blood, the dew and the flood.
We breathe in thy bed, at the foot and the head;
We cover thee warm, that thou take no harm:
And when thou dost wake,
Dame Earth shall quake,
And the houses shake,
And her belly shall ake,
As her back were brake,
Such a birth to make,
As is the blue drake:[2]
Whose form thou shalt take."

Dame. Never a star yet shot!
Where be the ashes?

Hag Here i' the pot.

Dame. Cast[3] them up; and the flint-stone
Over the left shoulder bone;
Into the west.

[1] Here they speak as if they were creating some new feature shape which the devil persuades them to be able to do often by the pronouncing of words and pouring out of liquors on the earth.—JONSON.

[2] Dragon.

[3] This throwing of ashes and sand, with the flint-stone, cross-sticks, and burying of sage, &c., are all used (and believed by them) to the raising of storm and tempest.—JONSON.

Hag.   It will be best.

5 *Charm.*

"The sticks are across, there can be no loss,
The sage is rotten, the sulphur is gotten
Up to the sky, that was i' the ground.
Follow it then, with our rattles, round;
Under the bramble, over the brier,
A little more heat will set it on fire:
Put it in mind to do it kind,
Flow water and blow wind.
Rouncy is over, Robble is under,
A flash of light, and a clap of thunder,
A storm of rain, another of hail.
We all must home i' the eggshell sail;
The mast is made of a great pin,
The tackle of cobweb, the sail as thin,
And if we go through and not fall in—"

Dame. Stay[1], all our charms do nothing win
Upon the night; our labour dies,
Our magic feature[2] will not rise—
Nor yet the storm! we must repeat
More direful voices far, and beat
The ground with vipers till it sweat.

6 *Charm.*

"Bark dogs, wolves howl,
Seas roar, woods roule[3],
Clouds crack, all be black,
But the light our charms do make."

Dame. Not yet! my rage begins to swell;
Darkness, Devils, Night, and Hell,

---

[1] This stop, or interruption, shewed the better by causing that general
silence which made all the following noises, enforced in the next charm,
more direful.—JONSON.   [2] Shape.   [3] Roll.

Do not thus delay my spell.
I call you once, and I call you twice;
I beat you again, if you stay me thrice:
Through these crannies where I peep,
I 'll let in the light to see your sleep;[1]
And all the secrets of your sway
Shall lie as open to the day
As unto me.   Still are you deaf!
Reach me a bough that ne'er bare leaf,
To strike the air; and aconite,
To hurl upon this glaring light;
A rusty knife, to wound mine arm;
And as it drops I 'll speak a charm,
Shall cleave the ground, as low as lies
Old shrunk-up Chaos, and let rise
Once more his dark and reeking head,
To strike the world and nature dead,
Until my magic birth be bred.

7 *Charm.*

 " Black go in, and blacker come out;
  At thy going down, we give thee a shout."
   Hoo!
 " At thy rising again thou shalt have two,
  And if thou dost what we would have thee do,
  Thou shalt have three, thou shalt have four,
  Thou shalt have ten, thou shalt have a score."
   Hoo! Har! Har! Hoo!

8 *Charm.*

 "A cloud of pitch, a spur and a switch,
  To haste him away, and a whirlwind play,
  Before and after, with thunder for laughter,

---

[1] This is one of their common menaces, when their magic receives the least stop.—JONSON.

And storms for joy, of the roaring boy;
His head of a drake, his tail of a snake."

9 *Charm.*

" About, about, and about,
   Till the mist arise, and the lights fly out,
   The images neither be seen nor felt;
   The woollen burn and the waxen melt:
   Sprinkle your liquors upon the ground,
   And into the air; around, around.
         Around, around,
         Around, around,
         Till a music sound,
         And the pace be found,
         To which we may dance,
         And our charms advance."

At which, with a strange and sudden music, they fell into a magical dance, full of preposterous change and gesticulation, but most applying to their property: who at their meetings do all things contrary to the custom of men, dancing back to back, and hip to hip, their hands joined, and making their circles backward, to the left hand, with strange phantastic motions of their heads and bodies. All which were excellently imitated by the maker of the dance, M. Hierome Herne, whose right it is here to be named.

In the heat of their dance, on the sudden was heard a sound of loud music, as if many instruments had made one blast; with which not only the *Hags* themselves, but the hell into which they ran, quite vanished, and the whole face of the Scene altered, scarce suffering the memory of such a thing; but in the place of it appeared a glorious and magnificent building, figuring the HOUSE OF FAME, in the top of which were discovered the twelve *Masquers*, sitting upon a throne triumphal, erected in form of a pyramid, and circled with all store of light. From whom a person by this time descended, in the furniture[1] of *Perseus*, and expressing heroic and masculine *Virtue*, began to speak.

                 [1] Armour.

HEROIC VIRTUE.

So should at Fame's loud sound and Virtue's sight,
All dark and envious witchcraft fly the light.
I did not borrow Hermes' wings, nor ask
His crooked sword, nor put on Pluto's casque,
Nor on mine arm advanced wise Pallas' shield,
(By which, my face aversed, in open field
I slew the Gorgon) for an empty name:
When Virtue cut off Terror, he gat Fame.
And if, when Fame was gotten, Terror died,
What black Erynnis, or more hellish Pride,
Durst arm these hags, now she is grown and great,
To think they could her glories once defeat?
I was her parent, and I am her strength.
Heroic Virtue sinks not under length
Of years or ages; but is still the same,
While he preserves, as when he got Good Fame.
My daughter then, whose glorious house you see
Built all of sounding brass, whose columns be
Men-making poets, and those well-made men,
Whose strife it was to have the happiest pen
Renown them to an after-life, and not
With pride to scorn the Muse, and die forgot;
She, that enquireth into all the world,
And hath about her vaulted palace hurled
All rumours and reports, or true, or vain,
What utmost lands, or deepest seas contain,
But only hangs great actions on her file;
She, to this lesser world and greatest isle,
To-night sounds honour, which she would have seen
In yond' bright bevy, each of them a queen.
Eleven of them are of times long gone.
PENTHESILEA, the brave Amazon,
Swift-foot CAMILLA, Queen of Volscia,

Victorious THOMYRIS of Scythia,
Chaste ARTEMISIA, the Carian dame
And fair-haired BERONICE, Aegypt's fame,
HYPSICRATEA, glory of Asia,
CANDACE, pride of Aethiopia,
The Britain honour, VOADICEA,
The virtuous Palmyrene, ZENOBIA,
The wise and warlike Goth, AMALASUNTA,
And bold VALASCA, of Bohemia;
These, in their lives, as fortunes, crowned the choice
Of womankind, and 'gainst all opposite voice,
Made good to time, had after death the claim
To live eternized in the House of Fame.
Where hourly hearing (as what there is old?)
The glories of BEL-ANNA so well told,
Queen of the Ocean; how that she alone
Possest all virtues, for which one by one
They were so famed: and wanting then a head
To form that sweet and gracious pyramid
Wherein they sit, it being the sovereign place
Of all that palace, and reserved to grace
The worthiest queen: these without envy on her
In life desired that honour to confer,
Which with their death no other should enjoy.
She this embracing with a virtuous joy,
Far from self-love, as humbling all her worth
To him that gave it, hath again brought forth
Their names to memory; and means this night
To make them once more visible to light:
And to that light, from whence her truth of spirit
Confesseth all the lustre of her merit:
To you, most royal and most happy king,
Of whom Fame's house in every part doth ring
For every virtue, but can give no increase:
Not though her loudest trumpet blaze your peace:

To you, that cherish every great example
Contracted in yourself; and being so ample
A field of honour cannot but embrace
A spectacle so full of love and grace
Unto your court: where every princely dame
Contends to be as bounteous of her fame
To others, as her life was good to her.
For by their lives they only did confer
Good on themselves; but by their fame to yours,
And every age the benefit endures.

Here the throne wherein they sat, being *machina versatilis*, suddenly changed; and in the place of it appeared *Fama bona*, as she is described (in *Iconolog.*[1] di Cesare Ripa) attired in white, with white wings, having a collar of gold about her neck, and a heart hanging at it: which Orus Apollo, in his *hierogl.*[2] interprets the note of a good *Fame*. In her right-hand she bore a trumpet, in her left an olive-branch: and for her state, it was as Virgil describes her, at the full, her feet on the ground, and her head in the clouds. She, after the music had done, which waited on the turning of the machine, called from thence to *Virtue*, and spake this following speech.

FAME.

Virtue, my father and my honour; thou
That mad'st me good as great; and dar'st avow
No fame for thine but what is perfect: aid
To-night the triumphs of thy white-winged maid.
Do those renowned queens all utmost rites
Their states can ask. This is a night of nights.
In mine own chariots let them crowned ride;
And mine own birds and beasts, in geers applied
To draw them forth. Unto the first car tie
Far-sighted eagles, to note Fame's sharp eye,

---

[1] A work on emblems by Cesare Ripa, published at Rome in 1603.
[2] A work attributed to Orus Apollo or Horapollo, a Greek grammarian of the fourth century A.D.

Unto the second, griffons, that design
Swiftness and strength, two other gifts of mine.
Unto the last, our lions, that imply
The top of graces, state, and majesty.
And let those Hags be led as captives, bound
Before their wheels, whilst I my trumpet sound.

At which the loud music sounded as before, to give the *Masquers*
time of descending.

And here we cannot but take the opportunity to make
some more particular description of their scene, as also of
the persons they presented; which, though they were disposed rather by chance than election, yet it is my part to
justify them all: and then the lady that will own her presentation, may.

To follow therefore the rule of chronology, which I
have observed in my verse, the most upward in time was
PENTHESILEA. She was queen of the Amazons, and succeeded Otrera, or (as some will) Orithya; she lived and
was present at the siege of Troy, on their part against
the Greeks, and (as Justin gives her testimony) *Inter
fortissimos viros, magna eius virtutis documenta extitere.*
She is nowhere named but with the preface of honour
and virtue; and is always advanced in the head of the
worthiest women. Diodorus Siculus makes her the
daughter of Mars. She was honoured in her death to
have it the act of Achilles. Of which Propertius sings
this triumph to her beauty,

> Aurea cui postquam nudavit cassida frontem,
> Vicit victorem candida forma virum.

Next follows CAMILLA, Queen of the Volscians, celebrated by Virgil, than whose verses nothing can be
imagined more exquisite, or more honouring the person
they describe. They are these, where he reckons up
those that came on Turnus his part, against Aeneas:

> Hos super advenit Volsca de gente Camilla,
> Agmen agens equitum et florentis aere catervas,

Bellatrix. Non illa colo, calathisve Minervae
Foemineas assueta manus, sed praelia virgo
Dura pati cursuque pedum praevertere ventos.
Illa vel intactae segetis per summa volaret
Gramina, nec teneras cursu laesisset aristas:
Vel mare per medium fluctu suspensa tumenti
Ferret iter, celeris nec tingueret aequore plantas.

And afterwards tells her attire and arms, with the admiration that the spectators had of her. All which, if the poet created out of himself, without Nature, he did but shew how much so divine a soul could exceed her.

The third lived in the age of Cyrus, the great Persian monarch, and made him leave to live, THOMYRIS, Queen of the Scythians, or Massagets. A heroine of a most invincible and unbroken fortitude: who, when Cyrus had invaded her, and taking her only son (rather by treachery than war, as she objected), had slain him; not touched with the grief of so great a loss, in the juster comfort she took of a great revenge, pursued not only the occasion and honour of conquering so potent an enemy, with whom fell two hundred thousand soldiers; but (what was right memorable in her victory) left not a messenger surviving of his side to report the massacre. She is remembered both by Herodotus and Justin, to the great renown and glory of her kind, with this elogy: *Quod potentissimo Persarum Monarchae bello congressa est, ipsumque et vita et castris spoliavit, ad justè ulciscendum filii eius indignissimam mortem.*

The fourth was honoured to life in time of Xerxes, and present at his great expedition into Greece; ARTEMISIA, the Queen of Caria; whose virtue Herodotus, not without some wonder records: that a woman, a queen, without a husband, her son a ward, and she administering the government, occasioned by no necessity, but a mere excellence of spirit, should embark herself for such a war; and there so to behave her, as Xerxes, beholding her fight, should say: *Viri quidem extiterunt mihi feminae, feminae autem viri.* She is no less renowned for her chastity and love to her husband Mausolus, whose bones (after he was dead) she preserved in ashes and drunk in wine, making herself his tomb; and yet built to his memory a monument deserving a place among the seven wonders of the world, which could not be done by less than a wonder of women.

The fifth was the fair-haired daughter of Ptolomaeus Philadelphus by the elder Arsinoë; who, married to her brother Ptolomaeus, surnamed Euergetes, was after Queen of Egypt. I find her written both BERONICE and BERENICE. This lady, upon an expedition of her new-wedded lord into Assyria, vowed to Venus, if he returned safe, and conqueror, the offering of her hair: which vow of hers (exacted by the success) she afterward performed. But her father missing it, and therewith displeased, Conon, a mathematician who was then in household with Ptolomy, and knew well to flatter him, persuaded the king that it was taken up to heaven, and made a constellation; shewing him those seven stars, *ad caudam Leonis*, which are since called *Coma Berenices*. Which story then presently celebrated by Callimachus, in a most elegant poem, Catullus more elegantly converted: wherein they call her the magnanimous even from a virgin; alluding (as Hyginus says) to a rescue she made of her father in his flight, and restoring the courage and honour of his army, even to a victory. Their words are,

Cognôram à parva virgine magnanimam.

The sixth, that famous wife of Mithridates, and Queen of Pontus, HYPSICRATEA, no less an example of virtue than the rest; who so loved her husband, as she was assistant to him in all labours and hazard of the war in a masculine habit. For which cause (as Valerius Maximus observes) she departed with a chief ornament of her beauty. *Tonsis enim capillis, equo se et armis assuefecit, quo facilius laboribus et periculis eius interesset.* And afterward, in his flight from Pompey, accompanied his misfortune with a mind and body equally unwearied. She is solemnly registered by that grave author as a notable precedent of marriage loyalty and love: virtues that might raise a mean person to equality with a queen; but a queen to the state and honour of a deity.

The seventh, that renown of Ethiopia, CANDACE: from whose excellency the succeeding queens of that nation were ambitious to be called so. A woman of a most haughty spirit against enemies, and a singular affection to her subjects. I find her celebrated by Dion and Pliny, invading Egypt in the time of Augustus: who, though she were enforced to a peace by his lieutenant Petronius, doth not the less worthily hold her place here; when everywhere this elogy remains of her fame: that she was *maximi animi mulier, tantique in suos meriti, ut omnes deinceps Aethiopium reginae eius nomine fuerint appellatae.* She governed in Meroë.

The eighth, our own honour, VOADICEA, or BOADICEA; by some Bunduica, and Bunduca, Queen of the Iceni, a people that inhabited that part of our island which was called East Anglia, and comprehended Suffolk, Norfolk, Cambridge, and Huntingdon shires. Since she was born here at home, we will first honour her with a home-born testimony; from the grave and diligent Spenser:

> Bunduca Britoness,
> Bunduca, that victorious conqueress,
> That lifting up her brave heroic thought
> 'Bove woman's weakness, with the Romans fought;
> Fought, and in the field against them thrice prevailed, &c.

To which see her orations in story, made by Tacitus and Dion: wherein is expressed all magnitude of a spirit, breathing to the liberty and redemption of her country. The latter of whom, doth honest her beside with a particular description: *Bunduica Britannica foemina, orta stirpe regia, quae non solùm eis cum magna dignitate praefuit, sed etiam bellum omne administravit; cuius animus virilis potius quam muliebris erat.* And afterwards, *Foemina, forma honestissima, vultu severo,* &c. All which doth weigh the more to her true praise, in coming from the mouths of Romans and enemies. She lived in the time of Nero.

The ninth, in time, but equal in fame, and (the cause of it) virtue, was the chaste ZENOBIA, Queen of the Palmyrenes, who, after the death of her husband Odenatus, had the name to be reckoned among the thirty that usurped the Roman empire from Galienus. She continued a long and brave war against several chiefs; and was at length triumphed on by

Aurelian: but *ea specie, ut nihil pompabilius P. Rom. videre-tur.* Her chastity was such, *ut ne virum suum quidem sciret, nisi tentatis conceptionibus.* She lived in a most royal manner, and was adored to the custom of the Persians. When she made orations to her soldiers, she had always her casque on. A woman of a most divine spirit, and incredible beauty. In Trebellius Pollio read the most notable description of a queen and her that can be uttered with the dignity of an historian.

The tenth, succeeding, was that learned and heroic AMA-LASUNTA, Queen of the Ostrogoths, daughter to Theodoric, that obtained the principality of Ravenna and almost all Italy. She drave the Burgundians and Almaines out of Liguria, and appeared in her government rather an example than a second. She was the most eloquent of her age, and cunning in all languages of any nation that had commerce with the Roman empire. It is recorded of her, that *Sine veneratione eam viderit nemo, pro miraculo fuerit ipsam audire loquentem. Tantaque illi in discernendo gravitas, ut criminis convicti, cum plecterentur, nihil sibi acerbum pati viderentur.*

The eleventh was that brave Bohemian Queen, VALASCA, who for her courage had the surname of Bold: that to redeem herself and her sex from the tyranny of men, which they lived in under Primislaus, on a night, and at an hour appointed, led on the women to the slaughter of their barbarous husbands and lords. And possessing themselves of their horses, arms, treasure, and places of strength, not only ruled the rest, but lived many years after with the liberty and fortitude of Amazons. Celebrated by Raphael Volaterranus, and in an elegant tract of an Italian's in Latin, who names himself Philalethes, *Polytopiensis civis, inter praestantissimas foe-minas.*

The twelfth, and worthy sovereign of all, I make BEL-ANNA, royal Queen of the Ocean; of whose dignity and person the whole scope of the invention doth speak throughout: which, to offer you again here, might but prove offence to that sacred modesty which hears any testimony of others iterated with more delight than her own praise. She being placed above the need of such ceremony, and safe in her princely virtue

against the good or ill of any witness. The name of Bel-anna
I devised to honour hers proper by; as adding to it the
attribute of Fair: and is kept by me in all my poems wherein
I mention her majesty with any shadow or figure. Of which
some may come forth with a longer destiny than this age
commonly gives to the best births, if but helped to light by
her gracious and ripening favour.

But here I discern a possible objection arising against me,
to which I must turn: as *How I can bring persons of so dif-
ferent ages to appear properly together? or why (which is
more unnatural) with Virgil's Mezentius, I join the living
with the dead?* I answer to both these at once. Nothing
is more proper; nothing more natural. For these all live,
and together, in their fame: and so I present them. Besides,
if I would fly to the all-daring power of poetry, where could
I not take sanctuary? or in whose poem? For other objec-
tions let the looks and noses of judges hover thick; so they
bring the brains: or if they do not, I care not. When I
suffered it to go abroad, I departed with my right: and now,
so secure[1] an interpreter I am of my chance, that neither
praise nor dispraise shall affect me.

There rests only that we give the description we promised
of the scene, which was the House of Fame. The structure
and ornament of which (as is profest before) was entirely
Master Jones his invention and design. First, for the lower
columns, he chose the statues of the most excellent poets, as
Homer, Virgil, Lucan, &c., as being the substantial supporters
of Fame. For the upper, Achilles, Aeneas, Caesar, and those
great heroes which these poets had celebrated: all which
stood as in massy gold. Between the pillars underneath
were figured land-battles, sea-fights, triumphs, loves, sacrifices, and all magnificent subjects of honour, in brass, and
heightened with silver. In which he profest to follow that
noble description made by Chaucer of the place. Above
were sited[2] the masquers, over whose heads he devised two
eminent figures of Honour and Virtue for the arch. The
friezes both below and above were filled with several-coloured

---

[1] Without care, indifferent.   [2] Placed.

lights, like emeralds, rubies, sapphires, carbuncles, &c., the reflex of which, with other lights placed in the concave, upon the masquers' habits was full of glory. These habits had in them the excellency of all device and riches: and were worthily varied by his invention to the nations whereof they were queens. Nor are these alone his due; but divers other accessions to the strangeness and beauty of the spectacle: as the hell, the going about of the chariots, and binding the witches, the turning machine, with the presentation of Fame, All which I willingly acknowledge for him; since it is a virtue planted in good natures, that what respects they wish to obtain fruitfully from others they will give ingenuously themselves.

By this time imagine the masquers descended, and again mounted into three triumphant chariots, ready to come forth. The first four were drawn with eagles (whereof I gave the reason, as of the rest, in Fame's speech), their four torch-bearers attending on the chariot's sides, and four of the Hags bound before them. Then followed the second, drawn by griffons, with their torch-bearers, and four other Hags. Then the last, which was drawn by lions, and more eminent (wherein her Majesty was), and had six torch-bearers more, peculiar to her, with the like number of Hags. After which a full triumphant music, singing this SONG, while they rode in state about the stage:—

Help, help, all tongues, to celebrate this wonder:
The voice of Fame should be as loud as thunder.
  Her house is all of echo made,
    Where never dies the sound:
  And as her brows the clouds invade,
    Her feet do strike the ground.
Sing then, good Fame, that's out of Virtue born:
For who doth Fame neglect, doth Virtue scorn.

Here they lighted from their chariots, and danced forth their first dance: then a second immediately following it: both right curious, and full of subtle and excellent changes, and seemed performed with no less spirits than of those they personated. The first was to the cornets, the second to the violins. After which they took out the men, and danced the measures; entertaining the time, almost to the space of an hour, with singular variety: when, to give them rest, from the music which attended the chariots, by that most excellent tenor voice and exact singer (her Majesty's servant, M. Jo. Allin) this ditty was sung:—

SONG.

When[1] all the ages of the earth
Were crowned but in this famous birth;
And that when they would boast their store
Of worthy queens, they knew no more:
How happier is that age can give
A Queen in whom all they do live!

After it succeeded their third dance; than which a more numerous[2] composition could not be seen: graphically disposed into letters, and honouring the name of the most sweet and ingenious Prince, CHARLES, Duke of York.[3] Wherein, beside that principal grace of perspicuity, the motions were so even and apt, and their expression so just, as, if mathematicians had lost proportion, they might there have found it. The author was M. Tho. Giles. After this they danced galliards and corantos. And then their last dance, no less elegant in the place than the rest, with which they took their chariots again, and triumphing about the stage, had their return to the House of Fame celebrated with this last SONG; whose notes (as the former) were the work and honour of my excellent friend Alfonso Ferrabosco:—

SONG.

Who, Virtue, can thy power forget,
That sees these live, and triumph yet?
Th' Assyrian pomp, the Persian pride,
Greeks' glory, and the Romans' died:
    And who yet imitate

---

[1] Whereas.   [2] Harmonious.
[3] Charles, Duke of Albany, born November 29, 1600, had been created Duke of York, January 6, 1605, on the evening of which day Jonson's *Masque of Blackness* was performed.

Their noises tarry the same fate.
Force greatness all the glorious ways
   You can, it soon decays;
But so good Fame shall never:
Her triumphs, as their causes, are for ever.

To conclude which, I know no worthier way of epilogue than the
celebration of who were the celebraters:—

The QUEEN'S MAJESTY.
The CO. OF ARUNDEL.
The CO. OF DERBY.
The CO. OF HUNTINGDON.
The CO. OF BEDFORD.
The CO. OF ESSEX.

The CO. OF MONTGOMERY.
The VISC. CRANBORNE.
The LA. ELIZ. GUILFORD.
The LA. ANNE WINTER.
The LA. WINDSOR.
The LA. ANNE CLIFFORD.

IV

BEN JONSON.

(1572–1637.)

OBERON, THE FAIRY PRINCE:

A MASQUE OF PRINCE HENRY'S AT WHITEHALL,
JANUARY 1, 1611.

[Oberon is of course Prince Henry, born February 19, 1594,
died November 6, 1612.]

The first face of the scene appeared all obscure, and nothing perceived
but a dark rock, with trees beyond it, and all wildness that could be
presented: till, at one corner of the cliff, above the horizon, the moon
began to shew, and rising, a SATYR was seen by her light to put
forth his head and call.

> 1 *Satyr.* CHROMIS! Mnasil![1] none appear?
> See you not who riseth here?
> You saw Silenus late, I fear.[2]—
> I 'll prove if this can reach your ear.

He wound his cornet, and thought himself answered; but was
deceived by the echo.

> O, you wake then! come away,
> Times be short are made for play;
> The humorous[3] moon too will not stay:—

---

[1] They are the names of two young Satyrs, I find in Virgil *Eclog.* 6,
that took Silenus sleeping.—JONSON.

[2] A proverbial speech, when they will tax one the other of drinking or
sleepiness; alluding to that former place in Virgil:—

> *Chromis et Mnasilus in antro*
> *Silenum, pueri, somno videre iacentem,*
> *Inflatum hesterno venas, ut semper, Iaccho.*—JONSON.

[3] Capricious.

What doth make you thus delay?
Hath his tankard touched your brain?
    Sure, they 're fallen asleep again:
    Or I doubt it was the vain
    Echo did me entertain.
Prove again—

He wound the second time, and found it.

                I thought 't was she!
    Idle nymph, I pray thee be
    Modest, and not follow me:
    I nor love myself, nor thee.[1]

Here he wound the third time, and was answered by another *Satyr*,
who likewise shewed himself.

        Ay, this sound I better know;
        List! I would I could hear moe.

At this they came running forth severally, from divers parts of the
rock, leaping and making antick action and gestures to the number
of ten; some of them speaking, some admiring: and amongst them
a SILENE, who is ever the prefect of the *Satyrs*, and so presented in
all their chori and meetings.

    2 *Satyr*. Thank us, and you shall do so.
    3 *Satyr*. Ay, our number soon will grow.
    2 *Satyr.* See Silenus!
    3 *Satyr*.   CERCOPS[2] too!
    4 *Satyr*. Yes.   What is there now to do?
    5 *Satyr*. Are there any nymphs to woo?
    4 *Satyr*. If there be, let me have two.
    Silenus. Chaster language!   These are nights,
Solemn to the shining rites

---

[1] Respecting that known fable of Echo's following Narcissus; and his
self-love.—JONSON.
[2] One of the Cercopes, thievish gnomes who robbed Hercules when
asleep.

Of the Fairy Prince and knights:
While the moon their orgies lights.

 2 *Satyr.* Will they come abroad anon?

 3 *Satyr.* Shall we see young OBERON?

 4 *Satyr.* Is he such a princely one
As you spake him long agone?

 Silenus. Satyrs, he doth fill with grace
    Every season, every place;
    Beauty dwells but in his face:
    He's the height of all our race.
  Our Pan's father, god of tongue,
    Bacchus, though he still be young,
    Phœbus, when he crowned sung,
    Nor Mars, when first his armour rung,
  Might with him be named that day:
    He is lovelier than in May
    Is the spring, and there can stay
    As little as he can decay.

 Omnes. O, that he would come away!

 3 *Satyr.* Grandsire, we shall leave to play
With Lyaeus[1] now; and serve
Only OBERON.

 Silenus. He'll deserve
All you can, and more, my boys.

 4 *Satyr.* Will he give us pretty toys,
To beguile the girls withal?

 3 *Satyr.* And to make 'em quickly fall?

 Silenus. Peace, my wantons! he will do
More than you can aim unto.

 4 *Satyr.* Will he build us larger caves?

 Silenus. Yes, and give you ivory staves
When you hunt; and better wine—

 1 *Satyr.* Than the master of the vine?

---

[1] A name of Bacchus, Lyaeus, of freeing men's minds from cares: παρὰ τὸ λύω, *solvo.*—JONSON.

2 *Satyr.* And rich prizes, to be won,
When we leap, or when we run?

1 *Satyr.* Ay, and gild our cloven feet?

3 *Satyr.* Strew our heads with poulders[1] sweet?

1 *Satyr.* Bind our crooked legs in hoops
Made of shells with silver loops?

2 *Satyr.* Tie about our tawny wrists
Bracelets of the fairy twists?

4 *Satyr.* And, to spight the coy nymphs' scorns,
Hang upon our stubbed horns
Garlands, ribbands, and fine posies—

3 *Satyr.* Fresh as when the flower discloses?

1 *Satyr.* Yes, and stick our pricking ears
With the pearl that Tethys wears.

2 *Satyr.* And to answer all things else,
Trap our shaggy thighs with bells;
That as we do strike a time,
In our dance shall make a chime—

3 *Satyr.* Louder than the rattling pipes
Of the wood gods—

1 *Satyr.*   Or the stripes
Of the taber; when we carry
Bacchus up, his pomp to vary.

Silenus. O, that he so long doth tarry!

Omnes. See! the rock begins to ope,
Now you shall enjoy your hope;
'T is about the hour, I know.

There the whole scene opened, and within was discovered the frontispiece of a bright and glorious palace, whose gates and walls were
transparent. Before the gates lay two SYLVANS, armed with their
clubs, and drest in leaves, asleep. At this the *Satyrs* wondering,
Silenus proceeds:

Silenus. Look! does not his palace show
Like another sky of lights?

[1] Powders.

Yonder with him live the knights,
Once the noblest of the earth,
Quickened by a second birth:
Who for prowess and for truth,
There are crowned with lasting youth:
And do hold, by Fate's command,
Seats of bliss in Fairy land.
But their guards, methinks, do sleep!
Let us wake 'em.—Sirs, you keep
Proper watch, that thus do lie
Drowned in sloth!

 1 *Satyr.*   They 've ne'er an eye
To wake withal.

 2 *Satyr.*   Nor sense, I fear;
For they sleep in either ear.[1]

 3 *Satyr.* Holla, Sylvans!—sure they 're caves
Of sleep these, or else they 're graves.

 4 *Satyr.* Hear you, friends!—who keeps the keepers?

 1 *Satyr.* They are the eighth and ninth sleepers!

 2 *Satyr.* Shall we cramp 'em?

Silenus.   Satyrs, no.

 3 *Satyr.* Would we had Boreas here, to blow
Off their leavy[2] coats, and strip 'em.

 4 *Satyr.* Ay, ay, ay; that we might whip 'em.

 3 *Satyr.* Or that we had a wasp or two
For their nostrils.

 1 *Satyr.*   Hairs will do
Even as well: take my tail.

 2 *Satyr.* What d' you say to a good nail
Through their temples?

 2 *Satyr.*   Or an eel
In their guts, to make 'em feel?

---

[1] *i.e.* sleep soundly, a literal translation of the Latin phrase, *In utramvis aurem dormire.*
[2] Leafy.

4 *Satyr.* Shall we steal away their beards?
3 *Satyr.* For Pan's goat, that leads the herds?
2 *Satyr.* Or try whether is more dead,
His club or the other's head?
Silenus. Wags, no more: you grow too bold.
1 *Satyr.* I would fain now see 'em rolled
Down a hill, or from a bridge
Headlong cast, to break their ridge-
Bones: or to some river take 'em,
Plump; and see if that would wake 'em.
2 *Satyr.* There no motion yet appears.
Silenus. Strike a charm into their ears.

At which the *Satyrs* fell suddenly into this catch.

Buz, quoth the blue flie,
    Hum, quoth the bee:
Buz and hum they cry,
    And so do we.
In his ear, in his nose,
    Thus, do you see?—   [*They tickle them.*
He eat the dormouse;
    Else it was he.

The two *Sylvans* starting up amazed, and betaking themselves to
their arms, were thus questioned by *Silenus*:

Silenus. How now, Sylvans! can you wake?
I commend the care you take
In your watch! Is this your guise,
To have both your ears and eyes
Sealed so fast; as these mine elves
Might have stol'n you from yourselves?
3 *Satyr.* We had thought we must have got
Stakes, and heated 'em red-hot,

And have bored you through the eyes,
With the Cyclops, ere you 'ld rise.

    2 *Satyr.* Or have fetched some trees to heave
Up your bulks, that so did cleave
To the ground there.

    4 *Satyr.*   Are you free
Yet of sleep, and can you see
Who is yonder up aloof?

    1 *Satyr.* Be your eyes yet moon-proof?

    1 *Sylvan.* Satyrs, leave your petulance,
And go frisk about and dance;
Or else rail upon the moon:
Your expectance is too soon.
For before the second cock
Crow, the gates will not unlock;
And till then we know we keep
Guard enough, although we sleep.

    1 *Satyr.* Say you so? then let us fall
To a song, or to a brawl:
Shall we, grandsire? Let us sport,
And make expectation short.

    Silenus. Do, my wantons, what you please
I 'll lie down and take mine ease.

    1 *Satyr.* Brothers, sing then, and upbraid,
As we use, yond' seeming maid.

SONG.

Now, my cunning lady, moon,
Can you leave the side so soon
    Of the boy you keep so hid?
Midwife Juno sure will say
This is not the proper way,
    Of your paleness to be rid.
But perhaps it is your grace
To wear sickness in your face,

That there might be wagers laid
Still, by fools, you are a maid.

Come, your changes overthrow,
What your look would carry so;
   Moon, confess then what you are,
And be wise, and free to use
Pleasures that you now do lose;
   Let us Satyrs have a share:
Though our forms be rough and rude,
Yet our acts may be endued
    With more virtue: every one
    Cannot be ENDYMION.

The song ended, they fell suddenly into an antick dance full of gesture
and swift motion, and continued it till the crowing of the cock: at
which they were interrupted by *Silenus*.

Silenus. Stay! the cheerful Chanticleer
Tells you that the time is near:—
See, the gates already spread!
Every Satyr bow his head.

There the whole palace opened, and the nation of *Faies* were discovered, some with instruments, some bearing lights, others singing;
and within afar off in perspective, the knights masquers sitting in
their several sieges[1]: at the further end of all, OBERON, in a chariot,
which, to a loud triumphant music, began to move forward, drawn
by two white bears, and on either side guarded by three *Sylvans*, with
one going in front.

SONG.

Melt earth to sea, sea flow to air,
   And air fly into fire,
Whilst we in tunes to Arthur's chair
   Bear Oberon's desire;
    Than which there's nothing can be higher,

---

[1] Seats.

Save JAMES, to whom it flies:
But he the wonder is of tongues, of ears, of eyes.

Who hath not heard, who hath not seen,
  Who hath not sung his name?
The soul that hath not, hath not been;
  But is the very same
  With buried sloth, and knows not fame,
Which doth him best comprise:
For he the wonder is of tongues, of ears, of eyes.

By this time the chariot was come as far forth as the face of the
scene. And the *Satyrs* beginning to leap, and express their joy for
the unused state and solemnity, the foremost *Sylvan* began to speak.

  1 *Sylvan.* Give place, and silence; you were rude too
    late;
This is a night of greatness and of state,
Not to be mixt with light and skipping sport;
A night of homage to the British court,
And ceremony due to Arthur's chair,
From our bright master, OBERON the fair;
Who with these knights, attendants, here preserved
In Fairy land, for good they have deserved
Of yond' high throne are come of right to pay
Their annual vows; and all their glories lay
At 's feet, and tender to this only great,
True majesty, restored in this seat;
To whose sole power and magic they do give
The honour of their being; that they live
Sustained in form, fame, and felicity,
From rage of fortune, or the fear to die.

  Silenus. And may they well. For this indeed is he,
My boys, whom you must quake at when you see.
He is above your reach; and neither doth,
Nor can he think within a Satyr's tooth:

Before his presence you must fall or fly,
He is the matter of virtue, and placed high.
His meditations to his height are even;
And all their issue is akin to heaven.
He is a god o'er kings; yet stoops he then
Nearest a man, when he doth govern men;
To teach them by the sweetness of his sway,
And not by force.   He's such a king as they
Who're tyrants' subjects, or ne'er tasted peace,
Would in their wishes form for their release.
'T is he that stays the time from turning old,
And keeps the age up in a head of gold:
That in his own true circle still doth run;
And holds his course as certain as the sun.
He makes it ever day, and ever spring,
Where he doth shine, and quickens everything,
Like a new nature: so that true to call
Him by his title is to say, He's all.

 1 *Sylvan.* I thank the wise Silenus for this praise.
Stand forth bright Faies and Elves, and tune your lays
Unto his name; then let your nimble feet
Tread subtle circles, that may always meet
In point to him; and figures to express
The grace of him and his great emperess,
That all that shall to-night behold the rites
Performed by princely Oberon and these knights,
May without stop point out the proper heir
Designed so long to Arthur's crowns and chair.

SONG

BY TWO FAIES.

1 *Faie.* Seek you majesty, to strike?
     Bid the world produce his like.

2 *Faie.*   Seek you glory, to amaze?
              Here let all eyes stand at gaze.
Chorus.   Seek you wisdom, to inspire?
                  Touch then at no other's fire.

1 *Faie.*   Seek you knowledge, to direct?
              Trust to his without suspect.
2 *Faie.*   Seek you piety, to lead?
              In his footsteps only tread.
Chorus.   Every virtue of a king,
                  And of all in him we sing.

Then the lesser *Faies* dance forth their dance[1]; which ended, a full
SONG follows by all the voices.

> The solemn rites are well begun;
>   And though but lighted by the moon,
> They shew as rich as if the sun
>   Had made this night his noon.
> But may none wonder that they are so bright,
> The moon now borrows from a greater light.
>   Then, princely Oberon,
>   Go on,
>   This is not every night.

There OBERON and the knights dance out the first masque-dance;
which was followed with this

SONG.

> Nay, nay,
> You must not stay,
> Nor be weary yet;

[1] Gifford prints the following from Sir John Finet, Master of the
Ceremonies to James I.: "The little ladies performed their dance to
the amazement of all beholders, considering the tenderness of their years,
and the many intricate changes of the dance, which was so disposed
that, which way soever the changes went, the little duke [Charles] was
still found in the midst of these little dancers."

This's no time to cast away;
Or for Faies so to forget
The virtue of their feet.
Knotty legs and plants[1] of clay
Seek for ease, or love delay.
But with you it still should fare
As with the air of which you are.

After which they danced forth their second masque-dance, and were again excited by a

SONG.

1 *Faie.*　Nor yet, nor yet, O you in this night blest,
　　　　 Must you have will, or hope to rest.
2 *Faie.*　If you use the smallest stay,
　　　　 You'll be overta'en by day.
1 *Faie.*　And these beauties[2] will suspect
　　　　 That their forms you do neglect,
　　　　 If you do not call them forth.
2 *Faie.*　Or that you have no more worth
　　　　 Than the coarse and country Faerie,
　　　　 That doth haunt the hearth or dairy.

Then followed the measures, corantos, galliards, &c., till *Phosphorus*, the day-star, appeared, and called them away; but first they were invited home by one of the *Sylvans* with this

---

[1] Feet, from the Latin *planta*.

[2] "These light skirmishers," Sir John Finet continues, "the faies, having done their devoir, in came the princesses; first the Queen, next the lady Elizabeth's grace, then the lady Arbella, the countesses of Arundell, Derby, Essex, Dorset and Montgomery; the lady Hadington, the lady Elizabeth Grey, the lady Winsor, the lady Katharine Peter, the lady Elizabeth Guildford, and the lady Mary Wintoun. By that time these had done, it was high time to go to bed, for it was within half an hour of the sun's rising."

SONG.

Gentle knights,
Know some measure of your nights.
Tell the high graced Oberon
It is time that we were gone.
Here be forms so bright and airy,
And their motions so they vary,
As they will enchant the Faerie,
If you longer here should tarry.

Phosphorus. To rest, to rest! the herald of the day,
Bright Phosphorus, commands you hence; obey.
The moon is pale and spent; and winged night
Makes headlong haste to fly the morning's sight:
Who now is rising from her blushing wars,
And with her rosy hand puts back the stars.
Of which myself the last, her harbinger,
But stay to warn you, that you not defer
Your parting longer: then do I give way,
As Night hath done, and so must you, to Day.

After this they danced their last dance into the work. And with a
full SONG the star vanished, and the whole machine closed.

O yet how early, and before her time,
The envious Morning up doth climb,
    Though she not love her bed!
What haste the jealous Sun doth make,
His fiery horses up to take,
    And once more shew his head!
Lest, taken with the brightness of this night,
The world should wish it last, and never miss his light.

V.

THOMAS CAMPION.

(1567 ?–1620.)

THE DESCRIPTION, SPEECHES, AND SONGS, OF THE LORDS'
MASQUE, PRESENTED IN THE BANQUETING-HOUSE ON
THE MARRIAGE NIGHT OF THE HIGH AND MIGHTY
COUNT PALATINE, AND THE ROYALLY DESCENDED
THE LADY ELIZABETH.

[This is the first of three masques written in honour of this marriage.
It was presented, as its title indicates, by the noblemen of the Court on
the evening of the wedding-day, Sunday, February 14, 1613. The
other two were presented by the Inns of Court: the masque of the
Middle Temple and Lincoln's Inn, written by George Chapman, on
the evening of Monday, February 15, and the masque of the Inner
Temple and Gray's Inn, written by Francis Beaumont, on the evening
of Saturday, February 20.]

I HAVE now taken occasion to satisfy many, who long since
were desirous that the Lords' masque should be published,
which, but for some private lets, had in due time come forth.
The Scene was divided into two parts. From the roof to the
floor, the lower part being first discovered (upon the sound of
a double consort, exprest by several instruments, placed on
either side of the room) there appeared a wood in prospective, the innermost part being of relief, or whole round, the
rest painted. On the left hand from the seat was a cave, and
on the right a thicket, out of which came Orpheus, who was
attired after the old Greek manner, his hair curled and long,
a laurel wreath on his head, and in his hand he bare a silver
bird; about him tamely placed several wild beasts: and
upon the ceasing of the consort Orpheus spake.

Orpheus. Again, again, fresh kindle Phoebus' sounds,
T' exhale[1] Mania from her earthly den;

[1] Draw forth.

Allay the fury that her sense confounds,
And call her gently forth; sound, sound again.

The consorts both sound again, and Mania, *the goddess of madness,
appears wildly out of her cave. Her habit was confused and strange,
but yet graceful; she as one amazed speaks.*

Mania. What powerful noise is this importunes me,
T' abandon darkness which my humour fits?
Jove's hand in it I feel, and ever he
Must be obeyed ev'n of the frantic'st wits.

Orpheus. Mania!

Mania.   Hah!

Orpheus.   Brain-sick, why start'st thou so?
Approach yet nearer, and thou then shalt know
The will of Jove, which he will breathe from me.

Mania. Who art thou? if my dazzled eyes can see,
Thou art the sweet enchanter heav'nly Orpheus.

Orpheus. The same, Mania, and Jove greets thee thus:
Though several power to thee and charge he gave
T' enclose in thy dominions such as rave
Through blood's distemper, how durst thou attempt
T' imprison Entheus whose rage is exempt
From vulgar censure? it is all divine,
Full of celestial rapture, that can shine
Through darkest shadows: therefore Jove by me
Commands thy power straight to set Entheus free.

Mania. How can I? Frantics with him many more
In one cave are locked up; ope once the door,
All will fly out, and through the world disturb
The peace of Jove; for what power then can curb
Their reinless fury?

(M 372)   K

Orpheus.   Let not fear in vain
Trouble thy crazed fancy; all again,
Save Entheus, to thy safeguard shall retire,
For Jove into our music will inspire
The power of passion, that their thoughts shall bend
To any form or motion we intend.
Obey Jove's will then; go, set Entheus free.

Mania. I willing go, so Jove obeyed must be.

Orpheus. Let music put on Protean changes now;
Wild beasts it once tamed, now let Frantics bow.

At the sound of a strange music twelve *Frantics* enter, six men and six women, all presented in sundry habits and humours. There was the lover, the self-lover, the melancholic-man full of fear, the school-man, overcome with fantasy, the over-watched[1] usurer, with others that made an absolute medley of madness; in midst of whom *Entheus* (or poetic fury) was hurried forth, and tost up and down, till by virtue of a new change in the music, the Lunatics fell into a mad measure, fitted to a loud fantastic tune; but in the end thereof the music changed into a very solemn air, which they softly played, while *Orpheus* spake.

Orpheus. Through these soft and calm sounds, Mania, pass
With thy Fantastics hence; here is no place
Longer for them or thee; Entheus alone
Must do Jove's bidding now: all else be gone.

During this speech *Mania* with her *Frantics* depart, leaving *Entheus* behind them, who was attired in a close curace[2] of the antic fashion, bases[3] with labels[4], a robe fastened to his shoulders, and hanging down behind; on his head a wreath of laurels, out of which grew a pair of wings: in the one hand he held a book, and in the other a pen.

Entheus. Divinest Orpheus, O how all from thee

---

[1] Weary for want of sleep.
[2] Cuirass.   [3] Kilts.   [4] Lappets.

Proceed with wondrous sweetness! Am I free?
Is my affliction vanished?

Orpheus. Too, too long,
Alas, good Entheus, hast thou brooked this wrong
What! number thee with madmen! O mad age,
Senseless of thee, and thy celestial rage!
For thy excelling rapture, ev'n through things
That seem most light, is borne with sacred wings:
Nor are these musics, shows, or revels vain,
When thou adorn'st them with thy Phoebean brain.
Th' are palate-sick of much more vanity,
That cannot taste them in their dignity.
Jove therefore lets thy prisoned sprite obtain
Her liberty and fiery scope again;
And here by me commands thee to create
Inventions rare, this night to celebrate,
Such as become a nuptial by his will
Begun and ended.

Entheus. Jove I honour still,
And must obey. Orpheus, I feel the fires
Are ready in my brain, which Jove inspires.
Lo, through that veil I see Prometheus stand
Before those glorious lights which his false hand
Stole out of heav'n, the dull earth to inflame
With the affects [1] of Love and honoured Fame.
I view them plain in pomp and majesty,
Such as being seen might hold rivality
With the best triumphs. Orpheus, give a call
With thy charmed music, and discover all.

Orpheus. Fly, cheerful voices, through the air, and clear
These clouds, that yon hid beauty may appear.

[1] Dispositions, feelings, likely to result in *effects.*

A SONG.

I.

Come away; bring thy golden theft,
   Bring, bright Prometheus, all thy lights;
Thy fires from Heav'n bereft
   Show now to human sights.
Come quickly, come! Thy stars to our stars straight
      present,
For pleasure being too much deferred loseth her best
      content.
What fair dames wish, should swift as their own thoughts
      appear;
To loving and to longing hearts every hour seems a year.

II.

See how fair, O how fair, they shine!
   What yields more pomp beneath the skies?
Their birth is yet divine,
   And such their form implies.
Large grow their beams, their near approach afford them
      so;
By nature sights that pleasing are, cannot too amply
      show.
O might these flames in human shapes descend this
      place,
How lovely would their presence be, how full of grace!

In the end of the first part of this song, the upper part of the scene
was discovered by the sudden fall of a curtain; then in clouds of
several colours (the upper part of them being fiery, and the middle
heightened with silver) appeared eight stars of extraordinary bigness,
which so were placed, as that they seemed to be fixed between the
firmament and the earth. In the front of the scene stood *Prometheus*,
attired as one of the ancient heroes.

   Entheus. Patron of mankind, powerful and bounteous,
Rich in thy flames, reverend Prometheus,

In Hymen's place aid us to solemnise
These royal nuptials; fill the lookers' eyes
With admiration of thy fire and light,
And from thy hand let wonders flow to-night.

Prometheus. Entheus and Orpheus, names both dear to
    me,
In equal balance I your third will be
In this night's honour.   View these heav'n-born stars,
Who by my stealth are become sublunars;
How well their native beauties fit this place,
Which with a choral dance they first shall grace;
Then shall their forms to human figures turn,
And these bright fires within their bosoms burn.
Orpheus, apply thy music, for it well,
Helps to induce a courtly miracle.

Orpheus. Sound, best of musics, raise yet higher our
    sprites,
While we admire Prometheus' dancing lights.

A SONG.

1

Advance your choral motions now,
    You music-loving lights:
This night concludes the nuptial vow,
    Make this the best of nights:
So bravely crown it with your beams
    That it may live in fame
As long as Rhenus or the Thames
    Are known by either name.

II.

Once more again, yet nearer move
    Your forms at willing view;

Such fair effects of joy and love
   None can express but you.
Then revel midst your airy bowers
   Till all the clouds do sweat,
That pleasure may be poured in showers
   On this triumphant seat.

III.

Long since hath lovely Flora thrown
   Her flowers and garlands here;
Rich Ceres all her wealth hath shown,
   Proud of her dainty cheer.
Changed then to human shape, descend,
   Clad in familiar weed,
That every eye may here commend
   The kind delights you breed.

According to the humour of this song, the stars moved in an exceeding strange and delightful manner, and I suppose few have ever seen more neat artifice than Master Inigo Jones shewed in contriving their motion, who in all the rest of the workmanship which belonged to the whole invention shewed extraordinary industry and skill, which if it be not as lively exprest in writing as it appeared in view, rob not him of his due, but lay the blame on my want of right apprehending his instructions for the adorning of his art. But to return to our purpose; about the end of this song, the stars suddenly vanished, as if they had been drowned amongst the clouds, and the eight masquers appeared in their habits, which were infinitely rich, befitting states[1] (such as indeed they all were) as also a time so far heightened the day before with all the richest show of solemnity that could be invented. The ground of their attires was massy cloth of silver, embossed with flames of embroidery; on their heads, they had crowns, flames made all of gold-plate enameled, and on the top a feather of silk, representing a cloud of smoke. Upon their new transformation, the whole scene being clouds dispersed, and there appeared an element of artificial fires, with several circles of lights, in continual motion, representing the house of Prometheus, who then thus applies his speech to the masquers.

[1] Persons of rank.

They are transformed.

Prometheus. So pause awhile, and come, ye fiery sprites,
Break forth the earth like sparks t' attend these knights.

Sixteen pages, like fiery spirits, all their attires being alike composed
of flames, with fiery wings and bases, bearing in either hand a torch
of virgin wax, come forth below dancing a lively measure, and the
dance being ended, Prometheus speaks to them from above.

The Torch-bearers' Dance.

Prometheus. Wait, spirits, wait, while through the clouds
    we pace,
And by descending gain a higher place.

The pages return toward the scene, to give their attendance to the
masquers with their lights: from the side of the scene appeared a bright
and transparent cloud, which reached from the top of the heavens to
the earth: on this cloud the masquers, led by Prometheus, descended
with the music of a full song; and at the end of their descent, the
cloud brake in twain, and one part of it (as with a wind) was blown
overthwart the scene.

While this cloud was vanishing, the wood being the underpart of
the scene, was insensibly changed, and in place thereof appeared
four noble women-statues of silver, standing in several niches,
accompanied with ornaments of architecture, which filled all the end
of the house, and seemed to be all of goldsmith's work.   The first
order consisted of pilasters all of gold, set with rubies, sapphires,
emeralds, opals and such like.   The capitals were composed, and of
a new invention.   Over this was a bastard order with cartouches[1]
reversed coming from the capitals of every pilaster, which made the
upper part rich and full of ornament.   Over every statue was placed
a history in gold, which seemed to be of base relief; the conceits
which were figured in them were these.   In the first was Prometheus,
embossing in clay the figure of a woman, in the second he was represented stealing fire from the chariot-wheel of the sun; in the third
he is exprest putting life with this fire into his figure of clay; and in
the fourth square Jupiter, enraged, turns these new-made women into
statues.   Above all, for finishing, ran a cornice, which returned over
every pilaster, seeming all of gold and richly carved.

[1] Architectural ornaments in the shape of rolls of paper.

A FULL SONG.

> Supported now by clouds descend,
> Divine Prometheus, Hymen's friend:
> Lead down the new transformed fires
> And fill their breasts with love's desires,
> That they may revel with delight,
> And celebrate this nuptial night.
> So celebrate this nuptial night
>   That all which see may say
> They never viewed so fair a sight
>   Even on the clearest day.

Entheus. See, see, Prometheus, four of these first
    dames
Which thou long since out of thy purchased [1] flames,
Didst forge with heav'nly fire, as they were then
By Jove transformed to statues, so again
They suddenly appear by his command
At thy arrival.   Lo, how fixed they stand;
So did Jove's wrath too long, but now at last,
It by degrees relents, and he hath placed
These statues, that we might his aid implore,
First for the life of these, and then for more.

Prometheus. Entheus, thy counsels are divine and just,
Let Orpheus deck thy hymn, since pray we must.

THE FIRST INVOCATION IN A FULL SONG.

> Powerful Jove, that of bright stars,
> Now hast made men fit for wars,
> Thy power in these statues prove
> And make them women fit for love.

In the time of this invocation the first four statues are transformed
into women.

[1] Stolen.

Orpheus. See, Jove is pleased; statues have life and
  move!
Go, new-born men, and entertain with love
The new-born women, though your number yet
Exceeds theirs double, they are armed with wit
To bear your best encounters. Court them fair:
When words and music please, let none despair.

THE SONG.

I.

Woo her, and win her, he that can!
  Each woman hath two lovers,
So she must take and leave a man,
  Till time more grace discovers.
This doth Jove to shew that want
  Makes beauty most respected;
If fair women were more scant,
  They would be more affected.

II.

Courtship and music suit with love,
  They both are works of passion;
Happy is he whose words can move,
  Yet sweet notes help persuasion.
Mix your words with music then,
  That they the more may enter;
Bold assaults are fit for men,
  That on strange beauties venter.

While this song is sung, and the masquers court the four new transformed ladies, four other statues appear in their places.

Prometheus. Cease, cease your wooing strife! see, Jove
  intends
To fill your number up, and make all friends.
Orpheus and Entheus, join your skills once more,
And with a hymn the deity implore.

THE SECOND INVOCATION TO THE TUNE OF THE FIRST.

> Powerful Jove, that hast given four,
> Raise this number but once more,
> That complete, their numerous [1] feet
> May aptly in just measures meet.

The other four statues are transformed into women, in the time of this invocation.

Entheus. The number's now complete, thanks be to
    Jove!
No man needs fear a rival in his love;
For all are sped, and now begins delight
To fill with glory this triumphant night.

The masquers, having everyone entertained his lady, begin their first new entering dance: after it, while they breathe, the time is entertained with a dialogue song.

> Breathe you now, while Io Hymen
>   To the bride we sing:
> O how many joys and honours,
>   From this match will spring!
> Ever firm the league will prove,
> Where only goodness causeth love.
> Some for profit seek
> What their fancies most disleek [2];
> These love for virtue's sake alone:
> Beauty and youth unite them both in one.

CHORUS.

> Live with thy bridegroom happy, sacred bride;
> How blest is he that is for love envìed!

---

[1] Rhythmical, moving in time to the music.   [2] Dislike.

THE MASQUERS' SECOND DANCE.

Breathe again, while we with music
   Fill the empty space;
O but do not in your dances
   Yourselves only grace.
Ev'ry one fetch out your fere[1],
Whom chiefly you will honour here.
Sights most pleasure breed,
When their numbers most exceed.
Choose then, for choice to all is free;
Taken or left, none discontent must be.

CHORUS.

Now in thy revels frolic-fair delight,
To heap joy on this ever-honoured night.

The masquers during this dialogue take out others to dance with
them; men women, and women men; and first of all the princely
bridegroom and bride were drawn into these solemn revels,[2] which
continued a long space, but in the end were broken off with this
short song.

A SONG.

Cease, cease you revels, rest a space;
New pleasures press into this place,
Full of beauty and of grace.

The whole scene was now again changed, and became a prospective[3]
with porticoes on each side, which seemed to go in a great way; in
the middle was erected an obelisk, all of silver, and in it lights of
several colours; on the side of this obelisk, standing on pedestals,
were the statues of the bridegroom and bride, all of gold, in gracious
postures. This obelisk was of that height, that the top thereof touched
the highest clouds, and yet Sibylla did draw it forth with a thread of
gold. The grave sage was in a robe of gold tuckt up before to her
girdle, a kirtle gathered full and of silver; with a veil on her head,
being bare-necked, and bearing in her hands a scroll of parchment.

[1] Partner.   [2] See Introduction, p. xxxiv.   [3] Perspective, vista.

Entheus. Make clear the passage to Sibylla's sight,
Who with her trophy comes to crown this night;
And, as herself with music shall be led,
So shall she pull on with a golden thread
A high vast obelisk, dedicate to Fame,
Which immortality itself did frame.
Raise high your voices now; like trumpets fill
The room with sounds of triumph, sweet and shrill.

A SONG.

> Come triumphing, come with state,
>   Old Sibylla, reverend dame;
> Thou keep'st the secret key of fate,
>   Preventing swiftest Fame.
> This night breathe only words of joy,
> And speak them plain, now be not coy.

Sibylla.

Debetur alto iure principium Iovi,
Votis det ipse vim meis, dictis fidem.
Utrinque decoris splendet egregium iubar;
Medio triumphus mole stat dignus sua,
Coelumque summo capite dilectum petit.
Quam pulchra pulchro sponsa respondet viro!
Quam plena numinis!   Patrem vultu exprimit,
Parens futura masculae prolis, parens
Regum, imperatorum.   Additur Germaniae
Robur Britannicum: ecquid esse par potest?
Utramque iunget una mens gentem, fides,
Deique cultus unus, et simplex amor.
Idem erit utrique hostis, sodalis idem, idem
Votum periclitantium, atque eadem manus.
Favebit illis pax, favebit bellica
Fortuna, semper aderit adiutor Deus.
Sic, sic Sibylla; vocibus nec his deest

Pondus, nec hoc inane monumentum trahit.
Et aureum est, et quale nec flammas timet,
Nec fulgura, ipsi quippe sacratur Iovi.

> *Prometheus.* The good old sage is silenced, her free
> tongue
That made such melody, is now unstrung:
Then grace hèr trophy with a dance triumphant;
Where Orpheus is none can fit music want.

A SONG AND DANCE TRIUMPHANT OF THE MASQUERS.

I.

Dance, dance! and visit now the shadows of our joy,
All in height, and pleasing state, your changed forms
employ.
And as the bird of Jove salutes with lofty wing the
morn,
So mount, so fly, these trophies to adorn.
Grace them with all the sounds and motions of delight,
Since all the earth cannot express a lovelier sight.
View them with triumph, and in shades the truth adore:
No pomp or sacrifice can please Jove's greatness more.

II.

Turn, turn! and honour now the life these figures bear:
Lo, how heav'nly natures far above all art appear!
Let their aspects revive in you the fire that shined so
late,
Still mount and still retain your heavenly state.
Gods were with dance and with music served of old,
Those happy days derived their glorious style from gold:
This pair, by Hymen joined, grace you with measures
then,
Since they are both divine and you are more than men.

Orpheus. Let here Sibylla's trophy stand,
Lead her now by either hand,
That she may approach yet nearer,
And the bride and bridegroom hear her
Bless them in her native tongue,
Wherein old prophecies she sung,
Which time to light hath brought.
She speaks that which Jove hath taught:
Well may he inspire her now,
To make a joyful and true vow.

Sibylla. Sponsam sponse toro tene pudicam,
Sponsum sponsa tene toro pudicum.
Non haec unica nox datur beatis,
At vos perpetuo haec beabit una
Prole multiplici, parique amore.
Laeta, ac vera refert Sibylla; ab alto
Ipse Iuppiter annuit loquenti.

Prometheus. So be it ever; joy and peace,
And mutual love give you increase,
That your posterity may grow
In fame, as long as seas do flow.

Entheus. Live you long to see your joys,
In fair nymphs and princely boys;
Breeding like the garden flowers,
Which kind heav'n draws with her warm showers.

Orpheus. Enough of blessing, though too much
Never can be said to such;
But night doth waste, and Hymen chides,
Kind to bridegrooms and to brides.
Then, singing, the last dance induce,
So let good night present excuse.

THE SONG.

No longer wrong the night
Of her Hymenaean right;
A thousand Cupids call away,
Fearing the approaching day;
The cocks already crow:
    Dance then and go!

The last new dance of the masquers, which concludes all with a
lively strain at their going out.

FINIS.

VI.

FRANCIS BEAUMONT.
(1584-1616.)

THE MASQUE OF THE INNER-TEMPLE AND GRAY'S INN.

PRESENTED IN THE BANQUETING-HOUSE AT WHITEHALL, FEBRUARY 20, 1613.

TO THE WORTHY SIR FRANCIS BACON, HIS MAJESTY'S SOLICITOR-GENERAL, AND THE GRAVE AND LEARNED BENCH OF THE ANCIENTLY-ALLIED HOUSES OF GRAY'S INN AND THE INNER-TEMPLE, THE INNER-TEMPLE AND GRAY'S INN.

YE that spared no time nor travail in the setting forth, ordering and furnishing of this Masque (being the first fruits of honour in this kind which these two Societies have offered to his majesty) will not think much now to look back upon the effects of your own care and work; for that, whereof the success was then doubtful, is now happily performed and graciously accepted; and that which you were then to think of in straits of time, you may now peruse at leisure: and you, Sir Francis Bacon, especially, as you did then by your countenance and loving affection advance it, so let your good word grace it and defend it, which is able to add value to the greatest and least matters.

THE MASQUE OF THE INNER-TEMPLE AND GRAY'S INN, GRAY'S INN AND THE INNER-TEMPLE.

This Masque was appointed to have been presented the Shrove-Tuesday before, at which time the masquers, with their attendants, and divers others, gallant young gentlemen of both houses, as their convoy, set forth from Winchester-house (which was the rendezvous) towards the court, about seven of the clock at night.

This voyage by water[1] was performed in great triumph: the gentlemen-masquers being placed by themselves in the King's royal barge, with the rich furniture of state, and adorned with a great number of lights, placed in such order as might make the best show.

They were attended with a multitude of barges and gallies, with all variety of loud music, and several peals of ordnance; and led by two admirals.

Of this show his majesty was graciously pleased to take view, with the prince, the Count Palatine and the Lady Elizabeth their highnesses, at the windows of his privy gallery, upon the water, till their landing, which was at the privy stairs; where they were most honourably received by the lord-chamberlain, and so conducted to the vestry.

The hall was by that time filled with company of very good fashion, but yet so as a very great number of principal ladies and other noble persons were not yet come in, whereby it was foreseen that the room would be so scanted as might have been inconvenient; and thereupon his majesty was most graciously pleased, with the consent of the gentlemen-masquers, to put off the night[2] until Saturday following, with the special favour and privilege, that there should be no let as to the outward ceremony of magnificence until that time.

At the day that it was presented, there was a choice room reserved for the gentlemen of both their houses, who, coming in troop about seven of the clock, received that special honour and noble favour, as to be brought to their places by the Right Honourable the Earl of Northampton, Lord-Privy Seal.

---

[1] The masquers of the Middle Temple and Lincoln's Inn on the previous evening had come by land: their procession is minutely described by Chapman in his introduction to that masque.

[2] The king was not unnaturally fatigued after all the wedding festivities, including the masques of the two preceding nights, and did not feel disposed to sit out a third: " Sir Francis Bacon ventured to entreat his Majesty that by this disgrace [putting off the performance] he would not as it were bury them quick; and I hear the king should answer that they must bury him quick, for he could last no longer".—*Letter of Mr. Chamberlain to Sir Dudley Careleton* in Nichols ii. 589.

THE DEVICE OR ARGUMENT OF THE MASQUE.

Jupiter and Juno, willing to do honour to the marriage of the two famous rivers Thamesis and Rhine, employ their messengers severally, Mercury and Iris, for that purpose. They meet and contend: then Mercury, for his part, brings forth an anti-masque all of spirits and divine natures; but yet not of one kind or livery (because that had been so much in use heretofore), but, as it were, in consort, like to broken music[1]: and, preserving the propriety of the device,—for that rivers in nature are maintained either by springs from beneath or showers from above,—he raiseth four of the Naiades out of the fountains, and bringeth down five of the Hyades out of the clouds to dance. Hereupon Iris scoffs at Mercury, for that he had devised a dance but of one sex, which could have no life: but Mercury, who was provided for that exception, and in token that the match should be blessed both with love and riches, calleth forth out of the groves four Cupids, and brings down from Jupiter's altar four Statuas[2] of gold and silver to dance with the Nymphs and Stars: in which dance, the Cupids being blind, and the Statuas having but half life put into them, and retaining still somewhat of their old nature, giveth fit occasion to new and strange varieties both in the music and paces. This was the first anti-masque.

Then Iris, for her part, in scorn of this high-flying device, and in token that the match shall likewise be blessed with the love of the common people, calls to Flora, her confederate,—for that the months of flowers are likewise the months of sweet showers and rainbows,— to bring in a May-dance, or rural dance, consisting likewise not of any suited[3] persons, but of a confusion or commixture of all such persons as are natural and proper for country sports. This is the second anti-masque.

Then Mercury and Iris, after this vying one upon the other, seem to leave their contention; and Mercury, by the consent of Iris, brings down the Olympian Knights, intimating that Jupiter having, after a long discontinuance, revived the Olympian games, and summoned thereunto from all parts the liveliest and activest persons that were, had enjoined them, before they fell to their games, to do honour to these nuptials. The Olympian games portend to the match celebrity, victory, and felicity. This was the main masque.

[1] Concerted music.
[2] Statues, the Latin form of the word.
[3] Similar, of one kind.

The fabric was a mountain with two descents, and severed with two traverses.[1] At the entrance of the King,

The first traverse was drawn, and the lower descent of the mountain discovered, which was the pendant of a hill to life, with divers boscages[2] and grovets[3] upon the steep or hanging grounds thereof; and at the foot of the hill four delicate fountains, running with water and bordered with sedges and water-flowers.

Iris first appeared; and, presently after, Mercury, striving to overtake her. Iris apparelled in a robe of discoloured[4] taffeta, figured in variable colours, like the rainbow, a cloudy wreath on her head, and tresses. Mercury in doublet and hose of white taffeta, a white hat, wings on his shoulders and feet, his caduceus[5] in his hand, speaking to Iris as followeth:—

Mercury. Stay, stay!
Stay, light-foot Iris! for thou striv'st in vain;
My wings are nimbler than thy feet.

Iris.   Away,
Dissembling Mercury! my messages
Ask honest haste; not like those wanton ones
Your thundering father sends.

Mercury.   Stay, foolish maid!
Or I will take my rise upon a hill,
When I perceive thee seated in a cloud
In all the painted glory that thou hast,
And never cease to clap my willing wings,
Till I catch hold of thy discolour'd bow,
And shiver it beyond the angry power
Of your curst[6] mistress to make up again.

Iris. Hermes, forbear: Juno will chide and strike.
Is great Jove jealous that I am employ'd

---

[1] Curtains.   [2] Shrubberies.
[3] Little groves.   [4] Of various colours.
[5] A herald's staff, especially used to signify the wand of Mercury, the messenger of the gods.   [6] Cross, peevish.

On her love-errands? She did never yet
Clasp weak mortality in her white arms,
As he hath often done: I only come
To celebrate the long-wish'd nuptials
Here in Olympia, which are now perform'd,
Betwixt two goodly rivers, that have mix'd
Their gentle-rising waves, and are to grow
Into a thousand streams, great as themselves;
I need not name them, for the sound is loud
In heaven and earth; and I am sent from her,
The queen of marriage, that was present here,
And smil'd to see them join, and hath not chid
Since it was done. Good Hermes, let me go.

    Mercury. Nay, you must stay; Jove's message is the
      same:
Whose eyes are lightning, and whose voice is thunder,
Whose breath is any wind he will; who knows
How to be first in earth as well as heaven.

    Iris. But what hath he to do with nuptial-rites?
Let him keep state upon his starry throne,
And fright poor mortals with his thunderbolts,
Leaving to us the mutual darts of eyes.

    Mercury. Alas, when ever offered he to abridge
Your lady's power, but only now in these,
Whose match concerns the general government?
Hath not each god a part in these high joys?
And shall not he, the king of gods, presume
Without proud Juno's licence? Let her know,
That, when enamour'd Jove first gave her power
To link soft hearts in undissolving bands,
He then foresaw, and to himself reserv'd,
The honour of this marriage. Thou shalt stand
Still as a rock, while I, to bless this feast,
Will summon up with my all-charming rod

The Nymphs of fountains, from whose watery locks
(Hung with the dew of blessing and increase)
The greedy rivers take their nourishment.—
Ye Nymphs, who, bathing in your lovèd springs,
Beheld these rivers in their infancy,
And joy'd to see them, when their circled heads
Refresh'd the air, and spread the ground with flowers;
Rise from your wells, and with your nimble feet
Perform that office to this happy pair,
Which in these plains you to Alphëus did,
When passing hence, through many seas, unmixed,
He gained the favour of his Arethuse!

Immediately upon which speech, four Naiades arise gently out of
their several fountains, and present themselves upon the stage, attired
in long habits of sea-green taffeta, with bubbles of crystal, intermixt
with powdering of silver, resembling drops of water, bluish tresses,
on their heads garlands of water-lilies. They fall into a measure,
dance a little, then make a stand.

Iris. Is Hermes grown a lover? by what power,
Unknown to us, calls he the Naiades?

Mercury. Presumptuous Iris, I could make thee dance,
Till thou forgott'st thy lady's messages,
And rann'st back crying to her. Thou shalt know
My power is more; only my breath and this
Shall move fix'd stars, and force the firmament
To yield the Hyades, who govern showers
And dewy clouds, in whose dispersèd drops
Thou form'st the shape of thy deceitful bow.—
Ye maids, who yearly at appointed times
Advance with kindly tears the gentle floods,
Descend and pour your blessing on these streams,
Which rolling down from heaven-aspiring hills,
And now united in the fruitful vales,
Bear all before them, ravish'd with their joy,
And swell in glory, till they know no bounds!

Five Hyades descend softly in a cloud from the firmament to the middle part of the hill, apparelled in sky-coloured taffeta robes, spangled like the heavens, golden tresses, and each a fair star on their head; from thence descend to the stage; at whose sight the Naiades, seeming to rejoice, meet and join in a dance.

Iris. Great wit and power hath Hermes, to contrive
A lifeless dance, which of one sex consists!

Mercury. Alas, poor Iris! Venus hath in store
A secret ambush of her wingèd boys,
Who, lurking long within these pleasant groves,
First struck these lovers with their equal darts;
Those Cupids shall come forth and join with these,
To honour that which they themselves began.

Enter four Cupids from each side of the boscage, attired in flame-coloured taffeta close to their body, like naked boys, with bows, arrows, and wings of gold, chaplets of flowers on their heads, hood-winked with tiffiny scarfs; who join with the Nymphs and the Hyades in another dance. That ended, MERCURY speaks.

Mercury. Behold the Statuas, which wise Vulcan plac'd
Under the altar of Olympian Jove,
And gave to them an artificial life,
Shall dance for joy of these great nuptials;
See how they move, drawn by this heavenly joy,
Like the wild trees which follow'd Orpheus' harp!

The Statuas enter, supposed to be before descended from Jove's altar, and to have been prepared in the covert with the Cupids, attending their call.

These Statuas were attired in cases of gold and silver close to their body, faces, hands, and feet; nothing seen but gold and silver, as if they had been solid images of the metal; tresses of hair, as they had been of metal embossed, girdles and small aprons of oaken leaves, as if they likewise had been carved or moulded out of the metal: at their coming, the music changed from violins to hautboys, cornets, &c., and the air of the music was utterly turned into a soft time, with drawing notes, excellently expressing their natures, and the measure likewise was fitted unto the same, and the Statuas placed in such several postures, sometimes all together in the centre of the dance, and sometimes in the four utmost angles, as was very graceful, besides the novelty. And so concluded the first Anti-masque.

Mercury. And what will Juno's Iris do for her?

Iris. Just match this show, or my invention fails:
Had it been worthier, I would have invok'd
The blazing comets, clouds, and falling stars,
And all my kindred meteors of the air,
To have excell'd it; but I now must strive
To imitate confusion:—therefore, thou,
Delightful Flora, if thou ever felt'st
Increase of sweetness in those blooming plants
On which the horns of my fair bow decline,
Send hither all the rural company
Which deck the May-games with their clownish sports!
Juno will have it so.

The second Anti-masque rush in, dance their measure, and as rudely depart; consisting of a Pedant, May-Lord, May-Lady, Servingman, Chambermaid, a Country Clown or Shepherd, Country Wench; an Host, Hostess; a He-Baboon, She-Baboon; a He-Fool, She-Fool, ushering them in.

All these persons apparelled to the life, the men issuing out of one side of the boscage, and the women from the other. The music was extremely well fitted, having such a spirit of country jollity as can hardly be imagined; but the perpetual laughter and applause was above the music.

The dance likewise was of tne same strain; and the dancers, or rather actors, expressed every one their part so naturally and aptly, as when a man's eye was caught with the one, and then passed on to the other, he could not satisfy himself which did best. It pleased his Majesty to call for it again at the end, as he did likewise for the first Anti-masque; but one of the Statuas by that time was undressed.

Mercury.   Iris, we strive,
Like winds at liberty, who should do worst

Ere we return.   If Juno be the queen
Of marriage, let her give happy way
To what is done in honour of the state
She governs.

 Iris. Hermes, so it may be done
Merely in honour of the state, and these
That now have prov'd it; not to satisfy
The lust of Jupiter, in having thanks
More than his Juno; if thy snaky rod
Have power to search the heavens, or sound the sea,
Or call together all the ends of earth,
To bring in any thing that may do grace
To us and these; do it, we shall be pleas'd.

 Mercury. Then know, that from the mouth of Jove
  himself,
Whose words have wings, and need not to be borne,
I took a message, and I bare it through
A thousand yielding clouds, and never stay'd
Till his high will was done: the Olympian games,
Which long had slept, at these wish'd nuptials
He pleas'd to have renew'd, and all his knights
Are gather'd hither, who within their tents
Rest on this hill; upon whose rising head,
Behold, Jove's altar, and his blessèd priests
Moving about it!—Come, you holy men,
And with your voices draw these youths along,
That, till Jove's music call them to their games,
Their active sports may give a blest content
To those, for whom they are again begun.

The Main Masque.—The second traverse is drawn, and the higher
ascent of the mountain is discovered; wherein, upon a level, after a
great rise of the hill, were placed two pavilions, open in the front of
them: the pavilions were to sight as of cloth of gold, and they were
trimmed on the inside with rich armour and military furniture, hanged

up as upon walls; and behind the tents there were represented in prospective the tops of divers other tents, as if it had been a camp. In these pavilions were placed fifteen Olympian Knights, upon seats a little embowed near the form of a croisant; and the Knights appeared first, as consecrated persons, all in veils, like to copes, of silver tiffiny, gathered, and falling a large compass about them, and over their heads high mitres, with long pendants behind falling from them; the mitres were so high that they received their hats and feathers, that nothing was seen but veil. In the midst between both the tents, upon the very top of the hill, being a higher level than that of the tents, was placed Jupiter's altar, gilt, with three great tapers upon golden candle-sticks burning upon it; and the four Statuas, two of gold, and two of silver, as supporters, and Jupiter's Priests in white robes about it. Upon the sight of the King, the veils of the Knights did fall easily from them, and they appeared in their own habit.

The Knights' Attire.—Arming doublets[1] of carnation satin, embroidered with blazing stars of silver plate, with powderings of smaller stars betwixt; gorgets of silver mail; long hose of the same, with the doublets laid with silver lace spangled, and enriched with embroidery between the lace; carnation silk stockings embroidered all over; garters and roses[2] suitable; pumps of carnation satin embroidered as the doublets; hats of the same stuff and embroidery, cut like a helmet before, the hinder part cut into scallops answering the skirts of their doublets; the bands of the hats were wreaths of silver in form of garlands of wild olives; white feathers, with one fall of carnation; belts of the same stuff, and embroidered with the doublet; silver swords; little Italian bands and cuffs embroidered with silver; fair long tresses of hair.

The Priests' Habits.—Long robes of white taffeta; long white heads of hair; the High-Priest a cap of white silk shag close to his head, with two labels at the ears, the midst rising in form of a pyramis, in the top thereof a branch of silver; every Priest playing upon a lute; twelve in number.

The Priests descend, and sing this song following; after whom the Knights likewise descend, first laying aside their veils, belts and swords.

---

[1] Doublets used in military accoutrement.
[2] Rosettes, knots of ribands on the shoes.

THE FIRST SONG.

Shake off your heavy trance,
And leap into a dance,
Such as no mortals use to tread,
  Fit only for Apollo
To play to, for the moon to lead,
  And all the stars to follow!

The Knights by this time are all descended and fallen into their
place, and then dance their first measure.

THE SECOND SONG.

On, blessed youths! for Jove doth pause
Laying aside his graver laws
  For this device;
And at the wedding such a pair,
Each dance is taken for a prayer,
  Each song a sacrifice.

The Knights dance their second measure.

THE THIRD SONG.

Single.

More pleasing were these sweet delights,
If ladies mov'd as well as knights:
Run every one of you, and catch
A nymph, in honour of this match;
And whisper boldly in her ear,—
Jove will but laugh, if you forswear.

All.

And this day's sins he doth resolve
That we his priests should all absolve.

The Knights take their Ladies to dance with them galliards, durets[1],
corantos, etc., and lead them to their places; then loud music sounds,
supposed to call them to their Olympian games.

[1] See p. 112, note.

THE FOURTH SONG.

Ye should stay longer, if we durst:
Away!   Alas, that he that first
Gave Time wild wings to fly away,
Hath now no power to make him stay!
And though these games must needs be play'd,
I would this pair, when they are laid,
    And not a creature nigh 'em,
Could catch his scythe, as he doth pass,
And clip his wings, and break his glass,
    And keep him ever by 'em.

The Knights dance their parting measure, and ascend, put on their
swords and belts; during which time the Priests sing

THE FIFTH AND LAST SONG.

Peace and silence be the guide
To the man, and to the bride!
If there be a joy yet new
In marriage, let it fall on you,
    That all the world may wonder!
If we should stay, we should do worse,
And turn our blessing to a curse,
    By keeping you asunder.

VII.

ANONYMOUS.

THE MASQUE OF FLOWERS,

BY THE GENTLEMEN OF GRAY'S INN.

AT THE COURT OF WHITEHALL, IN THE BANQUETING HOUSE, UPON TWELFTH NIGHT, 1614. BEING THE LAST OF THE SOLEMNITIES AND MAGNIFICENCES WHICH WERE PERFORMED AT THE MARRIAGE OF THE RIGHT HONOURABLE THE EARL OF SOMERSET AND THE LADY FRANCES, DAUGHTER OF THE EARL OF SUFFOLK, LORD CHAMBERLAIN.

[The marriage of Robert Carr, Earl of Somerset, with the divorced wife of the Earl of Essex took place on December 26, 1613. The masque for the evening of that day was written by Campion. For the Countess' first marriage eight years previously Jonson had written his *Hymenaei*. The authors of the following masque are probably the three gentlemen of the Inn whose initials are appended to the dedication. To this masque belongs the unique distinction of a modern revival: it was performed at Gray's Inn on July 7, 1887, the year of the Queen's Jubilee.]

TO THE VERY HONOURABLE KNIGHT, SIR FRANCIS BACON, HIS MAJESTY'S ATTORNEY-GENERAL.

HONOURABLE SIR; this last masque, presented by the gentlemen of Gray's Inn, before his Majesty, in honour of the marriage and happy alliance between two such principal persons of the kingdom, as are the Earl of Suffolk and the Earl of Somerset, hath received such grace from his Majesty, the Queen, and Prince, and such approbation from the general, as it may well deserve to be repeated to those that were present, and represented to those that were absent, by committing the same to the press as others have been.

The dedication of it could not be doubtful, you having been

the principal, and in effect the only person[1] that did both encourage and warrant the gentlemen to shew their good affection towards so noble a conjunction in a time of such magnificence, wherein we conceive without giving you false attributes, which little need where so many are true, that you have graced in general all the Societies of the Inns of Court, in continuing them still as third persons with the Nobility and Court, in doing the King honour. And particularly Gray's Inn, which as you have formerly brought to flourish both in the ancienter and younger sort, by countenancing virtue in every quality; so now you have made a notable demonstration thereof in the later and less serious kind, by this, that one Inn of Court by itself in time of a vacation, and in the space of three weeks, could perform that which hath been performed; which could not have been done, but that every man's exceeding love and respect to you gave him wings to overtake time, which is the swiftest of things. This which we allege for our honour, we may allege indifferently for our excuse, if anything were amiss or wanting; for your times did scarce afford moments, and our experience went not beyond the compass of some former employment of that nature, which our graver studies ought have made us by this time to have forgotten. And so, wishing you all increase of honour, we rest, humbly to do you service,   J. G.   W. D.   T. B.

THE DEVICE OF THE MASQUE.

The Sun, willing to do honour to a marriage between two noble persons of the greatest island of his universal empire, writeth his letter of commission to the two seasons of the year, the Winter and the Spring, to visit and present them on his part; directing the Winter to present them with sports, such as are commonly called by the name of Christmas sports, or Carnival sports; and the Spring with other sports of more magnificence.

And more especially, that Winter for his part take knowledge of a certain challenge which had been lately sent and accepted between Silenus and Kawasha upon this point, that Wine was more worthy than Tobacco, and did more cheer and relieve the spirits of man.

---

[1] Bacon would not allow anyone to share the expense of this masque with him. Chamberlain writes: "Sir Francis Bacon prepares a masque to honour this marriage, which will stand him in above £2000".

This to be tried at two weapons, at song and at dance, and requiring the Winter to give order that the same challenge be performed in the days of the solemnity of the same marriage.

The same letter containeth a second special direction to the Spring, that whereas of ancient time certain beautiful youths had been transformed from men to flowers, and had so continued till this time; that now they should be returned again into men, and present themselves in Masque at the same marriage.

All this is accordingly performed, and first the two Seasons Invierno and Primavera come in, and receive their dispatch from the Sun by Gallus, the Sun's messenger; thereupon Winter brings in the challenge, consisting of two Antick-masques, the Antick-masque of the Song, and the Antick-masque of the Dance.

Then the Spring brings in the Masque itself, and there is first seen in the fabric a fair garden upon a descending ground, and at the height thereof there is a stately long arbour or bower arched upon pillars, wherein the Masquers are placed, but are not discovered at the first, but there appear only certain great tufts of flowers betwixt the columns. Those flowers upon the charm do vanish, and so the Masquers appear every one in the space inter-column of his arch.

THE MASQUE.

At the entrance of the King, at the lower end of the Banqueting House appeared a traverse painted in perspective, like the wall of a city with battlements, over which were seen the tops of houses. In the middle whereof was a great gate, and on either side a temple, the one dedicated to SILENUS, and the other to KAWASHA,[1] in either of which opened a little gate.

Out of the great gate, in the middle of the city, entered INVIERNO or WINTER, attired like an old man, in a short gown of silk shag[2], like withered grass all frosted and snowed over, and his cap, gown, gamashes[3], and mittens, furred crimson, with long white hair and beard, hung with icicles. He marcheth up to the middle of the hall, and looks round about him.

Invierno. Why thus it should be; such a night as this
Puts down a thousand weary longsome days

[1] In De Bry's collection of voyages (*America*, Part I., Frankfort, 1590) we are informed that the inhabitants of Virginia had an idol called KIWASA "in templo oppidi Secota repositum, tanquam custos Regiorum cadaverum".   [2] A kind of rough cloth.   [3] Gaiters.

Of Summer, when a sun, and moon, and stars
Are met within the palace of a King,
In several glory shining each on other
With rays of comfort and benign aspects;
When hearts are warm.   'T is for the seely[1] birds
To sacrifice their pipes unto the Spring,
And let the pilgrim bless the Summer's day;
But courts, and youth, and ladies needs must praise
The Winter's reign.

While *Invierno* was thus speaking, entereth the SPRING or PRIMA-
VERA attired like a Nymph, a high tire on her head, antick with
knots of fair hair and cobweb lawns rising one above another, garnished with flowers to some height, and behind falling down in a
pendant; an upper-body of cloth of silver florie[2]; naked neck and
breast, decked with pearls; a kirtle of yellow cloth of gold, branched
with leaves; a mantle of green and silver stuff cut out in leaves;
white buskins, with green ribands fringed with flowers.   She over-
taking INVIERNO claps him on the shoulder.

Primavera.   Well overtaken, Winter.

Invierno. Primavera!
What 's that I see? why, how dare you approach
In Janus' month?   D' ye mean to give the lie
To all the almanacks that are come forth,
As if they had not lied enough besides?
Provoke me not; fly hence, you wanton girl,
Stay not one minute!

   Primavera. Good old lad; I know you are a merry
     one
Within doors; bluster not, I 'll choose thee for
My Valentine, and tell thee tales and riddles
These livelong nights.   Thou 'rt ever borrowing

---

[1] Simple; the word, which originally meant 'timely', then 'lucky' or
'happy', has in the modern form *silly* taken another step downwards.
[2] Perhaps 'floried' or 'florid', *i.e.* covered with flowers.

Some days of me, then let this one day pass,
Good frost-beard, now.   But stay, methinks I see
The trumpet of the Sun, he 'll stint [1] this strife.

GALLUS comes in first, attired like a Post in yellow damask doublet
and bases[2]; the doublet with close wings, cut like feathers; a pouch
of carnation satin, wherein was his packet hung in a baldric of the
same; a pair of yellow boots; spurs with one long prick like a cock;
a little hat of yellow damask, with a plume of red feathers like a
crest.

> *Invierno.* Gallus, mine own brave bird! welcome in
>   troth!
> Thou art no peeping creature that attends
> This gaudy wench, thou wak'st the feathered hours,
> And call'st to labour; tell us, what 's the news?

> *Primavera.* What, Crest-and-spur! welcome, thou
>   com'st in time,
> Winter hath almost giv'n me the ague, faith,
> He is so bitter; but thou shalt end our quarrel.

> *Gallus.* Seasons both, God save you in your times,
> I know you both so well, as if I should
> Give leave for you to chirp, and you to chat,—
>   How you make all things green,
>   And you make all things fat,—
> Time would away; peace, then, read this dispatch,
> For I must back to my accustomed watch.

WINTER reads the letter.   The letter superscribed:

To our faithful and never-failing Quarter-waiters, Invierno and Primavera.

We have taken knowledge of a marriage to be solem-
nized between two noble persons, in the principal Island
of our universal Empire, unto which we are pleased to
do honour, and thereupon have directed our several letters
to you the Seasons of the year to visit and present them

---

[1] Cut short.   [2] Kilt.

on your part. To this purpose we would have you, Invierno, to present them with such sports as are commonly
known by the name of Christmas sports, or Carnival
sports; and you, Primavera, with sports of a more delicate nature; either of you according to your quality.
And for your better instruction and enablement towards
the due execution of this your commission, we require
you, Invierno, that, whereas we understand that Silenus
hath lately sent a challenge to Kawasha upon this point,
to maintain that wine is more worthy than tobacco, and
cheereth man's spirit more, the same to be tried at two
several weapons, song and dance; which challenge the
said Kawasha hath also accepted;—you take order that
the said challenge be performed at this marriage, taking
your convenient time.   And we require you, Primavera,
for your part, that whereas of ancient time there were
certain fair youths turned into flowers, which have so
continued until this time,—that you deal with Flora by
virtue of this commission, that they be now re-turned
to men, and present a dance at this marriage.   Hereof
fail you not.

Given at our Palace, your Lord and Master, The SUN.

Postscript. We have also directed our letters to the
Summer and the Harvest, the one to present them with
length of days, and the other with fruit, but those letters
come with the next dispatch.

ANTICK-MASQUE OF THE SONG.

Hereupon they depart all three, and presently entered SILENUS
at a little gate on the right-hand, mounted upon an artificial ass,
which sometimes being taken with the strain of the music, did bow
down his ears, and listen with great attention; the trappings were of
ivy, attended by a Satyr for his palfreveir[1] who led the ass.

---

[1] Apparently a form of *palfrey*, nearer to the Latin *paraveredus*, an
extra post-horse.

At the same instant entered KAWASHA at the other little gate, riding upon a cowl-staff[1], covered with a foot-cloth of pied stuff, borne upon two Indians' shoulders attired like Floridans.

SILENUS, an old fat man, attired in a crimson satin doublet, without wings, collar, or skirts; a great paunch, so as his doublet, though drawn with a lace, would not meet together by a handful; sleeves of cloth of gold, bases and gamashes of the same; a red swollen face with a bunched nose, grey beard, bald head, prick-ears, and little horns.

KAWASHA had on his head a night-cap of red-cloth of gold, close to his skull, tied under his chin, two holes cut in the top, out of which his ears appeared, hung with two great pendants; on the crown of his cap a chimney; a glass chain about his neck; his body and legs of olive-colour stuff, made close like the skin; bases of tobacco-colour stuff, cut like tobacco leaves, sprinkled with orcedure[2]; in his hand an Indian bow and arrows.

Before either of these went a sergeant. The sergeant of SILENUS carried a copper mace, and a bunch of grapes carved at the upper end; the sergeant of KAWASHA carried on his shoulder a great tobacco-pipe as big as a caliver[3].

Before SILENUS marched four singers, and behind him five fiddlers; before and behind KAWASHA as many of each kind. The singers on SILENUS' part were a miller, a wine cooper, a vintner's boy, a brewer. His music, a tabor and pipe, a base violin, a treble violin, a sackbut[4], a mandora[5]. KAWASHA's singers, a skipper, a fencer, a pedlar, a barber. His music, a bobtail[6], a blind harper and his boy, a base violin, a tenor cornet, a sackbut.

Upon their entrance, the music on both sides played till they came to the middle of the stage. Then SILENUS' singers began his catch, and so marched forward towards the State.

---

[1] A stout stick for passing through the handles of a tub called a *cowl*, which was thus carried on the shoulders of two men, one walking in front of the other.

[2] Can this be a misprint for *ochre-dust*?

[3] A light musket.   [4] Trombone or bass-trumpet.   [5] Mandoline.

[6] Is this the name of the instrument or of the person who played it? If the former, it must signify a "kit" or small fiddle, so called probably from its curtailed shape, for there is no other treble instrument in the group of Kawasha's music.

The Catch.

Silenus. Ahey for and a ho,
    Let's make this great Potan[1]
    Drink off Silenus' can;
    And when that he well drunk is,
    Return him to his munkies
      From whence he came.

Then Kawasha's side answered:

Kawasha. Ahey for and a ho,
    We'll make Silen fall down
    And cast him in a sowne[2],
    To see my men of ire,
    All snuffing, puffing, smoke, and fire,
      Like fell dragon.

The Freeman's Song.

Silenus. Kawasha comes in majesty,
    Was never such a God as he;
    He is come from a far country
    To make our nose a chimney.

Chorus. Silenus' asse doth leer to see
    His well-appointed company.

The Fiddlers of SILENUS frumpled[3] over the last verses.

Kawasha. The wine takes the contrary way
      To get into the hood;
    But good tobacco makes no stay,
      But seizeth where it should.

    More incense hath burned
      At great Kawasha's foot,
    Than to Silen and Bacchus both,
      And take in Jove to boot.

[1] Potentate?   [2] Swoon.
[3] Played a tune expressive of mockery or contempt.

Chorus.   Therefore do yield,
                 And quit the field,
                    Or else I 'll smoke ye!

These verses frumpled over by the music of KAWASHA.

Silenus.   The Worthies they were nine, 't is true,
              And lately Arthur's Knights I knew;
              But now are come up worthies new,
              The roaring boys, Kawasha's crew.

Chorus.   But if Silenus' asse should bray,
              'T would make them roar and run away!

Kawasha. Silenus toppes[1] the barrel, but
               Tobacco toppes the brain,
             And makes the vapours fine and soote[2]
               That man revives again.

             Nothing but fumigation
               Doth chase away ill spirits,
             Kawasha and his nation
               Found out these holy rites.

Chorus.   Therefore do yield,
                 And quit the field,
                    Or else I 'll smoke ye!

This Song all join and sing:

             Ahey for and a ho,
             The ass still looks askance-a;
             But strife in song,
             It is too long,
               Let 's end it in a dance-a.

After the song ended, they marched all out in the same order they came in, their music playing.

            [1] Taps.   [2] Sweet.

ANTICK-MASQUE OF THE DANCE.

Then entered the antick-masque of Dance, consisting, on SILENUS'
side, of Pantaloon, Courtezan; Swiss and his Wife; Usurer, Midwife; Smug and his Wench. On KAWASHA'S, of Fretelyne[1], Bawd;
Roaring Boy, Citizen[2]; Mountebank, Jewess of Portugal; Chimney
Sweeper and his Wench.

The Dance ended, the loud music sounded. The traverse being
drawn, was seen a garden of a glorious and strange beauty, cast into
four quarters, with a cross-walk and alleys, compassing each quarter.
In the middle of the cross-walk stood a goodly fountain raised on
four columnes of silver; on the tops whereof stood four statues of
silver, which supported a bowl, in circuit containing four-and-twenty
foot, and was raised from the ground nine foot in height; in the middle
whereof, upon scrolls of silver and gold, was plac'd a globe, garnished
with four golden mask-heads, out of the which issued water into the
bowl; above stood a golden Neptune, in height three foot, holding
in his hand a trident, and riding on a dolphin so cunningly framed
that a river seemed to stream out of his mouth.

The garden-walls were of brick artificially painted in perspective,
all along which were placed fruit-trees with artificial leaves and fruit.
The garden within the wall was railed about with rails of three foot
high, adorned with balusters of silver, between which were placed
pedestals, beautified with transparent lights of variable colours; upon
the pedestals stood silver columns, upon the tops whereof were personages of gold, lions of gold, and unicorns of silver; every personage
and beast did hold a torchet burning, that gave light and lustre to
the whole fabrique.

Every quarter of the garden was finely hedged about with a low
hedge of cypress and juniper; the knots[3] within set with artificial
green herbs, embellished with all sorts of artificial flowers. In the
two first quarters were two pyramids garnished with gold and silver,
and glistering with transparent lights, resembling carbuncles, sapphires, and rubies. In every corner of each quarter were great pots
of gilly-flowers, which shadowed certain lights placed behind them,
and made a resplendent and admirable lustre.

---

[1] We might have expected "Harlequin" to balance "Pantaloon" on
Silenus' side. The French *frétiller*, however, means "to frisk", and in
thieves' argot "to dance": Littré also gives "*frétillon*, personne qui
s'agit sans cesse".

[2] As the other couples consist of a man and a woman, this should
probably be Citizen's wife. [3] Beds.

The two further quarters were beautified with tulips of divers colours, and in the corners of the said quarters were set great tufts of several kinds of flowers, receiving lustre from several lights placed behind them.

At the further end of the garden was a mount raised by degrees resembling banks of earth covered with grass; on the top of the mount stood a goodly arbour substantially made, and covered with artificial trees and with arbour-flowers, as eglantine, honeysuckles, and the like.

The arbour was in length three-and-thirty foot, in height one-and-twenty, supported with terms[1] of gold and silver; it was divided into six double arches, and three doors answered to the three walks of the garden. In the middle part of the arbour rose a goodly large turret, and at either end a smaller.

Upon the top of the mount on the front thereof was a bank of flowers curiously painted, behind which, within the arches, the Masquers sat unseen. Behind the garden over the top of the arbour were set artificial trees, appearing like an orchard joining to the garden, and over all was drawn in perspective a firmament like the skies in a clear night. Upon a grassy seat under the arbour sat the Garden-gods, in number twelve, apparelled in long robes of green rich taffeta, caps on their heads, and chaplets of flowers. In the midst of them sat PRIMAVERA, at whose entreaty they descended to the stage, and marching up to the King, sung to lutes and theorboes[2] the song that induced the charm:

CANTUS I.

Give place, you ancient Powers,
That turned men to flowers;
For never writer's pen
Yet told of flowers re-turned to men.

Chorus.   But miracles of new event
Follow the great Sun of our firmament.

---

[1] Termini, rectangular pillars of stone terminating in a human bust.

[2] A large double-necked lute with two sets of tuning pegs. It remained in occasional use until the end of the 18th century. A figure of it is given in Grove's *Dictionary of Music.*

The Charm.

Hearken, ye fresh and springing Flowers,
    The Sun shines full upon your earth;
Disclose out of your shady bowers,
    He will not blast your tender birth.
        Descend you from your hill,
        Take spirit at his will,
        No Flowers, but flourish still.

The Charm ended, the Gods retire to their places, the loud music
again sounding. The banks of flowers softly descending and vanishing, the Masquers, in number thirteen, appeared, seated in their
arches, apparelled in doublets and round hose of white satin; long
white silk stockings; white satin pumps; the doublet richly embroidered in curious panes with embossed flowers of silver, the panes
bordered with embroidery of carnation silk and silver; the hose cut
in panes answerable to the embroidery of the doublets: the skirts of
the doublets embroidered and cut into lily-flowers, and the wings set
forth with flowers of several colours, made in silk and frosted with
silver; ruff-bands edged with a lace of carnation silk and silver,
spangled very thick and stuck full of flowers of several kinds; fair
vizards and tresses; delicate caps of silk and silver flowers of sundry
kinds, with plumes of the same, in the top whereof stuck a great
bunch of egrets; every Masquer's pump fastened with a flower
suitable to his cap; on their left arms a white scarf fairly embroidered
sent them by the Bride, and on their hands a rich pair of embroidered
gloves, sent them by the Bridegroom.

The loud music ceasing, the Masquers descend in a gallant march
through three several doors of the arbour to the three several alleys
of the garden, marching till they all met in the middle alley under
the fountain, and from thence to the stage, where they fell into their
first measure.

That ended, the priests descend again, and sing the second song,
referring to the Device of the Transforming.

Cantus II.

Thrice happy Flowers!
Your leaves are turned into fine hair,

Your stalks to bodies straight and fair,
Your sprigs to limbs, as once they were,
Your verdure to fresh blood, your smell
To breath, your blooms, your seedy cell
All have a lovely parallel.

Chorus.

The Nymphs that on their heads did wear you,
Henceforth in their hearts will bear you.

That done, they dance their second measure, after which follows the
third song, referring to the Ladies:

Cantus III.

Of creatures are the Flowers, fair Ladies,
    The prettiest, if we shall speak true;
The earth's coronet, the sun's babies,
    Enamelled cups of heaven's sweet dew;
Your fairer hands have often blest them,
When your needles have exprest them.

Chorus.

Therefore though their shapes be changed,
Let not your favours be estranged.

This ended, they took their Ladies, with whom they danced measures,
corantos, durettos[1], moriscos, galliards.   Then was sung the fourth
song, having reference to the King.

Cantus IV.

All things return with time,
But seldom do they higher climb;
Yet virtue sovereign
Mends all things as they come again.

---

[1] The Italian *duretto* (French *duret*) signifies "somewhat stiff or hard",
and the dance in question was therefore in all probability of a stiff and
formal character.

This Isle was Britain in times past,
But then was Britain rude and waste;
But now is Britain fit to be
A seat for a fifth monarchy.

Chorus.   Offer we to his high deserts,
Praises of truth, incense of hearts,
By whom each thing with gain reverts.

Then they danced their parting measure, at the end whereof followed
this last song, having reference to the married couple:

CANTUS V.

Lovely couple, Seasons two
Have performed what they can do;
If the gods inspire our song,
The other two will not stay long.
Receive our Flowers with gracious hand,
As a small wreath to your garland;
Flowers of honour, Flowers of beauty
    Are your own; we only bring
Flowers of affection, Flowers of duty.

The Masque ended, it pleased his Majesty to call for the Antick-
Masque of song and dance, which was again presented; and then
the Masquers uncovered their faces, and came up to the State, and
kissed the King's, and Queen's, and Prince's hands with a great deal
of grace and favour, and so were invited to the banquet.

VIII.

BEN JONSON.

(1572–1637.)

THE GOLDEN AGE RESTORED.

IN A MASQUE AT COURT [WHITEHALL, JANUARY 1 AND 6],
1616, BY THE LORDS AND GENTLEMEN THE
KING'S SERVANTS.

[The second performance of this masque took place in consequence
of some punctilio on the part of the French ambassador, which had
rendered it necessary to defer his invitation. He now condescended to
attend together with the representatives of Venice and of Savoy. The
jealousies prevailing between the various ambassadors were a constant
source of anxiety to the Lord Chamberlain and the other officials whose
duty it was to make arrangements for Court ceremonials. At this
second performance the ambassadors, says Sir John Finet (*Philoxenis*,
1656, p. 31), "were all three placed . . . on the King's right-hand
(not right out, but byas forward); first and next to the King the French,
next him the Venetian, and next him the Savoyard. At his Majestie's
left-hand sate the Queene, and next her the Prince."]

Loud music: PALLAS in her chariot descending to a softer music.

L OOK, look! rejoice and wonder
  That you, offending mortals, are
 (For all your crimes) so much the care
Of him that bears the thunder.

Jove can endure no longer,
  Your great ones should your less invade;
  Or that your weak, though bad, be made
A prey unto the stronger.[1]

And therefore means to settle
  Astraea in her seat again;

[1] The proceedings against the murderers of Sir Thomas Overbury had
been commenced in the previous October.

And let down in his golden chain
The Age of better metal.

Which deed he doth the rather,
    That even Envy may behold
    Time not enjoyed his head of gold
Alone beneath his father.

But that his care conserveth,
    As time, so all time's honours too,
    Regarding still what heaven should do,
And not what earth deserveth.
            [*A tumult and clashing of arms heard within.*

But hark! what tumult from yond' cave is heard?
    What noise, what strife, what earthquake and alarms,
As troubled Nature for her maker feared;
    And all the Iron Age were up in arms!

Hide me, soft cloud, from their profaner eyes,
    Till insolent Rebellion take the field;
And as their spirits with their counsels rise,
    I frustrate all with showing but my shield.
                    [*She retires behind a cloud.*

    The IRON AGE presents itself, calling forth the EVILS.

Iron Age. Come forth, come forth, do we not hear
    What purpose, and how worth our fear,
        The king of gods hath on us?
    He is not of the Iron breed
    That would, though Fate did help the deed,
        Let Shame in so upon us.

    Rise, rise then up, thou grandame vice
    Of all my issue, Avarice,
        Bring with thee Fraud and Slander,

Corruption with the golden hands,
Or any subtler Ill that stands
  To be a more commander.

Thy boys, Ambition, Pride, and Scorn,
Force, Rapine, and thy babe last born,
  Smooth Treachery,[1] call hither.
Arm Folly forth, and Ignorance,
And teach them all our Pyrrhic dance:
  We may triumph together

Upon this enemy so great,
Whom if our forces can defeat,
  And but this once bring under,
We are the masters of the skies,
Where all the wealth, height, power lies,
  The sceptre and the thunder.

Which of you would not in a war
Attempt the price of any scar,
  To keep your own states even?
But here which of you is that he,
Would not himself the weapon be,
  To ruin Jove and heaven?

About it then, and let him feel
The Iron Age is turned to steel,
  Since he begins to threat her:
And though the bodies here are less
Than were the giants, he'll confess
  Our malice is far greater.

The EVILS enter for the Antimasque and dance to two drums,
trumpets, and a confusion of martial music. At the end of which
PALLAS re-appears, shewing her shield. The EVILS are turned to
Statues.

---

[1] Another allusion to the Somerset and Overbury affair.

Pallas. So change, and perish, scarcely knowing how
That 'gainst the gods do take so vain a vow,
And think to equal with your mortal dates,
Their lives that are obnoxious to no fates.—
'T was time t' appear, and let their folly see
'Gainst whom they fought, and with what destiny.
Die all that can remain of you but stone,
And that be seen awhile, and then be none!
Now, now descend, you both beloved of Jove,
And of the good on earth no less the love;

> [*The scene changes; and she calls*

ASTRAEA *and the* GOLDEN AGE.

Descend, you long, long wished and wanted pair,
And as your softer times divide the air,
So shake all clouds off with your golden hair;
For Spite is spent: the Iron Age is fled,
And with her power on earth, her name is dead.

ASTRAEA and the GOLDEN AGE descending with a

SONG.

Astraea, Golden Age. And are we then
　　　　　　　　To live agen
　　　　　　　　With men?

Astraea. Will Jove such pledges to the earth restore
As justice?
　Golden Age. Or the purer ore?
　Pallas. 　　　　　　　　Once more.
　Golden Age. 　But do they know
　　　　　　　How much they owe
　　　　　　　Below?
Astraea. And will of grace receive it, not as due?
Pallas. If not, they harm themselves, not you.

Astraea. True.

Golden Age. True.

Quire. Let narrow natures, how they will, mistake,
The great should still be good for their own sake.

                                        [*They come forward.*

Pallas. Welcome to earth, and reign.

Astraea, Golden Age. But how, without a train
                        Shall we our state sustain?

Pallas. Leave that to Jove: therein you are
No little part of his Minerva's care.

                    Expect awhile.——

You far-famed spirits of this happy isle,
That for your sacred songs have gained the style
Of Phoebus' sons, whose notes the air aspire[1]
Of th' old Egyptian or the Thracian lyre,
That CHAUCER, GOWER, LIDGATE, SPENSER, hight,
Put on your better flames and larger light,
To wait upon the Age that shall your names new nourish,
Since Virtue prest[2] shall grow, and buried Arts shall
        flourish.

Chaucer, Gower. We come.

Lidgate, Spenser.   We come.

Omnes.   Our best of fire,
    Is that which Pallas doth inspire.   [*They descend.*

Pallas. Then see you yonder souls, set far within the
        shade,
That in Elysian bowers the blessed seats do keep,
That for their living good now semi-gods are made,
    And went away from earth, as if but tamed with
        sleep.
These we must join to wake; for these are of the strain
That justice dare defend, and will the age sustain.

----

[1] Breathe forth.   [2] Speedily, vigorously.

Quire. Awake, awake, for whom these times were kept,
O wake, wake, wake, as you had never slept!
Make haste and put on air, to be their guard,
Whom once but to defend, is still reward.
    Pallas. Thus Pallas throws a lightning from her shield.
                    [The scene of light discovered.
    Quire. To which let all that doubtful darkness yield.
    Astraea. Now Peace,
    Golden Age.   And Love,
    Astraea.   Faith,
    Golden Age.   Joys,
    Astraea, Golden Age.   All, all increase. *[A pause.*
    Chaucer. And Strife,
    Gower.   And Hate,
    Lidgate.   And Fear,
    Spenser.   And Pain,
    Omnes.   All cease.
    Pallas. No tumour of an iron vein.
The causes shall not come again. *[The Masquers descend.*
    Quire. But, as of old, all now be gold.
Move, move then to these sounds;
And do not only walk your solemn rounds,
But give those light and airy bounds,
That fit the Genii of these gladder grounds.

                The first DANCE.

    Pallas. Already do not all things smile?
    Astraea. But when they have enjoyed a while
        The Age's quickening power:
    Golden Age. That every thought a seed doth bring,
        And every look a plant doth spring,
        And every breath a flower:

    Pallas. Then earth unploughed shall yield her crop,
        Pure honey from the oak shall drop,

The fountain shall run milk:
The thistle shall the lily bear,
And every bramble roses wear,
And every worm make silk.

Quire. The very shrub shall balsam sweat,
And nectar melt the rock with heat,
   Till earth have drunk her fill:
That she no harmful weed may know,
Nor barren fern, nor mandrake low,
   Nor mineral to kill.

Here the main DANCE.

After which:

Pallas. But here's not all: you must do more,
   Or else you do but half restore
      The Age's liberty.
Poets. The male and female used to join,
   And into all delight did coin
      That pure simplicity.

Then Feature[1] did to Form[2] advance,
And Youth called Beauty forth to dance,
   And every Grace was by:
It was a time of no distrust,
So much of love had nought of lust,
   None feared a jealous eye.

The language melted in the ear,
Yet all without a blush might hear,
   They lived with open vow.
Quire. Each touch and kiss was so well placed,
   They were as sweet as they were chaste,
      And such must yours be now.

[1] Comeliness.   [2] Shapeliness.

Here they dance with the *Ladies*.

Astraea. What change is here?   I had not more
    Desire to leave the earth before
        Than I have now to stay;
    My silver feet, like roots, are wreathed
    Into the ground, my wings are sheathed,
        And I cannot away.

    Of all there seems a second birth,
    It is become a heaven on earth,
        And Jove is present here.
    I feel the god-head; nor will doubt
    But he can fill the place throughout,
        Whose power is everywhere.

    This, this, and only such as this,
    The bright Astraea's region is,
        Where she would pray to live,
    And in the midst of so much gold,
    Unbought with grace, or fear unsold,[1]
        The law to mortals give.

Here they dance the Galliards and Corantos.

Pallas [*ascending and calling the* Poets].
    'T is now enough; behold you here,
    What Jove hath built to be your sphere,
        You hither must retire.
    And as his bounty gives you cause
    Be ready still without your pause,
        To shew the world your fire.

    Like lights about Astraea's throne,
    You here must shine, and all be one,
        In fervour and in flame;

[1] Unsold with fear; bribery and intimidation will be unknown.

That by your union she may grow,
And, you sustaining her, may know
  The Age still by her name.

Who vows, against or heat or cold,
To spin your garments of her gold,
  That want may touch you never;
And making garlands ev'ry hour,
To write your names in some new flower,
  That you may live for ever.

Quire. To Jove, to Jove, be all the honour given,
That thankful hearts can raise from earth to heaven.

IX.

BEN JONSON.

(1572–1637.)

LOVERS MADE MEN.

A MASQUE PRESENTED IN THE HOUSE OF THE RIGHT
HONOURABLE THE LORD HAY, BY DIVERS OF NOBLE
QUALITY HIS FRIENDS; FOR THE ENTERTAINMENT OF
MONSIEUR LE BARON DE TOUR, EXTRAORDINARY
AMBASSADOR FOR THE FRENCH KING, ON SATURDAY,
FEBRUARY 22, 1617.

Quid titulum poscis? versus duo tresve legantur.—MART.

[Lord Hay, afterwards Viscount Doncaster and Earl of Carlisle, had
been sent on a splendid embassy to France in the previous July, osten-
sibly to congratulate the young king, Louis XIII., on his marriage with
the Infanta of Spain, but in reality to ascertain whether the hand of his
sister, Henrietta Maria, could be secured for Prince Charles. He had
been magnificently entertained in Paris, and was now entertaining the
French ambassador in return with a supper and a masque; "the very
provision of cates for this supper", writes Mr. Chamberlain, "arising
to more than £600, wherein we are too apish to imitate the French
monkies in such monstrous waste. . . . Sir Edward Sackville, Sir Henry
Rich, Sir George Goring, and Sir Thomas Badger, are the principal
persons in the Masque." Lord Hay was also under an old obligation
to the Baron de Tour, for it was the Baron who, in 1603, first introduced
him to the notice of King James. The title "Lovers made Men" is
from the quarto of 1617: Gifford, who was not aware of this edition,
called it "The Masque of Lethe". A peculiarity of this masque is that
the masquers and the antimasquers are identical.]

The FRONT before the SCENE was an ARCH-TRIUMPHAL.

On the top of which, HUMANITY, placed in figure, sat with her lap
full of flowers, scattering them with her right hand, and holding a

golden chain in her left hand, to show both the freedom and the bond of courtesy, with this inscription:

SUPER OMNIA VULTUS.

On the two sides of the arch, CHEERFULNESS and READINESS, her servants.

CHEERFULNESS, in a loose flowing garment, filling out wine from an antique piece of plate; with this word:

ADSIT LAETITIAE DATOR.

READINESS, a winged maid, with two flaming bright lights in her hands; and her word,

AMOR ADDIDIT ALAS.

The SCENE discovered is, on the one side, the head of a boat, and in it CHARON putting off from the shore, having landed certain imagined ghosts, whom MERCURY there receives, and encourageth to come on towards the river LETHE, who appears lying in the person of an old man. The FATES sitting by him on his bank; a grove of myrtles behind them, presented in perspective, and growing thicker to the outer side of the scene. *Mercury*, perceiving them to faint, calls them on, and shows them his golden rod. And the whole masque was sung after the Italian manner, *stylo recitativo*, by Master Nicholas Lanier[1]; who ordered and made both the scene and the music.

Mercury. Nay, faint not now, so near the fields of rest.
   Here no more Furies, no more torments dwell
Than each hath felt already in his breast;
   Who hath been once in love, hath proved his hell.

Up then, and follow this my golden rod,
   That points you next to aged Lethe's shore,
Who pours his waters from his urn abroad,
   Of which but tasting, you shall faint no more.

---

[1] Nicholas Lanier was one of the royal musicians, and also a painter and engraver. In Italy the use of recitative in the place of spoken dialogue dates from the end of the sixteenth century; at the date of the present masque (Feb. 22, 1617) it was evidently a novelty in England. It had been already employed in *The Vision of Delight*, the court masque at Twelfth Night in this same year.

Lethe. Stay; who or what fantastic shades are these
That Hermes leads?
Mercury.   They are the gentle forms
Of lovers, tost upon those frantic seas
    Whence Venus sprung.
Lethe.   And have rid out her storms?

Mercury. No.
Lethe.   Did they perish?
Mercury.   Yes.
Lethe.   How?
Mercury.   Drowned by Love,
    That drew them forth with hopes as smooth as were
Th' unfaithful waters he desired them prove.
    Lethe. And turned a tempest when he had them there?

Mercury. He did, and on the billow would he roll,
    And laugh to see one throw his heart away;
Another sighing, vapour forth his soul;
    A third, to melt himself in tears, and say,

"O love, I now to salter water turn
    Than that I die in"; then a fourth, to cry
Amid the surges, "Oh! I burn, I burn".
    A fifth laugh out, "It is my ghost, not I".

And thus in pairs I found them. Only one
    There is, that walks, and stops, and shakes his head.
And shuns the rest, as glad to be alone,
    And whispers to himself, he is not dead.

Fates. No more are all the rest.
Mercury.   No!
1 Fate.   No.
Mercury.   But why
Proceeds this doubtful voice from destiny?
    Fates. It is too sure.

Mercury.   Sure!

2 Fate.   Ay. Thinks Mercury,

That any things or names on earth do die,

That are obscured from knowledge of the Fates,

Who keep all rolls?

3 Fate.   And know all nature's dates?

Mercury. They say themselves, they are dead.

1 Fate.   It not appears

Or by our rock[1],

2 Fate.   Our spindle,

3 Fate.   Or our shears.

Fates. Here all their threads are growing, yet none cut.

Mercury. I 'gin to doubt, that Love with charms hath put

This phant'sy in them; and they only think

That they are ghosts.

1 Fate.   If so, then let them drink

Of Lethe's stream.

2 Fate.   'T will make them to forget

Love's name.

3 Fate.   And so, they may recover yet.

Mercury. Go, bow unto the reverend lake:

                          [*To the* Shades.

And having touched there, up and shake

The shadows off, which yet do make

Us you, and you yourselves mistake.

Here they all stoop to the water, and dance forth their Antimasque in several gestures, as they lived in love: and retiring into the grove, before the last person be off the stage, the first Couple appear in their posture between the trees, ready to come forth changed.

Mercury. See! see! they are themselves agen.

1 Fate. Yes, now they are substances and men.

[1] Distaff.

2 Fate. Love at the name of Lethe flies.

Lethe. For in oblivion drowned he dies.

3 Fate. He must not hope, though other states
He oft subdue, he can the Fates.

Fates. 'T were insolence to think his powers
Can work on us, or equal ours.

    Chorus. Return, return,
        Like lights to burn
          On earth
           For others' good:
        Your second birth
     Will fame old Lethe's flood;
        And warn a world,
         That now are hurled
   About in tempest, how they prove
         Shadows for Love.
  Leap forth: your light it is the nobler made,
      By being strook out of a shade

Here they dance forth their entry, or first dance: after which CUPID
—appearing, meets them.

    Cupid. Why, now you take me! these are rites
That grace Love's days, and crown his nights!
These are the motions I would see,
And praise in them that follow me!
Not sighs, nor tears, nor wounded hearts,
Nor flames, nor ghosts; but airy parts
Tried and refined as yours have been,
And such they are I glory in.

    Mercury. Look, look unto this snaky rod,
And stop your ears against the charming god;
His every word falls from him is a snare;
Who have so lately known him, should beware.

    Here they dance their Main DANCE, which ended,

Cupid. Come, do not call it Cupid's crime,
You were thought dead before your time;
If thus you move to Hermes' will
Alone, you will be thought so still.
Go, take the ladies forth, and talk,
And touch, and taste too: ghosts can walk.
'Twixt eyes, tongues, hands, the mutual strife
Is bred that tries the truth of life.
They do, indeed, like dead men move,
That think they live, and not in love!

Here they take forth the *Ladies,* and the REVELS[1] follow.   After
which,

Mercury. Nay, you should never have left off;
But stayed, and heard your Cupid scoff,
To find you in the line you were.
   Cupid. Your too much wit breeds too much fear.
   Mercury. Good fly, good night.
   Cupid.   But will you go?
Can you leave Love, and he entreat you so?
   Here, take my quiver and my bow,
My torches too; that you by all may know
   I mean no danger to your stay:
This night I will create my holiday,
   And be yours naked and entire.

   Mercury. As if that Love disarmed were less a fire!
                  Away, away.

They dance their going out: which done,

Mercury. Yet lest that Venus' wanton son
Should with the world be quite undone,
For your fair sakes (you brighter stars,
Who have beheld these civil wars)

----

[1] See Introduction, p. xxxiv.

Fate is content these lovers here
Remain still such; so Love will swear
Never to force them act to do,
But what he will call Hermes to.

Cupid. I swear; and with like cause thank Mercury,
As these have to thank him and Destiny.

Chorus. All then take cause of joy; for who hath not?
Old Lethe, that their follies are forgot:
We, that their lives unto their fates they fit;
They, that they still shall love, and love with wit.

And thus it ended.

X.

BEN JONSON.

(1572–1637.)

NEWS FROM THE NEW WORLD DISCOVERED IN THE MOON.

A MASQUE, AS IT WAS PRESENTED AT COURT [WHITE-HALL] BEFORE KING JAMES, JANUARY 6 AND FEBRUARY 11, 1621.

Nascitur è tenebris: et se sibi vindicat orbis.

[This is the first of the series of masques written by Jonson, 1621–24, in which the antimasque is preceded by a clever scene of low comedy, ridiculing the follies of the day. Mr. Fleay identifies the Chronicler with Anthony Munday, the continuator of Stow's *Survey of London*, and the Printer with Nathaniel Butler, the chief news-vendor of the day, and the "Cymbal" of *The Staple of News*. To the first performance on Twelfth-day the only ambassador invited was the representative of the French monarch, the Marshal de Cadenet. At the second performance on Shrove Sunday the Spanish ambassador was present, and that in spite of a general expectation that he "would have held it an indignity, and wrong to his Master, to be present at a Maske seen before by a French Ambassador" (Sir John Finet, *Philoxenis*, p. 73).]

Enter two HERALDS, a PRINTER, CHRONICLER, and FACTOR.

1 Herald. News, news, news!

2 Herald. Bold and brave news!

1 Herald. New as the night they are born in.

2 Herald. Or the phant'sie that begot 'em.

1 Herald. Excellent news!

2 Herald. Will you hear any news?

Printer. Yes, and thank you too, sir: what's the price of 'em?

1 Herald. Price, coxcomb! what price, but the price o' your ears? As if any man used to pay for anything here.

2 Herald. Come forward; you should be some dull tradesman by your pig-headed sconce now, that think there's nothing good anywhere but what's to be sold.

Printer. Indeed I am all for sale, gentlemen, you say true: I am a printer, and a printer of news; and I do hearken after 'em wherever they be, at any rates; I'll give anything for a good copy now, be it true or false, so 't be news.

1 Herald. A fine youth!

Chronicler. And I am for matter of state, gentlemen, by consequence,—story;[1] to fill up my great book—my Chronicle, which must be three ream of paper at least; I have agreed with my stationer aforehand to make it so big, and I want for ten quire yet. I ha' been here ever since seven o'clock i' the morning to get matter for one page, and I think I have it complete; for I have both noted the number and the capacity of the degrees[2] here; and told twice over how many candles there are i' the room lighted, which I will set you down to a snuff precisely, because I love to give light to posterity in the truth of things.

1 Herald. This is a finer youth!

Factor. Gentlemen, I am neither printer nor chronologer, but one that otherwise take pleasure i' my pen: a factor of news for all the shieres[3] of England; I do write my thousand letters a week ordinary, sometime twelve hundred, and maintain the business at some charge both to hold up my reputation with mine own ministers in town and my friends of correspondence in the country; I have friends of all ranks and of all religions, for which

---

[1] History.   [2] Tiers of seats.
[3] Shires: the spelling of the original is preserved to indicate the pronunciation.

I keep an answering catalogue of dispatch; wherein I have my puritan news, my protestant news, and my pontificial news.

2 Herald. A superlative this!

Factor. And I have hope to erect a Staple for News ere long,[1] whither all shall be brought and thence again vented under the name of Staple-news, and not trusted to your printed conundrums[2] of the serpent in Sussex,[3] or the witches bidding the devil to dinner at Derby: news that when a man sends them down to the shieres where they are said to be done, were never there to be found!

Printer. Sir, that's all one, they were made for the common people; and why should not they ha' their pleasure in believing of lies are made for them, as you have in Paul's, that make 'em for yourselves.

1 Herald. There he speaks reason to you, sir.

Factor. I confess it; but it is the printing I am offended at, I would have no news printed; for when they are printed they leave to be news; while they are written, though they be false, they remain news still.

Printer. See men's divers opinions! It is the printing of 'em makes 'em news to a great many who will indeed believe nothing but what's in print. For those I do keep my presses, and so many pens going to bring forth wholesome relations, which once in half a score years, as the age grows forgetful, I print over again with a new date, and they are of excellent use.

Chronicler. Excellent abuse rather.

---

[1] Jonson's comedy *The Staple of News* was produced in 1626.

[2] Crotchets, absurdities.

[3] *True and Wonderfull. A discourse relating a strange and monstrous serpent or dragon lately discovered and yet living. To the great annoyance and divers slaughters both of men and cattell; by his strong and violent poyson: in Sussex, two miles from Horsam, in a woode called St. Leonards Forrest, and thirtie miles from London, this present month of August, 1614. With the true generation of serpents.* Printed at London, by John Trundle, 1614.

Printer. Master Chronicler, do not you talk, I shall—

1 Herald. Nay, gentlemen, be at peace one with another, we have enough for you all three, if you dare take upon trust.

Printer. I dare, I assure you.

Factor. And I, as much as comes.

Chronicler. I dare too, but nothing so much as I have done; I have been so cheated with false relations i' my time, as I ha' found it a far harder thing to correct my book, than collect it.

Factor. Like enough; but to your news, gentlemen, whence come they?

1 Herald. From the MOON, ours, sir.

Factor. From the Moon! which way? by sea or by land?

1 Herald. By moonshine; a nearer way, I take it.

Printer. Oh, by a trunk![1] I know it, a thing no bigger than a flute-case: a neighbour of mine, a spectacle-maker, has drawn the moon through it at the bore of a whistle, and made it as great as a drum-head twenty times, and brought it within the length of this room to me, I know not how often.

Chronicler. Tut, that's no news: your perplexive glasses[2] are common. No, it will fall out to be Pythagoras's way,[3] I warrant you, by writing and reading i' the moon.

Printer. Right, and as well read of you, i' faith: for Cornelius Agrippa[4] has it, *in disco lunae*; there 't is found.

---

[1] A tube, *i.e.* a telescope; called "perspicil" a few lines below.

[2] Usually called "perspective glasses", but perhaps intentionally misnamed by the chronicler.

[3] According to the scholiast on Aristophanes, *Nubes* 750, Pythagoras discovered a method of writing with blood on a polished mirror; and this being held opposite to the moon, what was written on the glass would be reflected on the orb of the moon, and would appear to be written upon it.

[4] Henricus Cornelius Agrippa, writer of works on magic and the occult sciences, born at Cologne 1486, died at Grenoble 1535.

1 Herald. Sir, you are lost, I assure you; for ours came to you neither by the way of Cornelius Agrippa nor Cornelius Drible.[1]

2 Herald. Nor any glass of—

1 Herald. No philosopher's phantasie.

2 Herald. Mathematician's perspicil.

1 Herald. Or brother of the Rosy Cross's intelligence, no forced way, but by the neat and clean power of poetry.

2 Herald. The mistress of all discovery.

1 Herald. Who, after a world of these curious uncertainties, hath employed thither a servant of hers in search of truth: who has been there—

2 Herald. In the moon.

1 Herald. In person.

2 Herald. And is this night returned.

Factor. Where? which is he? I must see his dog at his girdle, and the bush of thorns at his back, ere I believe it.

1 Herald. Do not trouble your faith then, for if that bush of thorns should prove a goodly grove of oaks, in what case were you and your expectation?

2 Herald. Those are stale ensigns o' the stage's man i' the moon,[2] delivered down to you by musty antiquity, and are of as doubtful credit as the maker's.

Chronicler. Sir, nothing again antiquity, I pray you, I must not hear ill of antiquity.

1 Herald. Oh! you have an old wife belike, or your

---

[1] Cornelis Drebbel (1572–1634), a Dutch savant who came to England about the year 1604 and was patronised by James I. He invented a machine for producing perpetual motion alluded to by Jonson in *The Silent Woman*, act v., and in Epigram xcvii.

[2] As for instance in *A Midsummer-Night's Dream*, v. 1. 136:

> This man, with lanthorn, dog, and bush of thorn,
> Presenteth Moonshine.

venerable jerkin there—make much of 'em. Our relation, I tell you still, is news.

2 Herald. Certain and sure news.

1 Herald. Of a new world.

2 Herald. And new creatures in that world.

1 Herald. In the orb of the moon.

2 Herald. Which is now found to be an earth inhabited.

1 Herald. With navigable seas and rivers.

2 Herald. Variety of nations, polities, laws.

1 Herald. With havens in 't, castles, and port-towns.

2 Herald. Inland cities, boroughs, hamlets, fairs, and
markets.

1 Herald. Hundreds and wapentakes! forests, parks,
coney-ground, meadow pasture, what not?

2 Herald. But differing from ours.

Factor. And has your poet brought all this?

Chronicler. Troth, here was enough: 't is a pretty piece
of poetry as 't is.

1 Herald. Would you could hear on, though!

2 Herald. Gi' your minds to 't a little.

Factor. What inns or ale-houses are there there? does
he tell you?

1 Herald. Truly, I have not asked him that.

2 Herald. Nor were you best, I believe.

Factor. Why in travel a man knows these things without
offence; I am sure if he be a good poet he has discovered
a good tavern in his time.

1 Herald. That he has, I should think the worse of his
verse else.

Printer. And his prose too, i' faith.

Chronicler. Is he a man's poet, or a woman's poet,[1] I
pray you?

---

[1] Middleton calls his *Inner Temple Masque* (1619) "an entertainment
for many worthy ladies", and writes "Being made for ladies, ladies

2 Herald. Is there any difference?

Factor. Many, as betwixt your man's tailor and your woman's tailor.

1 Herald. How, may we beseech you?

Factor. I'll show you; your man's poet may break out strong and deep i' the mouth, as he said of Pindar, *Monte decurrens velut amnis*: but your woman's poet must flow, and stroke the ear, and, as one of them said of himself sweetly—

> Must write a verse as smooth and calm as cream,
> In which there is no torrent, nor scarce stream.[1]

2 Herald. Ha' you any more on't?

Factor. No, I could never arrive but to this remnant.

1 Herald. Pity! would you had had the whole piece for a pattern to all poetry.

Printer. How might we do to see your poet? did he undertake this journey, I pray you, to the moon o' foot?

1 Herald. Why do you ask?

Printer. Because one of our greatest poets (I know not how good a one) went to Edinburgh o' foot,[2] and came back; marry, he has been restive[3], they say, ever since;

---

understood". Perhaps he is the poet glanced at in the text. Mr. Fleay, however, suggests that it is Campion who, in the address to the reader at the end of his *Masque at Lord Hay's Marriage* (1607), had written:

> "a Lady's praise
> Shall content my proudest hope,
> Their applause was all my scope;
> And to their shrines properly
> Revels dedicated be,
> Whose soft ears none ought to pierce
> But with smooth and gentle verse".

[1] Is this couplet the Factor's version of the last two lines quoted in the preceding note, or is it, as Mr. Fleay conjectures, taken verbally from the (now lost) Twelfth-Night masque of 1619, perhaps written by Campion?

[2] Jonson started on his memorable walk to Scotland in the summer of 1618, and was back again in London by May 1619.

[3] Lazy.

for we have had nothing from him[1]: he has set out nothing, I am sure.

1 Herald. Like enough, perhaps he has not all in; when he has all in, he will set out, I warrant you, at least those from whom he had it; it is the very same party that has been i' the moon now.

Printer. Indeed! has he been there since? belike he rid thither then?

Factor. Yes, post, upon the poet's horse, for a wager.

1 Herald. No, I assure you, he rather flew upon the wings of his muse. There are in all but three ways of going thither: one is Endymion's way, by rapture in sleep, or a dream. The other Menippus's way, by wing, which the poet took. The third, old Empedocles' way, who, when he leapt into Aetna, having a dry sear[2] body and light, the smoke took him and whift him up into the moon, where he lives yet, waving up and down like a feather, all soot and embers, coming out of that coal-pit: our poet met him and talked with him.

Chronicler. In what language, good sir?

2 Herald. Only by signs and gestures, for they have no articulate voices there, but certain motions to music: all the discourse there is harmony.

Factor. A fine lunatic language, i' faith; how do their lawyers then?

2 Herald. They are Pythagoreans, all dumb as fishes,[3] for they have no controversies to exercise themselves in.

Factor. How do they live then?

1 Herald. On the dew o' the moon, like grasshoppers, and confer with the doppers.[4]

---

[1] Jonson had written no masque since *Pleasure reconciled to Virtue,* January 6 and February 17, 1618.

[2] Withered.

[3] The story went that the Pythagoreans had to pass through a noviciate of five years' silence.

[4] Dippers, *i.e.* Anabaptists.

Factor. Ha' you doppers?

2 Herald. A world of doppers! but they are there as lunatic persons, walkers only: that have leave only to HUM and HA, not daring to prophesy, or start up upon stools to raise doctrine.

1 Herald. The brethren of the Rosy Cross have their college within a mile of the moon; a castle i' the air that runs upon wheels with a winged lanthorn—

Printer. I ha' seen 't in print.

2 Herald. All the fantastical creatures you can think of are there.

Factor. 'T is to be hoped there are women there, then.

1 Herald. And zealous women, that will outgroan the groaning wives of Edinburgh.

Factor. And lovers as fantastic as ours.

2 Herald. But none that will hang themselves for love, or eat candles' ends, or drink to their mistresses' eyes till their own bid 'em good night, as the sublunary lovers do.

Factor. No, sir?

2 Herald. No, some few you shall have that sigh or whistle themselves away; and those are presently hung up by the heels like meteors, with squibs i' their tails, to give the wiser sort warning.

Printer. Excellent!

Factor. Are there no self-lovers there?

2 Herald. There were; but they are all dead of late for want of tailors.

Factor. 'S light, what luck is that! we could have spared them a colony from hence.

2 Herald. I think some two or three of them live yet, but they are turned moon-calves by this.

Printer. O ay, moon-calves! what monster is that, I pray you?

2 Herald. Monster! none at all, a very familiar thing, like our fool here on earth.

1 Herald. The ladies there play with them instead of little dogs.

Factor. Then there are ladies?

2 Herald. And knights and squires.

Factor. And servants and coaches?

1 Herald. Yes, but the coaches are much o' the nature of the ladies, for they go only with wind.

Chronicler. Pretty, like China waggons.

Factor. Ha' they any places of meeting with their coaches, and taking the fresh open air, and then covert when they please, as in our Hyde Park or so?

2 Herald. Above all the Hyde Parks in Christendom, far more hiding and private; they do all in clouds there; they walk i' the clouds, they sit i' the clouds, they lie i' the clouds, they ride and tumble i' the clouds, their very coaches are clouds.

Printer. But ha' they no carmen to meet and break their coaches?

2 Herald. Alas, carmen! they will over a carman there, as he will do a child here: you shall have a coachman with cheeks like a trumpeter, and a wind in his mouth, blow him afore him as far as he can see him; or skirr[1] over him with his bat's wings a mile and a half ere he can steer his wry neck to look where he is.

Factor. And they ha' their New Wells[2] too, and physical waters, I hope, to visit all time of year?

1 Herald. Your Tunbridge, or the Spaw itself, are mere puddle to 'em: when the pleasant months o' the year come, they all flock to certain broken islands which are called there the Isles of Delight.

Factor. By clouds still?

1 Herald. What else! their boats are clouds too.

---

[1] Scour.
[2] Epsom probably, where the mineral springs were discovered about 1618.

2 Herald. Or in a mist; the mists are ordinary i' the moon; a man that owes money there needs no other protection; only buy a mist, and walk in 't, he 's never discerned; a matter of a baubee does it.

1 Herald. Only one island they have is called the isle of the Epicoenes, because there under one article both kinds are signified, for they are fashioned alike, male and female the same; not heads[1] and broad hats, short doublets and long points; neither do they ever untruss for distinction, but laugh and lie down in moonshine, and stab with their poniards; you do not know the delight of the Epicoenes in moonshine.

2 Herald. And when they ha' tasted the springs of pleasure enough, and billed, and kist, and are ready to come away; the shees only lay certain eggs (for they are never with child there), and of those eggs are disclosed a race of creatures like men, but are indeed a sort of fowl, in part covered with feathers (they call them VOLATEES), that hop from island to island: you shall see a covey of 'em, if you please, presently.

1 Herald. Yes, faith, 't is time to exercise their eyes, for their ears begin to be weary.

2 Herald. Then know we do not move these wings so
    soon,
On which our poet mounted to the moon
Menippus like, but all 'twixt it and us
Thus clears and helps to the presentment, thus.

Enter the VOLATEES for the ANTIMASQUE, and DANCE. After which

2 Herald. We have all this while (though the muses' heralds) adventured to tell your majesty no news; for hitherto we have moved rather to your delight than your belief. But now be pleased to expect a more noble dis-

---

[1] Close-cropped heads.

covery worthy of your ear as the object will be your eye:
a race of your own, formed, animated, lightened, and
heightened by you, who, rapt above the moon far in
speculation of your virtues, have remained there intranced
certain hours with wonder of the piety, wisdom, majesty
reflected by you on them from the divine light to which
only you are less. These, by how much higher they
have been carried from earth to contemplate your greatness, have now conceived the more haste and hope in
this their return home to approach your goodness; and
led by that excellent likeness of yourself, the Truth,[1]—imitating Procrustes' endeavour, that all their motions be
formed to the music of your peace, and have their ends
in your favour, which alone is able to resolve and thaw
the cold they have presently contracted in coming through
the colder region. *[Music.*

Here the Scene opens, and discovers the Region of the Moon, from
which the MASQUERS descend, and shake off their icicles.

FIRST SONG.

Howe'er the brightness may amaze,
Move you, and stand not still at gaze,
   As dazzled with the light:
But with your motions fill the place,
And let their fulness win you grace,
   Till you collect your sight.

So while the warmth you do confess,
And temper of these rays no less
   To quicken than refine,
You may by knowledge grow more bold,
And so more able to behold
   The body whence they shine.

The first DANCE follows.

[1] Prince Charles.

SECOND SONG.

Now look and see in yonder throne,
How all those beams are cast from one!
   This is that orb so bright,
Has kept your wonder so awake;
Whence you as from a mirror take
   The sun's reflected light.

Read him as you would do the book
Of all perfection, and but look
   What his proportions be;
No measure that is thence contrived,
Or any motion thence derived,
   But is pure harmony.

      Here the MAIN DANCE and REVELS.

THIRD SONG.

Not that we think you weary be,
            For he
   That did this motion give,
   And made it so long live,
Could likewise give it perpetuity.[1]

Nor that we doubt you have not more,
          And store
   Of changes to delight,
   For they are infinite,
As is the power that brought forth those before.

But since the earth is of his name
         And fame
   So full, you cannot add,
   Be both the first and glad
To speak him to the region whence you came.

      The last DANCE.

[1] Perpetual motion! surely the force of flattery could no further go.

FOURTH SONG.

Look, look already where I am,
>   Bright Fame,
>   Got up unto the sky,
>   Thus high,
>   Upon my better wing,
>   To sing
>   The knowing king,
> And make the music here
> With yours on earth the same.

Chorus. Join then to tell his name,
>   And say but James is he:
>   All ears will take the voice,
>   And in the tune rejoice,
>   Or Truth hath left to breathe, and Fame hath
>   left to be.

1 Herald. See! what is that this music brings,
And is so carried in the air about?
  2 Herald. Fame, that doth nourish the renown of kings,
And keep that fair which Envy would blot out.

Thus it ended.

XI.

BEN JONSON.

(1572–1637.)

THE MASQUE OF AUGURS.

WITH THE SEVERAL ANTIMASQUES.

PRESENTED ON TWELFTH-NIGHT [JANUARY 6 AND MAY 6, AT WHITEHALL], 1622.

[The Spanish ambassador, the Count de Gondomar, was present at the Twelfth-night performance of this masque. On May 6 he was present again together with his successor, Don Carlos de Coloma. "The French Ambassador, Monsieur de Tillier, receiving a kind of invitation, by way of offer, to be present at this Maske, returned answer, that he most humbly kissed his Majestie's handes for the honour intended him; but his stomach would not, he said, agree with cold meat, and desired therefore his absence might be pardoned, hereby pointing at the invitation and presence of the Spanish Ambassador in the first place at the same Maske the Christmas before, now repeated" (Sir John Finet, *Philoxenis*, p. 104).]

The first ANTIMASQUE had for the scene the Court Buttery-hatch.

The Presenters were from St. Katharine's:

Notch, a brewer's clerk.	Groom of the Revels.
Slug, a lighterman.	*Lady Alewife.*
Vangoose, a rare artist.	Her two women.
Urson, the bear-ward.	Three dancing bears.

Enter NOTCH and SLUG.

Notch. Come, now my head's in, I'll even venture the whole: I ha' seen the lions ere now, and he that hath seen them may see the king.

Slug. I think he may; but have a care you go not too nigh, neighbour Notch, lest you chance to have a tally made of your pate, and be clawed with a cudgel; there is as much danger going too near the king, as the lions.

Enter *Groom* of the *Revels*.

Groom. Whither, whither now, gamesters[1]? what is the business, the affair? stop, I beseech you.

Notch. This must be an officer or nothing, he is so pert and brief in his demands: a pretty man! and a pretty man is a little o' this side nothing; howsoever we must not be daunted now, I am sure I am a greater man than he out of the court, and I have lost nothing of my size since I came to it.

Groom. Hey-da! what 's this? a hogshead of beer broke out of the king's buttery, or some Dutch hulk! whither are you bound? the wind is against you, you must back; do you know where you are?

Notch. Yes, sir, if we be not mistaken, we are at the court; and would be glad to speak with something of less authority and more wit, that knows a little in the place.

Groom. Sir, I know as little as any man in the place. Speak, what is your business? I am an officer, groom of the revels, that is my place.

Notch. To fetch bouge[2] of court, a parcel of invisible bread and beer for the players, for they never see it; or to mistake six torches from the chandry[3], and give them one.

Groom. How, sir?

Notch. Come, this is not the first time you have carried coals[4]—to your own house, I mean, that should have warmed them.

Groom. Sir, I may do it by my place, and I must question you farther.

Notch. Be not so musty, sir; our desire is only to know

---

[1] "Mad wags", merry fellows.

[2] A corruption of *bouche,* rations.

[3] The place where candles were kept.

[4] "To carry coals" was a common proverbial expression meaning to submit to insult.

whether the king's majesty and the court expect any disguise here to-night?

Groom. Disguise! what mean you by that? do you
think that his majesty sits here to expect drunkards?[1]

Notch. No; if he did, I believe you would supply that
place better than you do this. Disguise was the old
English word for a masque, sir, before you were an implement belonging to the revels.

Groom. There is no such word in the office now, I
assure you, sir. I have served here, man and boy, a
prenticeship or twain, and I should know. But by what
name soever you call it, here will be a masque, and shall
be a masque, when you and the rest of your comrogues
shall sit *disguised* in the stocks.

Notch. Sure, by your language you were never meant
for a courtier, howsoever it hath been your ill fortune to
be taken out of the nest young; you are some constable's
egg, some such widgeon of authority, you are so easily
offended! Our coming was to show our loves, sir, and
to make a little merry with his majesty to-night, and we
have brought a masque with us, if his majesty had not
been better provided.

Groom. Who, you! you, a masque! why you stink
like so many bloat-herrings newly taken out of the
chimney! In the name of ignorance, whence came you?
or what are you? you have been hanged in the smoke
sufficiently, that is smelt out already.

Notch. Sir, we do come from among the brewhouses
in St. Katharine's, that's true, there you have smoked
us; the dock comfort your nostrils! and we may have
lived in a mist there, and so mist our purpose; but for
mine own part, I have brought my properties with me,
to express what I am; the keys of my calling hang here

---

[1] "Disguised" was a cant term for "drunk".

at my girdle, and this, the register-book of my function, shows me no less than a clerk at all points, and a brewer's clerk, and a brewer's head-clerk.

Groom. A man of accompt, sir! I cry you mercy.

Slug. Ay, sir, I knew him a fine merchant, a merchant of hops, till all hopt into the water.[1]

Notch. No more of that; what I have been I have been; what I am I am. I, Peter Notch, clerk, hearing the Christmas invention was drawn dry at court; and that neither the king's poet nor his architect had wherewithal left to entertain so much as a baboon of quality, nor scarce the Welsh ambassador,[2] if he should come there: out of my allegiance to wit, drew in some other friends that have as it were presumed out of their own naturals to fill up the vacuum with some pretty presentation, which we have addressed and conveyed hither in a lighter at the general charge, and landed at the back door of the Buttery, through my neighbour Slug's credit there.

Slug. A poor lighterman, sir, one that hath had the honour sometimes to lay in the king's beer there: and I assure you I heard it in no worse place than the very Buttery, for a certain there would be no masque, and from such as could command a jack of beer, two or three.

Enter VANGOOSE.

Vangoose. Dat is all true, exceeding true, de inventors be barren, lost, two, dre, vour mile, I know that from my selven; dey have no ting, no ting van deir own, but vat

---

1 "When a man of worship, whose beere was better hopped then maulted asked him [John Heywood] at his table how he liked of his beere, and whether it were well hopped, yes by the faith of my body, said hee, it is very well hopped: but if it had hopped a little further it had hopped into the water" (Camden's *Remains*, ed. 1614, p. 300).

2 "Thy sound is like the cuckoo, the Welch embassador".—Middleton, *A Trick to Catch the Old One*, act iv. sc. 5.

dey take vrom de eard, or de zea, or de heaven, or de
hell, or de rest van de veir elementen, de place a! dat
be so common as de vench in the burdello. Now me
would bring in some dainty new ting, dat never was, nor
never sall be in de *rebus natura*; dat has never van de
materia, nor de *forma*, nor de hoffen, nor de voot, but
a mera *devisa* of de brain—

Groom. Hey-da! what Hans Flutterkin is this? what
Dutchman does build or frame castles in the air.

Notch. He is no Dutchman, sir, he is a Briton born,
but hath learned to misuse his own tongue in travel, and
now speaks all languages in ill English; a rare artist he
is, sir, and a projector of masques. His project in ours
is, that we should all come from the Three Dancing
Bears in St. Katharine's (you may hap know it, sir) hard
by where the priest fell in, which alehouse is kept by a
distressed lady, whose name, for the honour of knight-
hood, will not be known; yet she is come in person here
errant, to fill up the adventure, with her two women that
draw drink under her; gentlewomen born all three, I
assure you.

Enter the LADY, with her two Maids.

Slug. And were three of those gentlewomen that should
have acted in that famous matter of England's Joy[1] in six
hundred[2] and three.

Lady. What talk you of England's Joy, gentlemen?
you have another matter in hand I wis, England's Sport
and Delight, if you can manage it. The poor cattle
yonder are passing away the time with a cheat loaf[3]

---

[1] A dumb-show of the chief events in Elizabeth's reign, arranged by
Richard Vennard or Vennar.

[2] Slug of course means sixteen hundred.

[3] A brown loaf, as we should call it, made of coarser flour than that
used for the *manchet*, or bread of the finest quality.

and a bombard of broken beer,[1] how will ye dispose of them?

Groom. Cattle! what cattle does she mean?

Lady. No worse than the king's game, I assure you; the bears, bears both of quality and fashion, right bears, true bears.

Notch. A device only to express the place from whence we come, my lady's house, for which we have borrowed three very bears, that, as her ladyship aforesaid says, are well bred, and can dance to present the sign, and the bear-ward to stand for the sign-post.

Groom. That is pretty; but are you sure you have sufficient bears for the purpose?

Slug. Very sufficient bears as any are in the ground, the Paris-garden,[2] and can dance at first sight, and play their own tunes if need be. John Urson, the bear-ward, offers to play them with any city-dancers christened for a ground measure.

Notch. Marry, for lofty tricks, or dancing on the ropes, he will not undertake; it is out of their element, he says. Sir, all our request is, since we are come, we may be admitted, if not for a masque, for an antic-masque; and as we shall deserve therein, we desire to be returned with credit to the Buttery from whence we came, for reward, or to the porter's lodge with discredit, for our punishment.[3]

Groom. To be whipt with your bears! well, I could be willing to venture a good word in behalf of the game, if I were assured the aforesaid game would be cleanly, and not fright the ladies.

---

[1] A *bombard* was a leather jug, named from its resemblance to the cannon so called. *Broken beer*, remnants of beer drawn for others; so "broken victuals".

[2] The famous bear-garden on the Bankside, Southwark.

[3] The usual place of chastisement for the menials and humbler retainers of great families.

Notch. For that, sir, the bear-ward hath put in security
by warranting my lady and her women to dance the whole
changes with them in safety; and for their abusing the
place you shall not need to fear, for he hath given them
a kind of diet-bread to bind them to their good behaviour.

Groom. Well, let them come; if you need one, I'll
help you myself.

Enter JOHN URSON with his Bears, who dance while he sings the
following

BALLAD.

Though it may seem rude
For me to intrude,
　　With these my bears, by chance-a;
'T were sport for a king,
If they could sing
　　As well as they can dance-a.

Then to put you out
Of fear or doubt,
　　We came from St. Katharine-a,
These dancing three,
By the help of me,
　　Who am the post of the sign-a.

We sell good ware,
And we need not care
　　Though court and country knew it;
Our ale's o' the best,
And each good guest
　　Prays for their souls that brew it.

For any ale-house,
We care not a louse,
　　Nor tavern in all the town-a;

Nor the Vintry-Cranes,
Nor St. Clement's Danes,
 Nor the Devil[1] can put us down-a.

Who has once there been,
Comes thither again,
 The liquor is so mighty;
Beer strong and stale,
And so is our ale,
 And it burns like aqua-vitae.

To a stranger there,
If any appear,
 Where never before he has been:
We shew the iron gate,
The wheel of St. Kate,
 And the place where the priest fell in.

The wives of Wapping,
They trudge to our tapping.
 And still our ale desire:
And there sit and drink,
Till they spue and stink,
 And often piss out our fire.

From morning to night,
And about to daylight,
 They sit, and never grudge it;
Till the fishwives join
Their single coin,
 And the tinker pawns his budget.

If their brains be not well,
Or their bladders do swell,
 To ease them of their burden,

    [1] The Devil Tavern.

My lady will come
With a bowl and a broom,
   And her handmaid with a jorden.

From court we invite
Lord, lady, and knight,
   Squire, gentleman, yeoman, and groom;
And all our stiff drinkers,
Smiths, porters, and tinkers,
   And the beggars shall give ye room.

Vangoose. How like you, how like you?

Groom. Excellent! the bears have done learnedly and sweetly.

Vangoose. 'T is noting, 't is noting; vill you see someting? ick sall bring in de Turkschen, met all zin bashaws, and zin dirty towsand Yanitsaries met all zin whooren, eunuken, all met an ander, de sofie van Persia, de Tartar cham met de groat king of Mogull, and make deir men, and deir horse, and deir elephanten, be seen fight in de ayr, and be all killen, and aliven, and no such ting. And all dis met de *ars* van de Catropricks[1], by de refleshie van de glassen.

Notch. Oh, he is an admirable artist.

Slug. And a half, sir.

Groom. But where will he place his glasses?

Vangoose. Fow, dat is all ean, as it be two, dree, veir, vife towsand mile off: ick sall multipliren de vizioun, met an ander secret dat ick heb: Spreck, vat vil you haben?

Groom. Good sir, put him to 't, bid him do something that is impossible; he will undertake it, I warrant you.

Notch. I do not like the Mogul, nor the great Turk, nor the Tartar, their names are somewhat too big for the room; marry, if he could shew us some country-players,

---

[1] Catoptrics, that part of optics which treats of reflection.

strolling about in several shires, without licence from the office, that would please I know whom; or some Welsh[1] pilgrims—

Vangoose. Pilgrim! now yow talk of de pilgrim, it come in my head. Ick vill show yow all de whole brave pilgrim o' de world: de pilgrim dat go now, now at de instant, two, dre towsand mile to de great Mahomet, at de Mecha, or here, dere, everywhere, make de fine labyrints, and shew all de brave error in de vorld.

Slug. And shall we see it here?

Vangoose. Yaw, here, here, here in dis room, tis very room: vel vat is dat to yow, if ick do de ting? vat an devil, vera boten devil?

Groom. Nay, good sir, be not angry.

Notch. 'T is a disease that follows all excellent men, they cannot govern their passions; but let him alone, try him one bout.

Groom. I would try him; but what has all this to do with our mask?

Vangoose. O sir, all de better vor an antick-mask, de more absurd it be, and vrom de purpose, it be ever all de better. If it go from de nature of de ting, it is de more art: for dere is art, and dere is nature, yow sall see. *Hocos Pocos! paucos palabros !*

Here the second ANTIMASQUE,

Which was a perplexed DANCE of straying and deformed PILGRIMS taking several paths, till with the opening of the light above, and breaking forth of APOLLO, they were all frighted away, and the MAIN MASQUE begun:

APOLLO, descending, SUNG.

It is no dream; you all do wake and see.
Behold who comes! far-shooting Phoebus, he

---

[1] Perhaps an allusion to the antimasque of Welshmen, which Jonson had written for the second performance of *Pleasure reconciled to Virtue*, February 17, 1618.

That can both hurt and heal; and with his voice
Rear towns, and make societies rejoice;
That taught the muses all their harmony,
And men the tuneful art of augury.
Apollo stoops, and when a god descends,
May mortals think he hath no vulgar ends.

Being near the earth, he called these persons following, who came
forth as from their tombs.

Linus! and Orpheus! Branchus! Idmon![1] all,
My sacred sons, rise at your father's call,
From your immortal graves; where sleep, not death,
Yet binds your powers.

Linus.   Here.
Orpheus.   Here.
Branchus.   What sacred breath
Doth re-inspire us?
Idmon.   Who is this we feel?
Phoemonoë[2]. What heat creeps through me, as when
     burning steel
Is dipt in water?

---

[1] Linus, Apollinis et Terpsichores filius.—*Paus.*
Orpheus, Apollinis et Calliopes, de quibus Virg. in *Ecloga* inscript.
> Non me carminibus vincet, non Thracius Orpheus,
> Nec Linus, huic mater quamvis, atque huic pater adsit,
> Orphei Calliopea, Lino formosus Apollo.

Branchus, Apollinis et Jances filius, de quo vid. Strab. lib. 4, et
Statium *Thebaid.* lib. 3,——patrioque aequalis honori Branchus.
Idmon, Apollinis et Asteries filius. De illo vid. Val. Flac. *Argo-nautic.* lib. 1.
> Contra Phoebius Idmon
> Non pallore viris non ullo horrore comarum
> Terribilis, plenus fatis, Phoeboque quieto,
> Cui genitor tribuit monitu praenoscere Divum
> Omina, seu flammas, seu lubrica cominus exta,
> Seu plenum certis interroget aëra pennis.—JONSON.

[2] Phoemonoë filia Phoebi, quae prima carmen heroicum cecinit.—
Hesiod in *Theog.*—JONSON.

Apollo.   Ay, Phoemonoë,
          Thy father Phoebus' fury filleth thee:
          Confess my godhead, once again I call,
          Let whole Apollo enter in you all,
          And follow me.
Omnes.   We fly, we do not tread;
          The gods do use to ravish whom they lead.

APOLLO being descended, shewed them where the KING sat, and
sung forward.

          Behold the love and care of all the gods,
             Of the ocean and the happy isles;
          That whilst the world about him is at odds,[1]
             Sits crowned lord here of himself, and smiles,
Chorus. To see the erring mazes of mankind,
             Who seek for that doth punish them to find.

          Then he advanced with them to the KING.

Apollo. Prince of thy peace, see what it is to love
             The powers above!
          Jove hath commanded me
             To visit thee;
          And in thine honour with my[2] music rear
             A college here [3]

[1] The Thirty Years' war had begun in 1618.
[2] Allusio ad illud Ovidii *Epistol. Epist. Parid.*
          Ilion aspicies, firmataque turribus altis
          Moenia Apollineae structa canore lyrae.—JONSON.

[3] Augurandi scientia nobilis erat et antiqua, apud gentes praesertim
Hetruscos: quibus erat collegium et domicilium celeberrimum Augurum,
quorum summa fuit authoritas et dignitas per totam Italiam, potissimum
Romae. Romulus, urbe condita, collegium et Augures ibi instituit, ipse
nobilis, ut apud Liv. lib. 1, et Tull. lib. 1, optimus Augur. Eorum
officium fuit auspicia captare, et ex iis colligere signa futurarum rerum,
deorumque monita considerare de eventibus prosperis vel adversis.
Sacra erat Romanis et res regia habita, dignitasque penes patricios et
principes viros mansit, etiam apud imperatores obtinuit, unde ab Apol-
line nostro talis Praeses pulchrè designatus.—JONSON.

Of tuneful augurs, whose divining skill
    Shall wait thee still,
And be the heralds of his highest will.
    The work is done,
And I have made their president thy son;
    Great Mars too, on these nights,
    Hath added Salian rites.[1]
Yond, yond afar,
They closed in their temple are,[2]
And each one guided by a star.

Chorus. Haste, haste to meet them, and as they advance,
    'Twixt every dance,
Let us interpret their prophetic trance.

Here they fetched out the MASQUERS [*i.e.* the AUGURS]: and
came before them with the TORCHBEARERS along the stage, singing
this full

SONG.

Apollo. Which way and whence the lightning flew,
    Or how it burned bright and blue,
    Design and figure by your lights:
    Then forth, and shew the several flights
    Your birds have made, or what the wing,
    Or voice in augury doth bring:
    Which hand the crow cried on, how high
    The vulture, or the erne[3] did fly;

---

[1] Saltationes in rebus sacris adhibebantur apud omnes penè gentes:
et à saliendo, seu saltatione sacra ad saliare carmen instituta, Salii dicti
et Marti consecrati. Omnes etiam qui ad cantum et tibiam ludebant
Salii et Salisubsuli dicebantur. Salius ὑμνῳδὸς, *vet. gloss.*; et Pacuv.
Pro imperio sic Salisubsulus vestro excubet Mars; et Virg. *Aeneid*, lib. 8.
    Tum Salii ad cantus incensa altaria circum
    Populeis adsunt evincti tempora ramis.—JONSON.

[2] Auguria captaturi coelum eligebant purum et serenum, aëreque
nitido. Lituum (qui erat baculus incurvus, augurale signum) manu
tenebat augur. Eo coeli regiones designabat, et metas inter quas con-
tineri debebant auguria: et hae vocabantur templa.—JONSON.
    [3] Eagle.

What wing the swan made, and the dove,
The stork, and which did get above:
Show all the birds of food or prey,
But pass by the unlucky jay,
The night-crow[1], swallow, or the kite,
Let those have neither right,
Chorus. Nor part
In this night's art.

Here the TORCHBEARERS danced.

After which the AUGURS laid by their staves, and danced their entry; which done, APOLLO and the rest interpreted the Augury.

Apollo. The signs are lucky all, and right,[2]
There hath not been a voice, or flight,
Of ill presage—
Linus.   The bird that brings[3]
Her augury alone to kings,
The dove, hath flown.
Orpheus.   And to thy peace,
Fortunes and the Fates increase.
Branchus. Minerva's hernshaw, and her owl,
Do both proclaim thou shalt control
The course of things.
Idmon.   As now they be
With tumult carried—

---

[1] Night-heron.

[2] Habebant dextra et laeva omina; antica et postica; orientalia et occidentalia. Graeci, cum se ad septentrionem obverterent, ortum ad dextram habuere. Romani meridiem in auspicando cum tuerentur, ortum ad laevam habuere. Itaque sinistrae partes eadem sunt Romanis quae Graecis dextrae ad ortum. Sinistra igitur illis meliora, dextra pejora: Graecis contrà. Sinistra, pertinentia ad ortum, salutaria, quia ortus lucis index et auctor. Dextra, quia spectant occasum, tristia.—JONSON.

[3] Columbae auguria non nisi regibus dant: quia nunquam singulae volant: sicut rex nunquam solus incedit. Nuntiae pacis.—JONSON.

Apollo.   And live free
From hatred, faction, or the fear
To blast the olive thou dost wear.
  Chorus. More is behind, which these do long to show,
And what the gods to so great virtue owe.

Here the MAIN DANCE.

  Chorus. Still, still the auspice is so good,
    We wish it were but understood;
        It even puts Apollo
    To all his strengths of art, to follow
      The flights, and to divine
      What's meant by every sign.[1]
  Thou canst not less be than the charge
        Of every deity;
    That thus art left here to enlarge,
        And shield their piety!
  Thy neighbours at thy fortune long have gazed;
  But at thy wisdom all do stand amazed,
        And wish to be
    O'ercome, or governed by thee!
  Safety itself so sides thee where thou go'st,
  And Fate still offers what thou covet'st most.

Here the REVELS.

After which, APOLLO went up to the KING, and SUNG.

  Apollo. Do not expect to hear of all
        Your good at once, lest it forestal
        A sweetness would be new:
        Some things the Fates would have concealed

---

[1] Signa quae sese offerent, erant multifaria: nam si objiceretur avis aliqua, considerabatur quo volatu ferretur, an obliquo vel prono, vel supino motu corporis; quo flecteret, contorqueret, aut contraheret membra; qua in parte se occultaret; an ad dextram vel sinistram canerent oscines, &c.—JONSON.

From us the gods, lest being revealed,
Our powers shall envy you.
It is enough your people learn
The reverence of your peace,
As well as strangers do discern
The glories by th' increase;[1]
And that the princely augur here,[1] your son,
Do by his father's lights his courses run.
Chorus. Him shall you see triumphing over all,
Both foes and vices; and your young and tall
Nephews,[2] his sons, grow up in your embraces,
To give this island princes in long races.

Here the heaven opened, and JOVE, with the *Senate* of the *Gods*, was discovered, while APOLLO returned to his seat, and ascending, SUNG.

Apollo. See, heaven expecteth my return,
The forked fire begins to burn,
Jove beckons me to come.
Jove. Though Phoebus be the god of arts,
He must not take on him all parts;
But leave his father some.
Apollo. My arts are only to obey,
Jove. And mine to sway.
Jove is that one, whom first, midst, last, you call,
The power that governs and conserveth all;
Earth, sea, and air, are subject to our check,
And fate with heaven moving at our beck.
Till Jove it ratify
It is no augury,
Though uttered by the mouth of Destiny.
Apollo. Dear father, give the sign, and seal it then.

---

[1] Romulus augur fuit, et Numa, et reliqui reges Romani, sicut ante eos Turnus, Rhamnetes, et alii. Lacedaemonii suis regibus augurem assessorem dabant. Cilices, Lycii, Cares, Arabes, in summa veneratione habuerunt auguria.—JONSON. [2] Grandsons, Latin *nepotes*.

The EARTH riseth.

It is the suit of Earth and men.

Jove. What do these mortals crave without our wrong?

Earth, with the rest. That Jove will lend us this our
    sovereign long;

  Let our grand-children, and not we,

  His want or absence ever see.

Jove. Your wish is blest,

Jove knocks his chin against his breast,[1]

    And firms[2] it with the rest.

Full Chorus. Sing then his fame through all the orbs;
    in even

Proportions, rising still from earth to heaven;

And of the lasting of it leave to doubt;

The power of time shall never put that out.

    This done, the whole Scene shut, and the MASQUERS
        danced their last DANCE.

        And thus it ended.

---

[1] Mos Jovis, annuendo votis et firmandis ominibus. Apud Homer, &c.
—JONSON.   [2] Confirms.

XII.

BEN JONSON.

(1572–1637.)

PAN'S ANNIVERSARY; OR, THE SHEPHERD'S HOLYDAY.

AS IT WAS PRESENTED AT COURT BEFORE KING JAMES.

The Inventors, INIGO JONES; BEN JONSON.

[Both the date and the place of performance of this masque are uncertain. Requiring but little scenery, it would be independent of the stage apparatus of Whitehall: moreover, it is on the face of it a summer entertainment and connected with the rustic festival of sheep-shearing. It is not improbable therefore that, as Mr. Fleay suggests, it was written for King James's birthday, June 19: compare the Shepherd's 2nd speech, "what honours they may do to the great Pan, by increase of anniversary rites, fitted to the music of his peace". In the Folio of 1640 the month is not stated, but the year assigned is 1625; on March 27 of which year James died. In 1623 he kept his birthday either at Greenwich or at Wansted; in 1624 at Wansted.]

The SCENE Arcadia.

The Court being seated, the first presentation is of three NYMPHS, strewing several sorts of flowers, followed by an old SHEPHERD, with a censer and perfumes.

1 Nymph. Thus, thus begin the yearly rites
    Are due to Pan on these bright nights;
    His morn now riseth and invites
    To sports, to dances, and delights:
      All envious and profane, away,
      This is the shepherd's holyday.

2 Nymph. Strew, strew the glad and smiling ground
    With every flower, yet not confound:
    The primrose drop, the spring's own spouse,
    Bright day's-eyes, and the lips of cows,
      The garden-star, the queen of May,
      The rose, to crown the holyday.

3 Nymph. Drop, drop, you violets; change your hues,
    Now red, now pale, as lovers' use;
    And in your death go out as well
    As when you lived unto the smell:
      That from your odour all may say,
      This is the shepherd's holyday.

Shepherd. Well done, my pretty ones, rain roses still,
Until the last be dropt: then hence, and fill
Your fragrant prickles[1] for a second shower.
Bring corn-flag,[2] tulips, and Adonis' flower,
Fair ox-eye, goldy-locks, and columbine,
Pinks, goulands, king-cups, and sweet sops-in-wine,
Blue harebells, pagles, pansies, calaminth,
Flower-gentle, and the fair-haired hyacinth;
Bring rich carnations, flower-de-luces, lilies,
The checqued, and purple-ringed daffodillies,
Bright crown-imperial, kingspear, holyhocks,
Sweet Venus-navel, and soft lady-smocks;
Bring too some branches forth of Daphne's hair,
And gladdest myrtle for these posts to wear,
With spikenard weaved, and marjoram between,
And starred with yellow-golds, and meadows-queen,
That when the altar, as it ought, is drest,
More odour come not from the phoenix' nest;

---

[1] Light wicker baskets.
[2] *Corn-flag*, gladiolus; *goulands*, buttercups; *sops-in-wine*, pinks; *pagles*, cowslips; *flower-gentle*, amaranthus; *flower-de-luces*, yellow iris; *kingspear*, yellow asphodel; *yellow-golds*, corn marigolds; *meadows-queen*, meadow-sweet.

The breath thereof Panchaia[1] may envy,
The colours China[2], and the light the sky.

Loud Music.

The Scene opens, and in it are the MASQUERS discovered sitting about the Fountain of Light, the *Musicians* attired like the *Priests of Pan*, standing in the work beneath them, when entereth to the old shepherd

A FENCER, flourishing.

Fencer. Room for an old trophy of time; a son of the sword, a servant of Mars, the minion of the muses, and a master of fence! One that hath shown his quarters, and played his prizes at all the games of Greece in his time; as fencing, wrestling, leaping, dancing, what not? and hath now ushered hither by the light of my long sword, certain bold boys of Boeotia, who are come to challenge the Arcadians at their own sports, call them forth on their own holyday, and dance them down on their own green-swarth.

Shepherd. 'Tis boldly attempted, and must be a Boeotian enterprise, by the face of it, from all the parts of Greece else, especially at this time, when the best and bravest spirits of Arcadia, called together by the excellent Arcas, are yonder sitting about the Fountain of Light, in consultation of what honours they may do the great Pan, by increase of anniversary rites fitted to the music of his peace.

Fencer. Peace to thy Pan, and mum to thy music, swain: there is a tinker of Thebes a coming, called Epam, with his kettle, will make all Arcadia ring of him. What are

---

[1] Compare *Corona Minervae* (1636):
<blockquote>
" All breath's Panchaian here: nay only this
Is the cleare Westerne that Favonian is
Perpetual spring creating."
</blockquote>
Panchaia was the name of a mythical district in Arabia, the land of perfumes.

[2] China ware was now beginning to make its appearance in the London shops.

your sports for the purpose—say? If singing, you shall
be sung down; if dancing, danced down. There is no
more to be done with you, but know what;—which it is;
and you are in smoke, gone, vapoured, vanished, blown,
and, as a man would say in a word of two syllables,
nothing.

Shepherd. This is short, though not so sweet. Surely
the better part of the solemnity here will be dancing.

Fencer. Enough: they shall be met with instantly in
their own sphere, the sphere of their own activity, a dance.
But by whom, expect: no Cynaetheian,[1] nor Satyrs; but,
as I said, boys of Boeotia, things of Thebes, (the town is
ours, shepherd), mad merry Greeks, lads of life, that have
no gall in us, but all air and sweetness. A tooth-drawer
is our foreman, that if there be but a bitter tooth in the
company, it may be called out at a twitch: he doth command any man's teeth out of his head upon the point of
his poniard; or tickles them forth with his riding rod: he
draws teeth a horseback in full speed, yet he will dance a
foot, he hath given his word: he is yeoman of the mouth[2]
to the whole brotherhood, and is charged to see their gums
be clean and their breath sweet, at a minute's warning.
Then comes my learned Theban, the tinker I told you
of, with his kettledrum before and after, a master of music
and a man of metal, he beats the march to the tune of
Ticklefoot, Pam, Pam, Pam, brave Epam with a nondas.
That's the strain.

Shepherd. A high one!

Fencer. Which is followed by the trace and tract of an
excellent juggler, that can juggle with every joint about
him, from head to heel. He can do tricks with his toes,
wind silk and thread pearl with them, as nimble a fine
fellow of his feet as his hands: for there is a noble corn-

---

[1] Cynaetha was a town in Arcadia.
[2] There were officers in the royal household so called.

cutter, his companion, hath so pared and finified them—
Indeed he hath taken it into his care to reform the feet
of all, and fit all their footing to a form! only one splay
foot in the company, and he is a bellows-mender allowed[1],
who hath the looking to of all their lungs by patent, and
by his place is to set that leg afore still, and with his puffs
keeps them in breath during pleasure: a tinderbox-man,
to strike new fire into them at every turn, and where he
spies any brave spark that is in danger to go out, ply him
with a match presently.

Shepherd. A most politic provision!

Fencer. Nay, we have made our provisions beyond
example, I hope. For to these there is annexed a clock-
keeper, a grave person as Time himself, who is to see
that they all keep time to a nick, and move every elbow
in order, every knee in compass. He is to wind them up
and draw them down, as he sees cause: then is there a
subtle, shrewd-bearded sir, that hath been a politician,
but is now a maker of mouse-traps, a great inginer yet: and
he is to catch the ladies' favours in the dance with certain
cringes he is to make; and to bait their benevolence.
Nor can we doubt of the success, for we have a prophet
amongst us of that peremptory pate, a tailor or master
fashioner, that hath found it out in a painted cloth, or
some old hanging, (for those are his library), that we
must conquer in such a time, and such a half time; therefore bids us go on cross-legged, or however thread the
needles of our happiness, go through-stitch with all,[2] unwind
the clew of our cares; he hath taken measure of our minds,
and will fit our fortune to our footing. And to better
assure us, at his own charge brings his philosopher with
him, a great clerk, who, they say, can write, and it is
shrewdly suspected but he can read too. And he is to
take the whole dances from the foot by brachygraphy,

---

[1] Licensed. [2] *I.e.* go through with everything—a common phrase.

and so make a memorial, if not a map of the business. Come forth, lads, and do your own turns.

The BOEOTIANS enter for the ANTIMASQUE, which is danced.

After which,

Fencer. How like you this, shepherd? was not this gear gotten on a holyday?

Shepherd. Faith, your folly may deserve pardon because it hath delighted: but beware of presuming, or how you offer comparison with persons so near deities.[1] Behold where they are that have now forgiven you, whom should you provoke again with the like, they will justly punish that with anger which they now dismiss with contempt. Away!   [*They retire.*

To the MASQUERS.

And come, you prime Arcadians forth, that taught
   By Pan the rites of true society,
From his loud music all your manners wrought,
   And made your commonwealth a harmony;
Commending so to all posterity
   Your innocence from that fair fount of light,
As still you sit without the injury
   Of any rudeness folly can, or spite:
Dance from the top of the Lycaean mountain
   Down to this valley, and with nearer eye
Enjoy what long in that illumined fountain
   You did far off, but yet with wonder, spy.

HYMN I.

1 Nymph. Of Pan we sing, the best of singers, Pan,
   That taught us swains how first to tune our lays;
And on the pipe more airs than Phoebus can.
   Chorus. Hear, O you groves, and hills resound his praise.

---

[1] Persons of position about the court, who had been taken off in the Antimasque.

2 Nymph. Of Pan we sing, the best of leaders, Pan,
That leads the Naiads and the Dryads forth;
And to their dances more than Hermes can.
Chorus. Hear, O you groves, and hills resound his worth.

3 Nymph. Of Pan we sing, the best of hunters, Pan,
That drives the hart to seek unused ways;
And in the chase more than Sylvanus can.
Chorus. Hear, O you groves, and hills resound his praise.

2 Nymph. Of Pan we sing, the best of shepherds, Pan,
That keeps our flocks and us, and both leads forth
To better pastures than great Pales can.
Chorus. Hear, O you groves, and hills resound his worth.
And while his powers and praises thus we sing,
The valleys let rebound, and all the rivers ring.

The MASQUERS descend, and dance their Entry.

HYMN II.

Pan is our All, by him we breathe, we live,
We move, we are; 't is he our lambs doth rear,
Our flocks doth bless, and from the store doth give
The warm and finer fleeces that we wear.
He keeps away all heats and colds,
Drives all diseases from our folds;
Makes everywhere the spring to dwell,
The ewes to feed, their udders swell;
But if he frown, the sheep, alas!
The shepherds wither, and the grass.
Chorus. Strive, strive to please him then, by still
increasing thus
The rites are due to him, who doth all right for us.

The MAIN DANCE.

HYMN III.

If yet, if yet,
Pan's orgies you will further fit,
See where the silver-footed fays do sit,
    The nymphs of wood and water;
    Each tree's and fountain's daughter!
    Go take them forth, it will be good
To see some wave it like a wood,
And others wind it like a flood;
        In springs,
        And rings,
Till the applause it brings,
        Wakes Echo from her seat,
        The closes to repeat.
[*Echo. The closes to repeat.*]
Echo the truest oracle on ground,
        Though nothing but a sound.
[*Echo. Though nothing but a sound.*]
Beloved of Pan, the valleys' queen.
        [*Echo. The valleys' queen.*]
And often heard, though never seen.
        [*Echo. Though never seen.*]

Here the REVELS.

After which re-enter the *Fencer*.

Fencer. Room, room, there; where are you, shepherd?
I am come again, with my second part of my bold bloods,
the brave gamesters; who assure you by me, that they
perceive no such wonder in all is done here but that they
dare adventure another trial. They look for some sheepish
devices here in Arcadia, not these, and therefore a hall!
a hall! they demand.

Shepherd. Nay, then they are past pity, let them come,
and not expect the anger of a deity to pursue them, but

meet them. They have their punishment with their fact[1]: they shall be sheep.

Fencer. O spare me, by the law of nations, I am but their ambassador.

Shepherd. You speak in time, sir.

The THEBANS enter for the 2 ANTIMASQUE; which danced.

Shepherd. Now let them return with their solid heads, and carry their stupidity into Boeotia, whence they brought it, with an emblem of themselves and their country. This is too pure an air for so gross brains.　　　*[They retire.*

To the Nymphs.

End you the rites, and so be eased
Of these, and then great Pan is pleased.

HYMN IV.

Great Pan, the father of our peace and pleasure,
　Who givest us all this leisure,
Hear what thy hallowed troop of herdsmen pray
　For this their holyday,
And how their vows to thee they in Lycaeus[2] pay.
　Chorus. So may our ewes receive the mounting rams,
And we bring thee the earliest of our lambs:
So may the first of all our fells be thine,
And both the beestning[3] of our goats and kine;
　As thou our folds dost still secure,
　And keep'st our fountains sweet and pure;
Drivest hence the wolf, the tod,[4] the brock,
Or other vermin from the flock.
That we, preserved by thee, and thou observed by us,
May both live safe in shade of thy loved Maenalus.

---

[1] Crime.
[2] Lycaeus, a mountain in Arcadia where Pan was worshipped.
[3] The first milk given by a cow or goat.　　　[4] Fox.

Shepherd. Now each return unto his charge,
And though to-day you 've lived at large,
And well your flocks have fed their fill,
Yet do not trust your hirelings still.
See yond' they go, and timely do
The office you have put them to;
But if you often give this leave,
Your sheep and you they will deceive.

Thus it ended.

XIII.

BEN JONSON.

(1572–1637.)

NEPTUNE'S TRIUMPH FOR THE RETURN OF ALBION.

CELEBRATED IN A MASQUE AT THE COURT ON THE TWELFTH NIGHT 1624.

Omnis et ad reducem jam litat ara Deum.—MART. Lib. viii. Epig. xiv.

[Although the antimasques are distinct, *Neptune's Triumph* and *The Fortunate Isles* are two versions of the same masque, the difference between them being that in the one the leading motive is the safe return of Albion (Prince Charles) from Spain, while in the other it is the identification of the Fortunate Isles with the British Islands. The history of these two versions and the relationship between them is a puzzle which still awaits solution, but the facts are these:—On October 5, 1623, the Prince landed at Portsmouth on his return from Spain. A masque had been prepared for the following Twelfth-night, January 6, 1624, but was put off *sine die*, in consequence of the jealousies rife between the French and Spanish ambassadors, as to the place of honour at the performance. The marriage treaty with France was ratified by King James and his son in December 1624, but the arrival of the papal dispensation, which had been granted in November, was delayed for some time owing to certain conditions attached to it, and had not reached England by the end of January 1625. On December 29, 1624, "a new play called the masque", brought by Jonson to the licenser, was licensed both for performance at the Fortune and for publication. On Twelfth-night, 1625, "a masque of the Prince with certain lords and gentlemen" was to have been performed at Whitehall, and then being put off for three days, was actually performed on January 9. It may further be noted: (1) That in *Neptune's Triumph* an attempt is made to explain the performance of a masque celebrating the Prince's return more than a twelvemonth after the event, when the Cook asks, "But why not this till now?" and is told in reply, "It was not time", etc. (2) That lines alluding to

the approaching marriage of Prince Charles with the French princess
Henrietta Maria,

> "And sing the present prophecy that goes,
> Of joining the bright Lily and the Rose", etc.,

which occur in *The Fortunate Isles* are absent from *Neptune's Triumph*.
(3) That the mention of the *State*, *i.e.* the royal seat, in both versions of
the main masque, and Johphiel's address in *The Fortunate Isles*, "Great
King! your pardon if desire to please have trespass'd", etc., point to
a court performance actual or intended; and (4) That the incompatibility
of a masque from every point of view with the conditions of the public
stage of the day suggests that, whatever performance was given at the
Fortune, must have been considerably curtailed, or even confined to the
low comedy parts. The conclusion seems to be that in *Neptune's Triumph*
we have the masque as originally written, with the addition of the
apology above noticed, and in *The Fortunate Isles* a modified form of it
with a new antimasque, but which version it was that was produced either
at the Fortune in December 1624, or at Whitehall in January 1625, there
is not sufficient evidence to show.]

His Majesty being set, and the loud music ceasing. All that is discovered of a Scene are two erected pillars, dedicated to *Neptune*, with
this inscription upon the one,

NEP. RED.

On the other,

SEC. JOV.[1]

The POET entering on the stage to disperse the argument, is called
to by the MASTER COOK.

Cook. Do you hear, you creature of diligence and
business! what is the affair that you pluck for so under
your cloke?

Poet. Nothing but what I colour for,[2] I assure you; and
may encounter with, I hope, if luck favour me, the game-
ster's goddess.

Cook. You are a votary of hers, it seems, by your
language. What went you upon, may a man ask you?

Poet. Certainties, indeed, sir, and very good ones; the
presentation of a masque; you 'll see 't anon.

Cook. Sir, this is my room and region too, the Banquet-

---

[1] *Neptuno reduci, secundo Jove.*   [2] Profess.

ing-house.   And in matter of feast, the solemnity, nothing
is to be presented here but with my acquaintance and
allowance to it.

Poet. You are not his majesty's confectioner, are you?

Cook. No, but one that has as good title to the room,
his Master-cook.   What are you, sir?

Poet. The most unprofitable of his servants, I sir, the
Poet.   A kind of a Christmas ingine: one that is used at
least once a year, for a trifling instrument of wit or so.

Cook. Were you ever a cook?

Poet. A cook! no, surely.

Cook. Then you can be no good poet: for a good poet
differs nothing at all from a master-cook.   Either's art is
the wisdom of the mind.

Poet. As how, sir?

Cook. Expect.   I am by my place to know how to
please the palates of the guests; so you are to know the
palate of the times; study the several tastes, what every
nation, the Spaniard, the Dutch, the French, the Walloun,
the Neapolitan, the Briton, the Sicilian, can expect from
you.

Poet. That were a heavy and hard task, to satisfy
Expectation, who is so severe an exactress of duties; ever
a tyrannous mistress, and most times a pressing enemy.

Cook. She is a powerful great lady, sir, at all times, and
must be satisfied: so must her sister, Madam Curiosity,
who hath as dainty a palate as she; and these will
expect.

Poet. But what if they expect more than they understand?

Cook. That's all one, Master Poet, you are bound to
satisfy them.   For there is a palate of the understanding
as well as of the senses.   The taste is taken with good
relishes, the sight with fair objects, the hearing with
delicate sounds, the smelling with pure scents, the feeling

with soft and plump bodies, but the understanding with
all these; for all which you must begin at the kitchen.
There the art of Poetry was learned and found out, or
nowhere; and the same day with the art of Cookery.

Poet. I should have given it rather to the cellar, if my
suffrage had been asked.

Cook. O, you are for the oracle of the bottle, I see;
hogshead Trismegistus;[1] he is your Pegasus.   Thence
flows the spring of your muses, from that hoof.
Seduced Poet, I do say to thee—
A boiler, range, and dresser were the fountains
Of all the knowledge in the universe,
And that's the kitchen.   What! a master-cook!
Thou dost not know the man, nor canst thou know him,
Till thou hast served some years in that deep school,
That's both the nurse and mother of the arts,
And heard'st him read, interpret, and demonstrate.
A master-cook! why, he's the man of men
For a professor! he designs, he draws,
He paints, he carves, he builds, he fortifies,
Makes citadels of curious fowl and fish,
Some he dry-ditches, some motes round with broths;
Mounts marrow-bones; cuts fifty-angled custards;
Rears bulwark pies; and, for his outer works
He raiseth ramparts of immortal crust;
And teacheth all the tactics at one dinner:
What ranks, what files to put his dishes in,
The whole art military! then he knows
The influence of the stars upon his meats;
And all their seasons, tempers, qualities,
And so to fit his relishes and sauces!
He has Nature in a pot, 'bove all the chemists,
Or bare-breeched brethren of the Rosy-cross!

---

[1] A mythical Egyptian personage, to whom certain extant astrological
treatises were attributed.

He is an architect, an inginer,
A soldier, a physician, a philosopher,
A general mathematician!

   Poet.   It is granted.

   Cook. And that you may not doubt him for a Poet—

   Poet. This fury shows, if there were nothing else;
And 't is divine!

   Cook.   Then, brother poet.

   Poet.   Brother.

   Cook. I have a suit.

   Poet.   What is it?

   Cook.   Your device.

   Poet. As you came in upon me, I was then
Offering the argument, and this it is.

   Cook. Silence.

   Poet. [*reads.*] "The mighty Neptune, mighty in his
   styles,
And large command of waters and of isles;
Not as the 'lord and sovereign of the seas',
But 'chief in the art of riding,'[1] late did please
To send his Albion forth, the most his own,
Upon discovery to themselves best known,
Through Celtiberia; and, to assist his course,
Gave him his powerful Manager of Horse,[2]
With divine Proteus,[3] father of disguise,
To wait upon them with his counsels wise
In all extremes. His great commands being done,
And he desirous to review his son,
He doth dispatch a floating isle from hence
Unto the Hesperian shores, to waft him thence.

---

[1] Charles and Buckingham had travelled to Celtiberia (Spain) overland
through France; the return journey was made by sea.

[2] The Duke of Buckingham, Master of the Horse to the King, called
"loyal Hippius" below.

[3] Sir Francis Cottington, afterwards Lord Cottington, secretary to
Prince Charles.

Where, what the arts were, used to make him stay,
And how the Syrens wooed him by the way,
What monsters he encountered on the coast,
How near our general joy was to be lost,[1]
Is not our subject now; though all these make
The present gladness greater for their sake.
But what the triumphs are, the feast, the sport,
And proud solemnities of Neptune's court,
Now he is safe, and Fame 's not heard in vain,
But we behold our happy pledge again.
That[2] with him loyal Hippius is returned,
Who for it, under so much envy, burned
With his own brightness, till her starved snakes saw
What Neptune did impose, to him was law."

   Cook. But why not this till now?
   Poet.   It was not time
To mix this music with the vulgar's chime.
Stay, till the abortive and extemporal din
Of balladry were understood a sin,
Minerva cried; that what tumultuous verse,
Or prose could make, or steal, they might rehearse,
And every songster had sung out his fit;
That all the country and the city wit
Of bells and bonfires and good cheer was spent,
And Neptune's guard had drunk all that they meant;
That all the tales and stories now were old
Of the sea-monster Archy,[3] or grown cold:
The Muses then might venture undeterred,
For they love then to sing when they are heard.

   Cook. I like it well, 't is handsome; and I have
Something would fit this.   How do you present 'em?
In a fine island, say you?

---

[1] In a storm off the coast of Spain.   [2] Now that.
[3] Archie Armstrong, the Court Jester, who had been in Spain with the Prince; mentioned again below as Amphibion Archy.

Poet.   Yes, a Delos!
Such as when fair Latona fell in travail,
Great Neptune made emergent.
    Cook.   I conceive you.
I would have had your isle brought floating in now,
In a brave broth, and of a sprightly green,
Just to the colour of the sea; and then
Some twenty Syrens, singing in the kettle,
With an Arion mounted on the back
Of a grown conger, but in such a posture
As all the world should take him for a dolphin:
O, 't would ha' made such music!   Ha' you nothing
But a bare island?
    Poet.   Yes, we have a tree too,
Which we do call the tree of Harmony,
And is the same with what we read the sun
Brought forth in the Indian Musicana first,
And thus it grows: the goodly bole being got
To certain cubits height, from every side
The boughs decline, which taking root afresh,
Spring up new boles, and those spring new and newer,
Till the whole tree become a porticus,
Or arched arbor, able to receive
A numerous troop, such as our Albion,
And the companions of his journey are:
And this they sit in.
    Cook.   Your prime Masquers?
    Poet.   Yes.
    Cook. But where's your Antimasque now all this while?
I hearken after them.
    Poet.   Faith, we have none.
    Cook. None!
    Poet. None, I assure you, neither do I think them
A worthy part of presentation,
Being things so heterogene to all device,

Mere by-works, and at best outlandish nothings.

    Cook. O, you are all the heaven awry, sir!
For blood of poetry running in your veins,
Make not yourself so ignorantly simple.
Because, sir, you shall see I am a poet,
No less than cook, and that I find you want
A special service here, an antimasque,
I 'll fit you with a dish out of the kitchen,
Such as I think will take the present palates,
A metaphorical dish! and do but mark
How a good wit may jump with you.   Are you ready,
    child?
(Had there been masque, or no masque, I had made it.)
Child of the boiling-house!

Enter Boy.

    Boy.   Here, father.
    Cook. Bring forth the pot.   It is an olla podrida:
But I have persons to present the meats.
    Poet. Persons!
    Cook. Such as do relish nothing but *di stato*,
But in another fashion than you dream of,
Know all things the wrong way, talk of the affairs,
The clouds, the cortines[1], and the mysteries
That are afoot, and from what hands they have them,
The master of the elephant, or the camels:
What correspondences are held; the posts
That go and come, and know almost their minutes,
All but their business: therein they are fishes;
But ha' their garlic, as the proverb says.
They are our Quest of Enquiry after news.
    Poet. Together with their learned authors?
    Boy.   Yes, sir.
And of the epicoene gender, hees and shees:

[1] Curtains.

Amphibion Archy is the chief.
   Cook.   Good boy!
The child is learned too: note but the kitchen!
Have you put him into the pot for garlic?
   Boy. One in his coat shall stink as strong as he, sir,
And his friend Giblets with him.
   Cook.   They are two,
That give a part of the seasoning.
   Poet.   I conceive
The way of your gallimaufry[1].
   Cook.   You will like it,
When they come pouring out of the pot together.
   Boy. O, if the pot had been big enough!
   Cook.   What then, child?
   Boy. I had put in the elephant, and one camel
At least, for beef.
   Cook.   But whom ha' you for partridge?
   Boy. A brace of dwarfs, and delicate plump birds.
   Cook. And whom for mutton and kid?
   Boy.   A fine laced mutton[2]
Or two; and either has her frisking husband
That reads her the Corranto[3] every week.
Grave Master Ambler, newsmaster of Paul's,
Supplies your capon; and grown Captain Buz,[4]
His emissary, under-writes for turkey;
A gentleman of the Forest presents pheasant,
And a plump poulterer's wife in Grace's street,
Plays hen with eggs i' the belly, or a coney,
Choose which you will.
   Cook.   But where's the bacon, Tom?

[1] Hash.   [2] A wanton.
[3] Besides the dance so called, there were news-sheets of the day called *Corrantes* (Courants).
[4] In *The Staple of News* (1626), where the Cook reappears as Lickfinger, "master-cook and parcel-poet", master Ambler is "emissary Paul's" and Hans Buz "emissary Exchange".

Boy. Hogrel the butcher, and the sow his wife,
Are both there.
    Cook.   It is well; go dish 'em out.
Are they well boiled?
    Boy.   Podrida!
    Poet.   What's that, rotten?
    Cook. O, that they must be. There's one main in-
    gredient
We have forgot, the artichoke.
    Boy.   No, sir;
I have a fruiterer, with a cold red nose
Like a blue fig, performs it.
    Cook.   The fruit looks so.
Good child, go pour 'em out, shew their concoction.
They must be rotten boiled; the broth's the best on 't,
And that's the dance: the stage here is the charger.
And, brother poet, though the serious part
Be yours, yet envy not the cook his art.
    Poet. Not I: *nam lusus ipse Triumphus amat.*

Here the ANTIMASQUE is danced by the persons described, coming
out of the pot.

    Poet. Well, now expect the Scene itself; it opens!

The island of DELOS is discovered, the MASQUERS sitting in their
several sieges. The heavens opening, and APOLLO with MERCURY,
some of the MUSES and the goddess HARMONY, make the music; the
while the whole island moves forward, PROTEUS sitting below, and
APOLLO sings.

SONG.

Apollo. Look forth, the shepherd of the seas,
      And of the ports that keep'st the keys,
        And to your Neptune tell,
     His Albion, prince of all his isles,
     For whom the sea and land so smiles,
        Is home returned well.

Grand Chorus. And be it thought no common cause,
> That to it so much wonder draws,
>> And all the heavens consent
> With Harmony to tune their notes,
> In answer to the public votes [1]
>> That for it up were sent.

> It was no envious step-dame's rage,
> Or tyrant's malice of the age,
>> That did employ him forth;
> But such a wisdom that would prove
> By sending him their hearts and love,
>> That else might fear his worth.

By this time the island hath joined itself with the shore: and PROTEUS, PORTUNUS,[2] and SARON[3] come forth; and go up singing to the state, while the MASQUERS take time to land.

SONG.

Proteus. Ay, now the pomp of Neptune's triumph shines!
And all the glories of his great designs
Are read reflected in his son's return!
  Portunus. How all the eyes, the looks, the hearts here burn
At his arrival!
  Saron.   These are the true fires
Are made of joys!
  Proteus.   Of longing!
  Portunus.   Of desires!
  Saron. Of hopes!
  Proteus.   Of fears!
  Portunus.   No intermitted blocks.
  Saron. But pure affections, and from odorous stocks!
  Chorus. 'T is incense all that flames,
And these materials scarce have names!
  Proteus. My king looks higher, as he scorned the wars

[1] Prayers.   [2] The god of ports.   [3] The god of navigation.

Of winds, and with his trident touched the stars;
There is no wrinkle in his brow or frown,
But as his cares he would in nectar drown,
And all the silver-footed nymphs were drest
To wait upon him to the Ocean's feast.

Portunus. Or here in rows upon the banks were set,
And had their several hairs made into net
To catch the youths in as they come on shore.

Saron. How, Galatea sighing! O, no more:
Banish your fears.

Portunus.   And, Doris, dry your tears.
ALBION is come.

Proteus.   And Haliclyon[1] too,
That kept his side, as he was charged to do,
With wonder.

Saron.   And the Syrens have him not.

Portunus. Though they no practice, nor no arts forgot,
That might have won him, or by charm or song.

Proteus. Or laying forth their tresses all along
Upon the glassy waves.

Portunus.   Then diving.

Proteus.   Then,
Up with their heads, as they were mad of men.

Saron. And there the highest-going billows crown,
Until some lusty sea-god pulled them down.

Chorus. See, he is here!

Proteus.   Great master of the main,
Receive thy dear and precious pawn again.

Chorus. Saron, Portunus, Proteus bring him thus,
Safe as thy subjects' wishes gave him us:
And of thy glorious triumph let it be
No less a part, that thou their loves dost see,
Than that his sacred head's returned to thee.

---

[1] *I.e.* renowned at sea, the Duke of Buckingham again, Lord High
Admiral (Saron) and Lord Warden of the Cinque Ports (Portunus).

This sung, the island goes back, whilst the Upper Chorus takes it from them, and the MASQUERS prepare for their figure.

> *Chorus.* Spring all the graces of the age,
>   And all the loves of time:
>   Bring all the pleasures of the stage,
>   And relishes of rime:
>   Add all the softnesses of courts,
>   The looks, the laughters, and the sports:
>   And mingle all their sweets and salts,
>   That none may say the Triumph halts.

Here the MASQUERS dance their Entry.

Which done, the first prospective of a maritime palace, or the house of OCEANUS, is discovered with loud music; and the other above is no more seen.

> *Poet.* Behold the palace of Oceanus!
> Hail, reverend structure! boast no more to us
> Thy being able all the gods to feast;
> We have seen enough; our Albion was thy guest.

Then follows the Main Dance.

After which the second prospect of the sea is shown to the former music.

> *Poet.* Now turn and view the wonders of the deep,
> Where Proteus' herds and Neptune's orks[1] do keep,
> Where all is ploughed, yet still the pasture 's green,
> The ways are found, and yet no paths are seen.

There PROTEUS, PORTUNUS, SARON, go up to the Ladies with this *Song.*

> *Proteus.* Come, noble nymphs, and do not hide
> The joys for which you so provide.
>   *Saron.* If not to mingle with the men,
> What do you here? go home agen.
>   *Portunus.*   Your dressings do confess,

[1] A marine animal of some kind, perhaps the narwhal.

By what we see so curious parts
Of Pallas' and Arachne's arts,
  That you could mean no less.
 Proteus. Why do you wear the silkworm's toils,
Or glory in the shell-fish' spoils,
Or strive to shew the grains of ore
That you have gathered on the shore,
  Whereof to make a stock
To graft the greener emerald on,
Or any better-watered stone?
 Saron. Or ruby of the rock?
 Proteus. Why do you smell of amber-grise,[1]
Of which was formed Neptune's niece,
The queen of love; unless you can,
Like sea-born Venus, love a man?
 Saron. Try, put yourselves unto 't.
 Chorus. Your looks, your smiles, and thoughts that
 meet,
Ambrosian hands and silver feet,
  Do promise you will do 't.

The REVELS follow.

Which ended, the fleet is discovered, while the three cornets play.

 Poet. 'T is time your eyes should be refreshed at length
With something new, a part of Neptune's strength:
See yond' his fleet, ready to go or come,
Or fetch the riches of the ocean home,
So to secure him, both in peace and wars,
Till not one ship alone, but all be stars. [*A shout within.*

Re-enter the COOK, followed by a number of *Sailors.*

 Cook. I have another service for you, brother Poet; a
dish of pickled sailors, fine salt sea-boys, shall relish like

---

[1] Ambergris = gray amber, an odoriferous wax-like substance of
marbled ashy colour: *ambergrease* was a favourite, but erroneous, seventeenth-century form of the word.

anchovies or caveare, to draw down a cup of nectar in the skirts of a night.

Sailors. Come away, boys, the town is ours; hey for Neptune and our young master!

Poet. He knows the compass and the card,
While Castor sits on the main yard,
And Pollux too to help your hales[1];
And bright Leucothoë fills your sails:
Arion sings, the dolphins swim
And all the way, to gaze on him.

The ANTIMASQUE of Sailors.

Then the last *Song* to the whole Music, five lutes, three cornets, and ten voices.

SONG.

Proteus. Although we wish the Triumph still might last
For such a prince, and his discovery past;
Yet now, great lord of waters and of isles,
Give Proteus leave to turn unto his wiles.

Portunus. And whilst young Albion doth thy labours
ease,
Dispatch Portunus to thy ports.

Saron.   And Saron to thy seas:
To meet old Nereus with his fifty girls,
From aged Indus laden home with pearls,
And orient gums, to burn unto thy name.

Grand Chorus. And may thy subjects' hearts be all on
flame,
Whilst thou dost keep the earth in firm estate,
And 'mongst the winds dost suffer no debate;
But both at sea and land our powers increase
With health and all the golden gifts of peace.

The last Dance.

With which the whole ended.

[1] Hauls, hauling.

(M 872)   R

XIV.

BEN JONSON.

(1572–1637.)

THE FORTUNATE ISLES, AND THEIR UNION.

CELEBRATED IN A MASQUE DESIGNED FOR THE
COURT, ON THE TWELFTH-NIGHT, 1624.[1]

Hic choreae, cantusque vigent.

His Majesty being set,

Entereth in, running, JOHPHIEL, an airy spirit, and (according to
the Magi) the intelligence of Jupiter's sphere: attired in light silks
of several colours, with wings of the same, a bright yellow hair, a
chaplet of flowers, blue silk stockings, and pumps, and gloves, with
a silver fan in his hand.

Johphiel. Like a lightning from the sky,
　　Or an arrow shot by Love,
　　Or a bird of his let fly,
　　　Be 't a sparrow, or a dove,
　　With that winged haste, come I,
　　　Loosed from the sphere of Jove,
　　　　To wish good-night
　　　　To your delight.

To him enters a melancholic student, in bare and worn clothes,
shrowded under an obscure cloke, and the eves of an old hat, fetching
a deep sigh, his name Mr. MEREFOOL.

Merefool. Oh, oh!
Johphiel. In Saturn's name, the father of my lord,
What over-charged piece of melancholy

[1] See prefatory note to *Neptune's Triumph.*

Is this, breaks in between my wishes thus
With bombing[1] sighs?
   Merefool.   No! no intelligence!
Not yet! and all my vows now nine days old!
Blindness of fate! puppies had seen by this time;
But I see nothing that I should, or would see!
What mean the brethren of the Rosy-cross,
So to desert their votary?
   Johphiel.   O! 't is one
Hath vowed himself unto that airy order,
And now is gaping for the fly[2] they promised him.
I 'll mix a little with him for my sport.   [*Steps aside.*
   Merefool. Have I both in my lodging and my diet,
My clothes, and every other solemn charge,
Observed 'em, made the naked boards my bed,
A faggot for my pillow, hungred sore!
   Johphiel. And thirsted after 'em!
   Merefool.   To look gaunt and lean!
   Johphiel. Which will not be.
   Merefool.   Who 's that?—Yes, and out-watched,
Yea, and outwalked any ghost alive
In solitary circle, worn my boots,
Knees, arms, and elbows out!
   Johphiel.   Ran on the score!
   Merefool. That have I—who suggests that?—and for more
Than I will speak of to abate this flesh,
And have not gained the sight—
   Johphiel.   Nay, scarce the sense.
   Merefool. Voice, thou art right—of anything but a cold
Wind in my stomach.
   Johphiel.   And a kind of whimsey—
   Merefool. Here in my head that puts me to the staggers,
Whether there be that brotherhood or no.

---

[1] Booming.   [2] Familiar spirit.

Johphiel. Believe, frail man, they be, and thou shalt see.

Merefool. What shall I see?

Johphiel.   Me.

Merefool.   Thee! where?

Johphiel. [*comes forward.*]   Here, if you
Be Master Merefool.

Merefool.   Sir, our name is Merryfool,
But by contraction Merefool.

Johphiel.   Then are you
The wight I seek; and, sir, my name is Johphiel,
Intelligence to the sphere of Jupiter,
An airy jocular spirit, employed to you
From Father Outis.[1]

Merefool.   Outis! who is he?

Johphiel. Know ye not Outis? then you know nobody:—
The good old hermit that was said to dwell
Here in the forest without trees, that built
The castle in the air where all the brethren
Rhodostaurotic[2] live.   It flies with wings,
And runs on wheels; where Julian de Campis[3]
Holds out the brandished blade.

Merefool.   Is't possible
They think on me?

Johphiel.   Rise, be not lost in wonder,
But hear me, and be faithful.   All the brethren
Have heard your vows, salute you, and expect you
By me this next return.   But the good father
Has been content to die for you.

Merefool.   For me?

Johphiel. For you.   Last New-year's day, which some
    give out,
Because it was his birth-day, and began
The year of jubilee, he would rest upon it,
Being his hundred five and twentieth year:

---

[1] Nobody.   [2] Rosicrucian.   [3] A pseudonym of Julius Sperber.

But the truth is, having observed your genesis,
He would not live, because he might leave all
He had to you.
  Merefool. What had he?
  Johphiel.   Had! an office,
Two, three, or four.
  Merefool. Where?
  Johphiel.   In the upper region;
And that you 'll find. The farm of the great customs
Through all the ports of the air's intelligences;
Then constable of the castle Rosy-cross,
Which you must be; and keeper of the keys
Of the whole Kabal, with the seals; you shall be
Principal secretary to the stars:
Know all their signatures and combinations,
The divine rods and consecrated roots,
What not? Would you turn trees up like the wind,
To show your strength? march over heads of armies,
Or points of pikes, to show your lightness? force
All doors of arts with the petard of your wit?
Read at one view all books? speak all the languages
Of several creatures? master all the learnings
Were, are, or shall be? or, to shew your wealth,
Open all treasures, hid by nature, from
The rock of diamond to the mine of sea-coal?
Sir, you shall do it.
  Merefool. But how?
  Johphiel.   Why, by his skill,
Of which he has left you the inheritance,
Here in a pot; this little gallipot
Of tincture, high rose tincture. There 's your order,
         [*He gives him a rose.*
You will ha' your collar sent you ere 't be long.
  Merefool. I looked, sir, for a halter. I was desperate.
  Johphiel. Reach forth your hand.

Merefool.   O, sir, a broken sleeve
Keeps the arm back, as 't is i' the proverb.

    Johphiel.   Nay,
For that I do commend you; you must be poor
With all your wealth and learning.   When you ha' made
Your glasses, gardens in the depth of winter,
Where you will walk invisible to mankind,
Talked with all birds and beasts in their own language,
When you have penetrated hills like air,
Dived to the bottom of the sea like lead,
And riss'[1] again like cork, walked in the fire,
An 't were a salamander, passed through all
The winding orbs like an Intelligence,
Up to the empyreum, when you have made
The world your gallery, can dispatch a business
In some three minutes with the antipodes,
And in five more negotiate the globe over;
You must be poor still.

    Merefool.   By my place I know it.

    Johphiel. Where would you wish to be now, or what to
      see,
Without the Fortunate Purse to bear your charges,
Or Wishing Hat? I will but touch your temples,
The corners of your eyes, and tinct the tip,
The very tip o' your nose, with this collyrium,
And you shall see i' the air all the ideas,
Spirits, and atoms, flies that buzz about
This way and that way, and are rather admirable
Than any way intelligible.

    Merefool.   O, come, tinct me,
Tinct me; I long; save this great belly, I long!
But shall I only see?

    Johphiel.   See, and command
As they were all your varlets or your foot-boys:

                  [1] Risen.

But first you must declare, (your Greatness must,
For that is now your style,) what you would see,
Or whom.

    Merefool. Is that my style? my Greatness then
Would see King Zoroastres.

    Johphiel.   Why, you shall;
Or any one beside. Think whom you please;
Your thousand, your ten thousand, to a million:
All 's one to me, if you could name a myriad.

    Merefool. I have named him.

    Johphiel.   You 've reason.

    Merefool.   Ay, I have reason;
Because he 's said to be the father of conjurors,
And a cunning man i' the stars.

    Johphiel.   Ay, that 's it troubles us
A little for the present: for, at this time,
He is confuting a French almanack,
But he will straight have done, ha' you but patience;
Or think but any other in mean time,
Any hard name.

    Merefool.   Then Hermes Trismegistus.

    Johphiel. O, ὁ τρισμέγιστος! why, you shall see him.
A fine hard name! Or him, or whom you will,
As I said to you afore. Or what do you think
Of Howleglass, instead of him?

    Merefool.   No, him
I have a mind to.

    Johphiel.   O, but Ulen-spiegle[1]
Were such a name!—but you shall have your longing.
What luck is this, he should be busy too!
He is weighing water but to fill three hour-glasses,
And mark the day in penn'orths like a cheese,
And he has done. 'T is strange you should name him

---

[1] Tyll Eulenspiegel or Ulenspiegel, *Anglice* Howleglass or Owlglass
the hero of a popular mediaeval German tale.

Of all the rest! there being Jamblicus,
Or Porphyry, or Proclus, any name
That is not busy.

Merefool.   Let me see Pythagoras.

Johphiel. Good.

Merefool. Or Plato.

Johphiel.   Plato is framing some ideas
Are now bespoken at a groat a dozen,
Three gross at least: and for Pythagoras,
He has rashly run himself on an employment
Of keeping asses from a field of beans,
And cannot be staved off.

Merefool.   Then Archimedes.

Johphiel. Yes, Archimedes!

Merefool.   Ay, or Aesop.

Johphiel.   Nay,
Hold your first man, a good man, Archimedes,
And worthy to be seen; but he is now
Inventing a rare mouse-trap with owl's wings
And a cat's-foot, to catch the mice alone:
And Aesop he is filing a fox-tongue
For a new fable he has made of court:
But you shall see 'em all, stay but your time
And ask in season; things asked out of season
A man denies himself. At such a time
As Christmas, when disguising is o' foot,
To ask of the inventions and the men,
The wits and the ingines that move those orbs!—
Methinks you should inquire now after Skelton,
Or Master Skogan.[1]

---

[1] Henry Scogan or Skogan, the friend of Chaucer (1361?-1407). Tradition vouched for the existence of a later John Scogan, court fool to Edward IV., to whom was ascribed a collection of jests very popular in the seventeenth century. Another collection of jests was fathered upon John Skelton (1460-1529), and this circumstance will help to explain the frequent association of the two poets, Skelton and the elder Scogan (who was confused with his namesake), in popular literature.

Merefool. Skogan! what was he?

Johphiel. O, a fine gentleman and master of arts
Of Henry the Fourth's time, that made disguises
For the king's sons, and writ in ballad-royal[1]
Daintily well.

Merefool. But wrote he like a gentleman?

Johphiel. In rime, fine tinkling rime, and flowand verse,
With now and then some sense! and he was paid for 't,
Regarded and rewarded; which few poets
Are now-a-days.

Merefool. And why?

Johphiel. 'Cause every dabbler
In rime is thought the same:—but you shall see him.
Hold up your nose. [*Anoints his eyes and temples.*

Merefool. I had rather see a Brachman[2]
Or a Gymnosophist[3] yet.

Johphiel. You shall see him, sir,
Is worth them both: and with him Domine Skelton,
The worshipful poet laureat to King Harry,
And *Tityre tu*[4] of those times. Advance quick Skogan,
And quicker Skelton, show your crafty[5] heads
Before this heir of arts, this lord of learning,
This master of all knowledge in reversion!

Enter SKOGAN and SKELTON, in like habits as they lived.

Skogan. Seemeth we are called of a moral intent,
If the words that are spoken as well now be meant.

Johphiel. That, Master Skogan, I dare you ensure.

Skogan. Then, son, our acquaintance is like to endure.

---

[1] Stanzas of seven or (afterwards) eight lines of ten syllables.
[2] Brahmin.
[3] A member of the first of the seven classes of Indian society described by Arrian.
[4] A cant name given to the roistering blades of the seventeenth century. This is perhaps the earliest instance of its occurrence in literature.
[5] Clever.

Merefool. A pretty game! like crambo[1], Master Skogan,
Give me thy hand: thou 'rt very lean, methinks.
Is 't living by thy wits?

Skogan.   If it had been that,
My worshipful son, thou hadst ne'er been so fat.

Johphiel. He tells you true, sir.   Here 's a gentleman,
My pair of crafty clerks, of that high caract[2]
As hardly hath the age produced his like,
Who, not content with the wit of his own times,
Is curious to know yours, and what hath been.

Merefool. Or is, or shall be.

Johphiel.   Note his latitude.

Skelton.   *O, vir amplissimus,*
            Ut scholis dicimus,
            Et gentilissimus!

Johphiel. The question-*issimus*
Is, should he ask a sight now, for his life,
I mean a person he would have restored
To memory of these times, for a playfellow,—
Whether you would present him with an Hermes,
Or with an Howleglass?

Skelton.   An Howleglass
            To come to pass
            On his father's ass;
            There never was,
            By day nor night,
            A finer sight,
            With feathers upright
            In his horned cap,
            And crooked shape,
            Much like an ape,
            With owl on fist,
            And glass at his wrist.

---

[1] A game in which one person names a word, to which another
endeavours to find a rhyme.   [2] *Carat,* refinement, excellence.

Skogan. Except the four knaves entertained for the
    guards
Of the kings and the queens that triumph[1] in the cards.
    Johphiel. Ay, that were a sight and a half, I confess,
To see 'em come skipping in, all at a mess[2]!
    Skelton.   With Elinor Rumming,
            To make up the mumming;
            That comely Gill,
            That dwelt on a hill,
            But she is not grill[3]:
            Her face all bowsy,
            Droopy and drowsy,
            Scurvy and lousy,
            Comely crinkled,
            Wondrously wrinkled,
            Like a roast pig's ear
            Bristled with hair.
    Skogan. Or, what do you say to Ruffian Fitz-Ale?
    Johphiel. An excellent sight, if he be not too stale.
But then we can mix him with modern Vapors,
The child of tobacco, his pipes, and his papers.
    Merefool. You talked of Elinor Rumming, I had rather
            See Ellen of Troy.
    Johphiel.   Her you shall see:
            But credit me,
            That Mary Ambree
            (Who marched so free
            To the siege of Gaunt,
            And death could not daunt,
            As the ballad doth vaunt,)
            Were a braver wight,
            And a better sight.
    Skelton.   Or Westminster Meg,
            With her long leg,

[1] Trump.   [2] A party of four.   [3] Hideous.

As long as a crane;
And feet like a plane:
With a pair of heels,
As broad as two wheels;
To drive down the dew,
As she goes to the stew:
And turns home merry,
By Lambeth ferry.
Or you may have come
In, Thomas Thumb,
In a pudding fat
With Doctor Rat.[1]

Johphiel.   Ay, that! that! that!
We 'll have 'em all,
To fill the hall.

The ANTIMASQUE follows, consisting of these twelve persons,
HOWLEGLASS, the four KNAVES, two RUFFIANS (FITZ-ALE and
VAPOR), ELINOR RUMMING, MARY AMBREE, LONG MEG of West-
minster, TOM THUMB, and Doctor RAT.

They DANCE, and withdraw.

Merefool. What, are they vanished! where is skipping
Skelton?
Or moral Skogan?   I do like their show,
And would have thanked them, being the first grace
The company of the Rosy-cross hath done me.
Johphiel. The company o' the Rosy-cross, you widgeon!
The company of players.   Go, you are,
And will be still yourself, a Merefool, in:
And take your pot of honey here, and hogs-grease,
See who has gulled you, and make one. [*Exit* Merefool.
Great king,
Your pardon, if desire to please have trespassed.
This fool should have been sent to Anticyra,

[1] One of the leading characters in *Gammer Gurton's Needle* (1563).

The isle of ellebore, there to have purged,
Not hoped a happy seat within your waters.
Hear now the message of the Fates, and Jove,
On whom these Fates depend, to you, as Neptune,
The great commander of the seas and isles.
That point of revolution being come,
When all the Fortunate Islands should be joined;
MACARIA one, and thought a principal,
That hitherto hath floated, as uncertain
Where she should fix her blessings, is to-night
Instructed to adhere to your Britannia:
That where the happy spirits live, hereafter
Might be no question made by the most curious,
Since the MACARII come to do you homage,
And join their cradle to your continent.

Here the Scene opens, and the MASQUERS are discovered sitting
in their several sieges. The air opens above, and APOLLO, with
HARMONY and the SPIRITS of Music, sing, the while the Island
moves forward, PROTEUS sitting below and hearkening.

SONG.

Look forth, the shepherd of the seas,
And of the ports that keep'st the keys,
    And to your Neptune tell,
Macaria, prince of all the isles,
Wherein there nothing grows but smiles,
    Doth here put in to dwell.

The winds are sweet and gently blow,
But Zephyrus, no breath they know,
    The father of the flowers:
By him the virgin violets live,
And every plant doth odours give,
    As new as are the hours.

Chorus. Then think it not a common cause,
That to it so much wonder draws,
And all the heavens consent
With harmony to tune their notes,
In answer to the public votes,
That for it up were sent.

By this time, the island having joined itself to the shore, PROTEUS,
PORTUNUS, and SARON come forth, and go up singing to the state,
while the MASQUERS take time to rank themselves.

SONG.

Proteus. Ay, now the heights of Neptune's honours
shine,
And all the glories of his greater style
Are read reflected in this happiest isle.
Portunus. How both the air, the soil, the seat combine
To speak it blessed!
Saron.   These are the true groves
Where joys are born.
Proteus.   Where longings,
Portunus.   And where loves!
Saron. That live!
Proteus.   That last!
Portunus.   No intermitted wind
Blows here, but what leaves flowers or fruit behind.
Chorus. 'T is odour all that comes!
And every tree doth give his gums.
Proteus. There is no sickness, nor no old age known
To man, nor any grief that he dares own.
There is no hunger here, nor envy of state,
Nor least ambition in the magistrate.
But all are even-hearted, open, free,
And what one is, another strives to be.
Portunus. Here all the day they feast, they sport and
spring,

Now dance the Graces' hay[1], now Venus' ring:
To which the old musicians play and sing.
 Saron. There is Arion, tuning his bold harp,
From flat to sharp,
 Portunus.   And light Anacreon,
He still is one!
 Proteus.   Stesichorus there too,
That Linus and old Orpheus doth outdo
To wonder.
 Saron.   And Amphion! he is there.
 Portunus. Nor is Apollo dainty to appear
In such a quire; although the trees be thick,
 Proteus. He will look in, and see the airs be quick,
And that the times be true.
 Portunus.   Then, chanting,
 Proteus.   Then,
Up with their notes they raise the Prince of Men,
 Saron. And sing the present prophecy that goes,
Of joining the bright Lily and the Rose.
 Chorus. See! all the flowers,
 Proteus.   That spring the banks along,
Do move their heads unto that under song.
 Chorus. Saron, Portunus, Proteus, help to bring
Our primrose in, the glory of the spring;
And tell the daffodil, against that day,
That we prepare new gyrlands fresh as May,
And interweave the myrtle and the bay.

This sung, the island goes back, whilst the Upper Chorus takes it
from them, and the Masquers prepare for their figure.

 Chorus. Spring all the graces of the age,
     And all the loves of time;
    Bring all the pleasures of the stage,
     And relishes of rime.

       [1] A country dance.

Add all the softnesses of courts,
The looks, the laughters, and the sports
And mingle all their sweets and salts,
That none may say the Triumph halts.

The MASQUERS dance their ENTRY, or FIRST DANCE.

Which done, the first prospective, a maritime palace, or the house
of OCEANUS, is discovered to loud music.   The other above is no
more seen.

Johphiel. Behold the palace of Oceanus!
Hail, reverend structure! boast no more to us
Thy being able all the gods to feast:
We saw enough when Albion was thy guest.

Here the MEASURES.

After which, the second prospective, a sea, is shown to the former
music.

Johphiel. Now turn, and view the wonders of the deep.
Where Proteus' herds, and Neptune's orks do keep,
Where all is ploughed, yet still the pasture's green,
New ways are found, and yet no paths are seen.

Here PROTEUS, PORTUNUS, SARON, go up to the Ladies with
this SONG.

Proteus. Come, noble nymphs, and do not hide
The joys for which you so provide:
Saron. If not to mingle with the men,
What do you here?   Go home agen.
Portunus.   Your dressings do confess,
By what we see, so curious parts
Of Pallas and Arachne's arts,
                That you could mean no less.
Proteus. Why do you wear the silkworm's toils,
Or glory in the shell-fish' spoils,
Or strive to show the grains of ore

That you have gathered on the shore,
        Whereof to make a stock
To graft the greener emerald on.
Or any better-watered stone?
    Saron.   Or ruby of the rock?
    Proteus. Why do you smell of amber-grise,
Of which was formed Neptune's niece,
The queen of love; unless you can,
Like sea-born Venus, love a man?
    Saron.   Try, put yourselves unto 't.
    Chorus. Your looks, your smiles, and thoughts that
    meet,
Ambrosian hands and silver feet,
        Do promise you will do 't.

The Revels follow.

Which ended, the fleet is discovered, while the three cornets play.

    Johphiel. 'T is time your eyes should be refreshed at
    length
With something new, a part of Neptune's strength:
See yond' his fleet, ready to go or come,
Or fetch the riches of the ocean home,
So to secure him, both in peace and wars,
Till not one ship alone, but all be stars.

Then the last

SONG.

    Proteus. Although we wish the glory still might last
Of such a night, and for the causes past:
Yet now, great lord of waters and of isles,
Give Proteus leave to turn unto his wiles.
    Portunus. And whilst young Albion doth thy labours
    ease,
Dispatch Portunus to the ports,

Saron.   And Saron to the seas,
To meet old Nereus with his fifty girls,
From aged Indus laden home with pearls
And orient gums, to burn unto thy name.
  Chorus. And may thy subjects' hearts be all on flame,
Whilst thou dost keep the earth in firm estate,
And 'mongst the winds dost suffer no debate;
But both at sea and land our powers increase
With health, and all the golden gifts of peace.

After which they danced their last DANCE,

And thus it ended.

XV.

JAMES SHIRLEY.

(1596–1666.)

THE TRIUMPH OF PEACE.

A MASQUE PRESENTED BY THE FOUR HONOURABLE HOUSES
OR INNS OF COURT BEFORE THE KING AND QUEEN'S
MAJESTIES IN THE BANQUETING-HOUSE AT WHITE-
HALL, FEBRUARY 3, 1634.

[This gorgeous spectacle cost the four Inns of Court upwards of
£21,000. A second performance before their majesties was given on
February 11, at Merchant Taylors' Hall. This was under the auspices
of the Lord Mayor. The Queen had been so delighted with the masque
on its first performance that she desired to see it over again. It was
designed as a rejoinder to the strictures of Prynne in his *Histriomastix*
(1633).]

TO THE FOUR EQUAL AND HONOURABLE SOCIETIES,
THE INNS OF COURT.

I WANT words to express your cheerful and active desires,
to present your duties to their royal Majesties, in this
Masque; to celebrate, by this humble tender of your hearts
and services, the happiness of our Kingdom, so blest in the
present government, and never so rich in the possession of so
many and great pledges of their Parents' virtue, our native
Princes.

Your clear devotions already offered and accepted, let not
me want an altar for my oblation to you. This entertainment,
which took life from your command, and wanted no motion
or growth it could derive from my weak fancy, I sacrifice
again to you, and under your smile to the world. Let it not
repent you to look upon, what is the second time made your
own, and with it, the heart of the sacrificer, infinitely bound
to acknowledge your free, and noble souls, that have left no
way for a poet to satisfy his ambition, how to thank you, but
with thinking, he shall never be able to satisfy it.

I dare not rack my preface to a length. Proceed to be
yourselves (the ornament of our nation), and when you have
leisure to converse with imaginations of this kind, it shall be
an addition to your many favours, to read these papers, and
oblige beside the seals of your other encouragement,

The humblest of your honourers

JAMES SHIRLEY.

SPEAKING CHARACTERS IN THE MASQUE.

OPINION.	CARPENTER.	IRENE.
CONFIDENCE.	TAYLOR.	EUNOMIA.
FANCY.	BLACKGUARD.	DICHE.
JOLLITY.	PAINTER.	GENIUS.
LAUGHTER.	TAYLOR'S WIFE.	AMPHILUCHE.
NOVELTY.	PROPERTY MAN'S WIFE.	THE HOURS.
ADMIRATION.	FEATHER MAKER'S WIFE.	CHORUS.
	EMBROIDERER'S WIFE.	
	GUARDS.	

THE MASQUE OF THE GENTLEMEN
OF THE
FOUR HONOURABLE SOCIETIES, OR INNS OF COURT.

At Ely and Hatton Houses, the gentlemen and their assistants met,
and in this manner prepared for the Court.

The Antimasquers were ushered by a hornpipe[1], and a shalm[2];
riding in coats and caps of yellow taffeta, spotted with silver, their
feathers red, their horses led by men in coats of blue taffeta, their
wings red, and part of their sleeves yellow, caps and feathers; all
the torch-bearers in the same habit appointed to attend, and give
plentiful light to the whole train.

Fancy in a suit of several-coloured feathers, hooded, a pair of bat's
wings on his shoulders, riding alone, as sole presenter of the Antimasques.

After him rode Opinion and Confidence together:

Opinion in an old fashioned doublet of black velvet, and trunk
hose, a short cloak of the same with an antique cape, a black velvet
cap pinched up, with a white fall, and a staff in his hand;

Confidence in a slashed doublet, parti-coloured, breeches suitable
with points at knees, favours upon his breast and arm, a broad-

---

[1] A wind-instrument, so called because the bell or open end was sometimes made of horn.   [2] A reed-instrument like the shepherd's pipe.

brimmed hat, tied up on one side, banded with a feather, a long
lock of hair, trimmed with several-coloured ribands, wide boots, and
great spurs with bells for rowels.

Next rode Jollity and Laughter:

Jollity in a flame-coloured suit, but tricked like a morice dancer,
with scarfs and napkins, his hat fashioned like a cone, with a little
fall;

Laughter in a long side coat of several colours, laughing, vizards
on his breast and back, a cap with two grinning faces, and feathers
between.

Then followed variety of antick music; after which rode six
Projectors,[1] one after another, their horses led by torch-bearers:

The first, a Jockey with a bonnet on his head, upon the top of it
a whip, he seeming much to observe and affect a bridle which he
had in his hand;[2]

---

[1] Compare *The Devil is an Ass*, act i. sc. 3:

Fitzdottrel.   But what is a projector?
     I would conceive.

Engine.   Why, one, sir, that projects
Ways to enrich men, or to make 'em great,
By suits, by marriages, by undertakings:
According as he sees they humour it.

[2] "First in this Antimasque rode a fellow upon a little horse, with a great
bit in his mouth, and upon the man's head was a bit, with headstall and
reins fastened, and signified a Projector who begged a patent that none
in the kingdom might ride their horses, but with such bits as they should
buy of him. Then came another fellow with a bunch of carrots upon
his head, and a capon upon his fist, describing a Projector who begged
a patent of monopoly, as the first inventor of the art to feed capons fat
with carrots, and that none but himself might make use of that invention, and have the privilege for fourteen years according to the statute.
Several other Projectors were in like manner personated in this Antimasque; and it pleased the spectators the more, because by it an infor-
mation was covertly given to the King of the unfitness and ridiculousness
of these projects against the law: and the Attorney Noy, who had most
knowledge of them, had a great hand in this Antimasque of the Projectors."—Whitelocke, *Memorials*, 1732, p. 20.

The arrangements for the masque were conducted by a committee of
eight, consisting of two members from each of the four societies. Bul-
strode Whitelocke and Edward Hyde, afterwards Earl of Clarendon,
represented the Middle Temple. Whitelocke had charge of the music,
which was composed under his direction by Simon Ives and Henry
Lawes, and with the help of the former he even composed an air himself,
which was henceforward known as "Whitelocke's coranto". In his
Memorials, pp. 19-22, he gives a full account of the whole masque.

The second, a Country fellow in a leather doublet and grey trunk hose, a wheel with a perpetual motion on his head, and in his hand a flail ;

The third, a grim Philosophical-faced fellow, in his gown, furred and girdled about him, a furnace upon his head, and in his hand a lamp ;

The fourth, in a case of black leather, vast to the middle, and round on the top, with glass eyes, and bellows under each arm ;

The fifth, a Physician, on his head a hat with a bunch of carrots, a capon perched upon his fist ;

The sixth, like a Seaman, a ship upon his head, and holding a line and plummet in his hand.

Next these, rode so many Beggars[1] in timorous looks and gestures, as pursued by two Mastives that came barking after them.

Here variety of other antick music, counterfeiting the voices of birds; and after these rode a Magpie, a Crow, a Jay, and a Kite, in a quadrangular figure, and in the midst an Owl ;[2] these were followed by three Satyrs, two abreast, and one single, sided with torch-bearers; then three Dotterels in the same manner and attendance.

After these a Windmill, against which a fantastic Knight with his lance, and his Squire armed, seemed to make their attempts.

These moving forward in ridiculous show and postures, a Drummer followed on horseback, in a crimson taffeta coat, a white hat and feather tipt with crimson, beating two kettle drums.

Then fourteen Trumpeters, in crimson satin coats, white hats and feathers, and rich banners.

The Marshal[3] followed these, bravely mounted; attended with ten horse and forty foot, in coats and hose of scarlet trimmed with silver lace, white hats and feathers, their truncheons tipt with silver; these upon every occasion moving to and fro, to preserve the order of their march, and restrain the rudeness of the people, that in such triumphs, are wont to be insolent, and tumultuary.

After these an hundred Gentlemen, gloriously furnished and gallantly mounted, riding two and two abreast, every gentleman having his two pages richly attired, and a groom to attend him.

---

[1] "The beggars had their musick of keys and tongs and the like, snapping, and yet playing in a consort before them. These Beggars were also mounted, but on the poorest, leanest jades that could be gotten out of the dirt carts or elsewhere."—Whitelocke, *ibid*.

[2] "These were little boys put into covers of the shapes of those birds, rarely fitted, and sitting on small horses."—Whitelocke, *ibid*.

[3] "Mr. Darrel, afterwards knighted by the King."—Whitelocke, *ibid*.

Next after these, a chariot drawn by four horses, two and two together, richly furnished and adorned with gold and silver, the charioteer in a Polonian coat of green cloth of silver. In this were advanced Musicians, like Priests and Sybills, sons and daughters of harmony, some with coronets, others with wreaths of laurel and myrtle, playing upon their lutes, three footmen on each side in blue satin wrought with silver, and everyone a flambeau in his hand.

In the next chariot of equal glory, were placed on the lowest stairs four in sky-coloured taffeta robes seeded with stars, mantles ash-coloured, adorned with fringe and silver lace, coronets with stars upon their heads. In a seat a little more elevate sat Genius and Amphiluche.[1]

On the highest seat of this chariot, sat the three Hours, or heavenly sisters, Irene, Diche, and Eunomia;[2] all whose habits shall be described in their proper places: this chariot attended as the former.

After these, came the Four Triumphals or Magnificent Chariots, in which were mounted the Grand Masquers, one of the four houses in every chariot, seated within an half oval,[3] with a glorious canopy over their heads, all bordered with silver fringe, and beautified with plumes of feathers on the top;

The first chariot, silver and orange,

The second, silver and watchet[4],

The third, silver and crimson,

The fourth, silver and white;

All after the Roman form, adorned with much embossed and carved works, and each of them wrought with silver, and his several colour; they were mounted on carriages, the spring-trees, pole and axle-trees, the charioteer's seat, and standers, wheels, with the fellies, spokes, and naves, all wrought with silver, and their several colour.

They were all drawn with four horses afront, after the magnificent Roman triumphs, their furniture, harness, headstall, bits, reins, and traces, chamfron, cronet, petronel, and barb,[5] of rich cloth of silver, of several works and colours, answerable to the linings of the chariots.

---

[1] The morning twilight.

[2] The three Horae, or goddesses of the seasons, Peace, Justice, and Good Order, or Law.

[3] This half-oval shape was intended to put all the seats in the chariot on an equality, and so avoid all disputes as to precedence between the representatives of the several Inns.　　　　　　[4] Pale blue.

[5] *Chamfron*, frontlet; *cronet*, what part of the armour this was is not known; *petronel*, poitral, armour for the breast of a horse; *barb*, the covering of the breast and flanks.

The charioteers in Polony coats of the same colour of the chariots, their caps, feathers, and buskins answerable.

The two out-horses of every chariot led by two men, in habits wrought with silver, and conformable to the colour of the other furniture; four footmen on either side of every chariot, in rich habits, also wrought with silver, answerable to the rest, every one carrying a flambeau in his hand.

Between every of these chariots, four musicians in their robes and garlands, were mounted, riding two abreast, attended with torch-bearers.

The habit of the Masquers gave infinite splendour to this solemnity; which more aptly shall be expressed in his place.

This Masque was presented in the Banqueting-house at Whitehall, before the King and Queen's Majesties, and a great assembly of lords and ladies, and other persons of quality, whose aspect, sitting on the degrees[1] prepared for that purpose, gave a great grace to this spectacle, especially being all richly attired.

At the lower end of the room, opposite to the State, was raised a stage with a descent of stairs in two branches landing into the room. This basement was painted in rustic work.

The border of the front and sides that enclosed all the scene, had first a ground of arbour-work, intermixed with loose branches and leaves; and in this was two niches; and in them two great figures standing in easy postures, in their natural colours, and much bigger than the life. The one, attired after the Grecian manner, held in one hand a sceptre, and in the other a scrowl, and a picked[2] antique crown on his head, his cuirass was of gold richly enchased, his robe blue and silver, his arms and thighs bare, with buskins enriched with ornaments of gold, his brown locks long and curled, his beard thick, but not long, and his face was of a grave and jovial aspect; this figure stood on a round pedestal, feigned of white marble, enriched with several carvings; above this in a compartment of gold was written MINOS. The figure on the other side was in a Roman habit, holding a table in one hand, and a pen in the other, and a white bend or diadem about his head, his robe was crimson and gold, his mantle yellow and silver, his buskins watchet trimmed with silver, his hair and beard long and white, with a venerable aspect, standing likewise on a round pedestal answerable to the other; and in the compartment over him was written NUMA. Above all this, in a

---

[1] Tiers of seats.
[2] Peaked, *i.e.* having peaks or points rising from the circle.

proportionate distance, hung two great festoons of fruits in colours, which served for finishing to these sides. The upper part, in manner of a large frieze, was adorned with several compartments with draperies hanging down, and the ends tied up in knots, with trophies proper to feasts and triumphs, composed of masking vizards and torches. In one of the lesser compartments, was figured a sharp-sighted eye, and in the other a golden yoke; in the midst was a more great and rich compartment, on the sides of which sat naked children in their natural colours, with silver wings, in action of sounding golden trumpets, and in this was figured a caduceus[1] with an olive branch, all which are hierogliphics of Peace, Justice, and Law.

A curtain being suddenly drawn up, the scene was discovered, representing a large street with sumptuous palaces, lodges, porticos, and other noble pieces of architecture, with pleasant trees and grounds; this going far from the eye, opens itself into a spacious place, adorned with public and private buildings seen afar of, representing the forum or piazza of Peace. Over all was a clear sky with transparent clouds, which enlightened all the scene.

The spectators having entertained their eyes awhile with the beauty and variety of this scene, from one of the sides of the street enters Opinion, etc.

Enter OPINION; CONFIDENCE meets him; they salute.

Confidence. Most grave Opinion!

Opinion. Confidence, most welcome!
Is Fancy come to court?

Confidence. Breaking his way
Thorough the guard.

Opinion. So violent?

Confidence. With jests
Which they 're less able to resist;
He 'll crack a halbert with his wit.

Opinion. A most
Strong Fancy! yet we ha' known a little engine
Break an ingenious head-piece. But your master—

Confidence. Companion, sir: Fancy will keep no servants,

[1] Wand.

And Confidence scorns to wait.

Opinion.   Cry mercy, sir;
But is this gentleman, this Signor Fancy,
So rare a thing, so subtle, as men speak him?

Confidence. He's a great prince of th' air, believe it,
    sir,
And yet a bird of night.

Opinion.   A bird!

Confidence.   Between
An owl and bat, a quaint hermaphrodite,
Begot of Mercury and Venus, Wit and Love:
He's worth your entertainment.

Opinion.   I am most
Ambitious to see him; he is not
So nimble as I wish him.   Where's my wife,
My Lady Novelty?

Enter NOVELTY.

Novelty.   Your wife! you might
Have fram'd a newer word; they can but call
Us so i' th' country.

Opinion.   No exception,
Dear Madam Novelty; I must prepare you,
To entertain a gentleman.   Where's Admiration,
Our daughter?

Enter ADMIRATION.

Admiration. Here, sir.   What gay man is this?

Opinion. Please you honour us, and bring in your
    friend, sir.

Confidence. I'll do't; but he prevents me.

Enter FANCY, JOLLITY, and LAUGHTER.

Opinion.   Sir, I am ignorant
By what titles to salute you, but you're welcome
To court.

Fancy. Save yourself, sir, your name 's Opinion.

Opinion. And your 's Fancy.

Fancy.   Right.

Jollity.   Mine Jollity.

Laughter. Mine Laughter; ha, ha, ha!

Novelty.   Here 's a strange shape!

Admiration. I never saw the like.

Fancy. I come to do you honour with my friends here,
And help the masque.

   Opinion.   You 'll do a special favour.

   Fancy. How many antimasques ha' they? of what
     nature?

For these are fancies that take most; your dull
And phlegmatic inventions are exploded;
Give me a nimble antimasque.

   Opinion.   They have none, sir.

   Laughter. No antimasque! I 'ld laugh at that, i' faith.

   Jollity. What make we here? No jollity!

   Fancy.   No antimasque!

Bid 'em down with the scene, and sell the timber,
Send Jupiter to grass, and bid Apollo
Keep cows again; take all their gods and goddesses,
For these must farce up[1] this night's entertainment,
And pray the court may have some mercy on 'em,
They will be jeer'd to death else for their ignorance.
The soul of wit moves here; yet there be some,
If my intelligence fail not, mean to show
Themselves jeer majors; some tall[2] critics have
Planted artillery and wit murderers.
No antimasque! let 'em look to 't.

   Opinion.   I have heard, sir;

Confidence made 'em trust, you 'ld furnish 'em:
I fear they should have made their address earlier
To your invention, but your brain 's nimble.

---

[1] Stuff, bolster up.   [2] Brave.

Pray, for the expectation that's upon 'em,
Lend them some witty fancies, set some engines
In motion that may conduce to the design.
I am their friend against the crowd that envy 'em,
And since they come with pure devotions
To sacrifice their duties to the king
And queen, I wish 'em prosper.
> *Fancy.*   You have charm'd me:
I 'll be their friend to-night; I have a fancy
Already.
> *Laughter.* Let it be ridiculous.
> *Confidence.* And confident.
> *Jollity.*   And jolly.
> *Fancy.*   The first antimasque
We will present ourselves in our own persons;
What think you on 't? Most grave Opinion,
You shall do well to lead the dance, and give it
Authority with your face; your lady may
Admire what she finds new.
> *Novelty.*   I shall applaud
The novelties.
> *Admiration.* And I admire.
> *Fancy.*   They tumble;
My skull's too narrow.
> *Laughter.*   Now his fancies caper.
> *Fancy.* Confidence, wait you upon Opinion;
Here Admiration, there Novelty;
This is the place for Jollity and Laughter;
Fancy will dance himself too.

> The first Antimasque, the dance expressing the natures
> of the presenters.

Fancy. How like you this device?
Opinion.   'T is handsome, but—
Laughter. Opinion will like nothing.

Novelty. It seems new.

Confidence. 'T was bold.

Jollity. 'T was jocund.

Laughter. Did not I do the fool well?

Admiration. Most admirably.

Laughter. Nay, and the ladies do but take
My part, and laugh at me, I am made, ha, ha!

Opinion. I could wish something, sir, of other nature,
To satisfy the present expectation.

Fancy. I imagine; nay, I 'm not ignorant of proprieties
And persons; 't is a time of peace, I 'll fit you,
And instantly make you a representation
Of the effects.

Opinion. Of peace? I like that well.

Fancy. And since in nothing they are more express'd
Than in good fellowship, I 'll present you with
A tavern.

The scene is changed into a tavern, with a flaming red lattice, several
drinking-rooms, and a back door, but especially, a conceited sign,
and an eminent bush.

Novelty. A spick and span new tavern!

Admiration. Wonderful! here was none within two
minutes.

Laughter. No such wonder, lady: taverns are quickly
up; it is but hanging out a bush at a nobleman's door,
or an alderman's gate, and 't is made instantly.

Confidence. Will 't please you, ladies, to accept the wine?

Jollity. Well said, Confidence.

Novelty. It will be new for ladies
To go to th' tavern; but it may be a fashion.
Follow me, Admiration.

Laughter. And the fool;
I may supply the absence of your fiddlers.

Jollity. If we can, let's leave Opinion behind us;
Fancy will make him drunk.

> [*Exeunt to the tavern*, CONFIDENCE, JOLLITY,
> LAUGHTER, NOVELTY, *and* ADMIRATION.

Another Antimasque of the MASTER of the tavern, his WIFE and
SERVANTS. After these a MAQUERELLE[1], two WENCHES, two
wanton GAMESTERS. These having danced and expressed their
natures, go into the TAVERN. Then enter a GENTLEMAN, and four
BEGGARS. The GENTLEMAN first danceth alone; to him the
BEGGARS; he bestows his charity; the CRIPPLES, upon his going
off, throw away their legs, and dance.

Opinion. I am glad they're off: are these effects of peace?
Corruption rather.

Fancy.   Oh, the beggars show
The benefit of peace.

Opinion.   Their very breath
Hath stifled all the candles, poison'd the
Perfumes: beggars—a fit presentment! how
They cleave still to my nostril! I must tell you,
I do not like such base and sordid persons,
And they become not here.

Fancy.   I apprehend,
If these distaste you, I can fit you with
Persons more cleanly;
What think you of projectors?

Opinion.   How, projectors?

Fancy. Here's one already.

Enter a JOCKEY.

                          This is a jockey:
He is to advance a rare and cunning bridle,
Made hollow in the iron part, wherein
A vapour subtly conveyed, shall so
Cool and refresh a horse, he shall ne'er tire;
And now he falls to his pace.   [*Jockey dances.*

[1] A bawd.

Enter a COUNTRY FELLOW.

Opinion.   This other?

Fancy.   His habit speaks him;
A country fellow, that has sold his acres
To purchase him a flail, which, by the motion
Of a quaint wheel, shall, without help of hands,
Thresh corn all day; and now he lays about him.

[*The Country Fellow dances.*]

Enter a third PROJECTOR.

This with a face philosophical and beard,
Hath with the study of twenty years found out
A lamp, which plac'd beneath a furnace, shall
Boil beef so thoroughly, that the very steam
Of the first vessel shall alone be able
To make another pot above seethe over.

Opinion. A most scholastic project! his feet follow

[*The third Projector dances.*]

The motions of his brain.

Enter a fourth PROJECTOR.

But what thing's this?
A chimera out of Rabelais?

Fancy.   A new project,
A case to walk you all day under water;
So vast for the necessity of air,
Which, with an artificial bellows cool'd,
Under each arm is kept still from corruption;
With those glass eyes he sees, and can fetch up
Gold or whatever jewels ha' been lost,
In any river o' the world.   [*The fourth Projector dances.*]

Opinion.   Strange water-rat!

Enter a fifth PROJECTOR.

Fancy. This grave man, some years past, was a physician,

A Galenist, and parcel Paracelsus;[1]
Thriv'd by diseases, but quite lost his practice,
To study a new way to fatten poultry
With scrapings of a carrot, a great benefit
To th' commonwealth.   [*The fifth Projector dances.*
Opinion.   He will deserve a monument.

Enter a sixth PROJECTOR.

Fancy. This is a kind of sea gull too, that will
Compose a ship to sail against the winds;
He 'll undertake to build a most strong castle
On Goodwin sands, to melt huge rocks to jelly,
And cut 'em out like sweetmeats with his keel;
And thus he sails.   [*The sixth Projector dances.*

All the Projectors dance after their antimasque. The MAQUERELLE,
WENCHES, GENTLEMAN, return, as from the tavern; they dance
together; the GALLANTS are cheated; and left to dance in, with a
drunken repentance.

Opinion. I know not, sir, how this may satisfy;
But might we be beholding to your fancy
For some more quaint variety, some other
Than human shapes, would happily delight
And reach the expectation; I ha' seen
Dainty devices in this kind, baboons
In quellios[2], and so forth.
Fancy.   I can furnish you.
Opinion. Fancy will much oblige us.
Fancy.   If these objects
Please not, Fancy can present a change.
What see you now?

The scene becomes a woody LANDSCAPE, with low grounds proper
for hunting, the furthest part more desert, with bushes and bye-ways

---

[1] Partly a disciple of Paracelsus.   [2] Ruffs, Spanish *cuello.*

representing a place fit for purse-taking. In the furthest part of the scene is seen an Ivy-bush, out of which comes an OWL.

Opinion.　　　A wood, a broad-fac'd ow*l*,
An ivy-bush, and other birds about her!
Fancy. These can imagination create.
Silence, observe.

An OWL, a CROW, a KITE, a JAY, a MAGPIE. The birds dance and wonder at the OWL. When these are gone, enter a MERCHANT a' Horseback with his portmanteau; two THIEVES set upon him and rob him: these by a CONSTABLE and OFFICERS are apprehended and carried off. Then four NYMPHS enter dancing, with their javelins; three SATYRS spy them and attempt their persons; one of the nymphs escapeth; a noise of hunters and their horns within, as at the fall of a deer; then enter four HUNTSMEN and one NYMPH; these drive away the SATYRS, and having rescued the NYMPHS, dance with them.

Opinion. This all you will present?
Fancy.　　　　　　　　You speak as if
Fancy could be exhaust; invention flows
From an immortal spring; you shall taste other
Variety, nimble as thought. We change the scene.

A LANDSCAPE, the scene; and enter three DOTTERELS, and three DOTTEREL-CATCHERS.

Opinion. What are these?
Fancy.　　　　　　Dotterels; be patient and expect.

After the DOTTERELS are caught by several imitations,[1] enter a WINDMILL, a fantastic KNIGHT and his SQUIRE armed. The fantastic adventurer with his lance makes many attempts upon the windmill, which his squire imitates: to them enter a COUNTRY-GENTLEMAN and his SERVANT. These are assaulted by the KNIGHT and his SQUIRE, but are sent off lame for their folly.

---

1 Dotterels were believed to be so fond of mimicry as to let themselves be caught while they were preoccupied with imitating the gestures of the fowler.

Then enter four BOWLERS, who shew much variety of sport in their game and postures, and conclude the ANTIMASQUE.

Enter CONFIDENCE, JOLLITY, LAUGHTER, NOVELTY, ADMIRATION.

Opinion. Madam, accuse your absence—
Novelty.   Come, we know
All your devices, sir; but I will have
An antimasque of my own, in a new place too.
Opinion. Hah, what's the matter?
Confidence, Jollity, Laughter, Admiration,
And Madam Novelty, all drunk! These are
Extremes indeed.
    Admiration.   Admirable opinion!
    Confidence. Be confident.
    Laughter.   And foolish.
    Jollity.   I am as light now!—
    Fancy. Let 'em enjoy their fancies.
    Opinion.   What new change
Is this? These strains are heavenly.
                    [FANCY *and the rest go off fearfully.*

The Antimasquers being gone, there appears in the highest and foremost part of the heaven, by little and little to break forth, a whitish cloud, bearing a chariot feigned of goldsmith's work; and in it sate IRENE, or Peace, in a flowery vesture like the spring, a garland of olives on her head, a branch of palm in her hand, buskins of green taffeta, great puffs about her neck and shoulders.

She sings.

SONG I.

Irene.   Hence, ye profane, far hence away!
            Time hath sick feathers while you stay.
                Is this delight
                For such a glorious night,
                Wherein two skies
                Are to be seen,

One starry, but an aged sphere,
　　Another here,
Created new and brighter from the eyes
　　Of king and queen?

Chorus.　Hence, ye profane, far hence away!
Time hath sick feathers while you stay.

SONG II.

Irene.　Wherefore do my sisters stay?
Appear, appear Eunomia!
'T is Irene calls to thee,
　　Irene calls;
　　Like dew that falls
　　Into a stream,
I 'm lost with them
That know not how to order me.

Chorus.　See where she shines, oh see
In her celestial gaiety!
Crown'd with a wreath of stars, to show
The evening's glory in her brow.

Here, out of the highest part of the opposite side, came softly
descending another cloud, of an orient colour, bearing a silver
chariot curiously wrought, and differing in all things from the first:
in which sate EUNOMIA or Law, in a purple satin robe, adorned
with golden stars, a mantle of carnation laced, and fringed with
gold, a coronet of light upon her head, buskins of purple, drawn
out with yellow. This chariot attended as the former.

SONG III.

Eunomia. Think not I could absent myself this night;
But Peace is gentle and doth still invite
Eunomia; yet should'st thou silent be,
The rose and lily which thou strowest

            All the cheerful way thou goest,
            Would direct to follow thee.

Irene.   Thou dost beautify increase,
            And chain security with peace

Eunomia. Irene fair, and first divine,
            All my blessings spring from thine.

Irene.   I am but wild without thee, thou abhorrest
            What is rude, or apt to wound,
            Canst throw proud trees to the ground,
            And make a temple of a forest.

Eunomia. No more, no more, but join
            Thy voice, and lute with mine.

Both.   The world shall give prerogative to neither;
            We cannot flourish but together.

Chorus.   Irene enters like a perfum'd spring,
            Eunomia ripens every thing,
            And in the golden harvest leaves
            To every sickle his own sheaves.

At this, a third cloud, of a various colour from the other two, begins to descend toward the middle of the scene with somewhat a more swifter motion; and in it sate a person representing DICHE or Justice, in the midst, in a white robe and mantle of satin, a fair long hair circled with a coronet of silver pikes, white wings and buskins, a crown imperial in her hand.

SONG IV.

Diche.   Swiftly, oh swiftly! I do move too slow,
            What holds my wing from making haste
            When every cloud sails by so fast?
            I heard my sisters' voice, and know
            They have forsaken heaven's bright gate,
            To attend another state,
            Of gods below.
            Irene, chaste Eunomia!

Irene, Eunomia. We,
   Diche, have stay'd expecting thee;
   Thou giv'st perfection to our glory
   And seal to this night's story;
   Astrea, shake the cold dew from thy wing.
Eunomia. Descend.
Irene.   Descend.
Eunomia. Descend, and help us sing
   The triumph of Jove's upper court abated,
   And all the deities translated.

Chorus. The triumph of Jove's upper court abated,
   And all the deities translated.

Eunomia. Now gaze, and when thy wonder will allow,
   Tell what thou hast beheld.
Diche.   Never, till now,
   Was poor Astrea blind; oh strange surprise,
   That too much sight should take away my eyes!
   Am I in earth or heaven?
Irene.   What throne is that,
   On which so many stars do wait?
Diche. My eyes are blest again, and now I see
   The parents of us three:
   'T is Jove and Themis; forward move,
   And sing to Themis, and to Jove.

Then the whole train of Musicians move in a comely figure
toward the King and Queen, and bowing to their State, this following ode is sung.

SONG V.

  To you, great king and queen, whose smile
  Doth scatter blessings through this isle,
    To make it best
    And wonder of the rest,

We pay the duty of our birth;
Proud to wait upon that earth
Whereon you move,
Which shall be nam'd,
And by your chaste embraces fam'd,
The paradise of love.
Irene, plant thy olives here;
Thus warm'd, at once they 'll bloom and bear;
Eunomia, pay thy light;
While Diche, covetous to stay,
Shall throw her silver wings away,
To dwell within your sight.

The scene is changed, and the Masquers appear sitting on the ascent of a hill, cut out like the degrees of a theatre; and over them a delicious arbour, with terms[1] of young men, their arms converted into scrowls[2], and under their waists a foliage with other carvings to cover the joining of the term from the naked, all feigned of silver; these bore up an architrave, from which was raised a light covering arched, and interwoven with branches through which the sky beyond was seen.

The Masquers were sixteen in number, the sons of Peace, Law and Justice, who sitting in a gracious but not set form, every part of the seats made a various composition, but all together tending to a pyramidal figure.

Their habits were mixed, between the ancient and modern; their bodies carnation, the shoulders trimmed with knots of pure silver, and scallops of white and carnation, under them the labels of the same, the under sleeves white, and a puffed sleeve full of gathering, falling down to the elbow; about their waist was a small scallop, and a slender girdle; their under bases[3] were carnation and white, with labels as at their shoulders, and all this in every part was richly embroidered with pure silver; their hats carnation low crowned, the brim double, and cut into several quarters lined with white, and all over richly embroidered, as the rest; about their hats were wreaths of olive, and plumes of white feathers, with several falls, the longest toward the back; their long stockings were white, with white shoes and roses.

---

[1] Termini.   [2] Scrolls.   [3] Kilts.

Beneath these a **Genius** or angelical person, with wings of several-coloured feathers, a carnation robe tucked up, yellow, long hair, bound with a silver coronet, a small white rod in his hand, white buskins; who descended to the stage speaketh.

Genius. No foreign persons I make known,
But here present you with your own,
The children of your reign, not blood:
Of age, when they are understood,
Not seen by faction or owl's sight,
Whose trouble is the clearest light;
But treasures to their eye and ear,
That love good for itself, not fear.
Oh, smile on what yourselves have made!
These have no form, no sun, no shade,
But what your virtue doth create;
Exalted by your glorious fate,
They 'll tower to heaven, next which, they know
And wish no blessedness but you.
That very look into each eye   [*The Masquers move.*
Hath shot a soul, I saw it fly.
Descend, move nimbly, and advance,
Your joyful tribute in a dance.

Here, with loud music, the Masquers descend and dance their entry to the violins; which ended, they retire to the scene, and then the Hours and Chori again move toward the State and sing.

SONG VI.

They that were never happy Hours
Till now, return to thank the powers
    That made them so.
    The Island doth rejoice,
And all her waves are echo to our voice,
Which, in no ages past, hath known
    Such treasures of her own.

Live, royal pair, and when your sands are spent
　　With heaven's and your consent,
　　Though late, from your high bowers
　　Look down on what was yours;
For, till old Time his glass hath hurl'd,
And lost it in the ashes of the world,
We prophesy, you shall be read and seen,
In every branch, a king or queen.

The song ended, and the Musicians returned, the Masquers dance
their main dance; after which they again retire to the scene; at
which they no sooner arrive, but there is heard a great noise, and
confusion of voices within, some crying, *They will come in*, others
Knock 'em down, Call the rest of the guard; then a crack is heard
in the works, as if there were some danger by some piece of the
machines falling; this continued a little time, there rush in a CAR-
PENTER, a PAINTER, one of the BLACK GUARD,[1] a TAILOR, the
TAILOR'S WIFE, an EMBROIDERER'S WIFE, a FEATHER-MAKER'S
WIFE, and a PROPERTY MAN'S WIFE.

Carpenter. D'ye think to keep us out?

1 Guard. Knock her down.

Tailor. Knock down my wife! I'ld see the tallest beef-
eater on you all but hold up his halberd in the way of
knocking my wife down, and I'll bring him a button hole
lower.

Tailor's Wife. Nay, let 'em, let 'em husband, at their
peril.

2 Guard. Complain to my lord chamberlain.

Property Man's Wife. My husband is somewhere in
the works; I'm sure I helped to make him an owl and
a hobby horse, and I see no reason but his wife may be
admitted in *forma paperis*, to see as good a masque as
this.

Black Guard. I never saw one afore: I am one of the
guard, though of another complexion, and I will see't,

---

[1] The lowest menials of the royal household.

now I am here, though I be turned out of the kitchen to-morrow for 't.

Painter. Ay, come, be resolute; we know the worst, and let us challenge a privilege; those stairs were of my painting.

Carpenter. And that timber I set up; somebody is my witness.

Feather-maker's Wife. I am sure my husband sold 'em most of the feathers; somebody promised me a fall[1] too, if I came to court, but let that pass.

Embroiderer's Wife. And mine embroidered two of the best habits: what though we be no ladies, we are Christians in these clothes, and the king's subjects, God bless us.

Tailor. Nay, now I am in, I will see a dance, though my shop windows be shut up for 't. Tell us?—hum? d' ye hear? do not they laugh at us? what were we best to do? The Masquers will do no feats as long as we are here; be ruled by me, hark every one; 't is our best course to dance a figary ourselves, and then they 'll think it a piece of the plot, and we may go off again with the more credit; we may else kiss the porter's lodge[2] for 't; let 's put a trick upon 'em in revenge, 't will seem a new device too.

Omnes. Content.

Tailor. And the musicians knew but our mind now!

[*The violins play.*

Hark, they are at it; now for a lively frisk. [*They dance.*

Now, let us go off cleanly, and somebody will think this was meant for an antimasque.

They being gone, the Masquers are encouraged by a song to their revels with the ladies.

---

[1] "Upon his [Mercury's] head a wreath, with small falls of white feathers."—Carew, *Coelum Britannicum*, p. 132, ed. Ebsworth.

[2] See *The Masque of Augurs*, p. 149, note 3.

SONG VII.

Why do you dwell so long in clouds,
  And smother your best graces?
'T is time to cast away those shrouds,
  And clear your manly faces.
Do not behave yourselves like spies
  Upon the ladies here;
On even terms go meet their eyes,
  Beauty and love shine there.
You tread dull measures thus alone,
  Not satisfy delight;
Go kiss their hands and make your own
  With every touch more white.

The Revels being passed, the scene is changed into a plain cham-
paign country, which terminates with the horizon, and above a
darkish sky, with dusky clouds, through which appeared the new
moon, but with a faint light by the approach of the morning; from
the furthest part of this ground, arose by little and little a great
vapour, which being come about the middle of the scene, it slackens
its motion, and begins to fall downward to the earth from whence
it came; and out of this rose another cloud of a strange shape and
colour, on which sate a young maid, with a dim torch in her hand;
her face was an olive colour, so was her arms and breast, on her
head a curious dressing, and about her neck a string of great pearl;
her garment was transparent, the ground dark blue, and sprinkled
with silver spangles, her buskins white, trimmed with gold; by these
marks she was known to be the forerunner of the morning, called
by the ancients AMPHILUCHE, and is that glimpse of light, which is
seen when the night is past, and the day not yet appearing.

SONG VIII.

Amphiluche. In envy to the Night,
      That keeps such revels here,
      With my unwelcome light
      Thus I invade her sphere;

Proclaiming wars
To Cynthia, and all her stars,
That, like proud spangles, dress
Her azure tress.
Because I cannot be a guest, I rise
To shame the Moon, and put out all her eyes.

Amphiluche ascending, the Masquers are called from their revels
by other voices.

SONG IX.

1. Come away, away, away,
See the dawning of the day,
Risen from the murmuring streams;
Some stars show with sickly beams
What stock of flame they are allow'd,
Each retiring to a cloud;
Bid your active sports adieu,
The morning else will blush for you.
2. Ye feather-footed Hours run
To dress the chariot of the Sun;
Harness the steeds, it quickly will
Be time to mount the eastern hill.
3. The lights grow pale with modest fears,
Lest you offend their sacred ears
And eyes, that lent you all this grace;
Retire, retire, to your own place.
4. And as you move from that blest pair,
Let each heart kneel, and think a prayer,
That all, that can make up the glory
Of good and great may fill their story.

Amphiluche hidden in the heavens, and the Masquers retired, the
scene closeth.

And thus concluded this Masque, which was, for the variety of
the shows, and richness of the habits, the most magnificent that
hath been brought to court in our time.

The scene and ornament was the act of Inigo Jones, Esquire, Surveyor of his Majesty's works.

The composition of the music was performed by Mr. William Lawes and Mr. Simon Ives, whose art gave an harmonious soul to the otherwise languishing numbers.

A Speech to the King and Queen's Majesties, when they were pleased to honour the city with their presence, and gave a gracious command the former Triumph should attend them.

Genius. Most great and glorious princes, once more, I
Present to your most sacred Majesty
The Sons of Peace, who tender you by me
Their joy-exalted heart and humble knee;
Happy in their ambition to wait,
And pay this second duty to your state,
Acknowledging no triumph but in you:
The honour you have done them is so new
And active in their souls, that it must grow
A part of them, and be immortal too.
These wonders you create, and every man
Receives as much joy as the island can;
Which shows you nearest heaven, that can let fall
Unequal, yet a perfect bliss to all.
Dwell still within yourselves, for other place
Is strait, and cannot circumscribe your grace;
Whilst men grow old with prayers for your blest reign,
Yet with your smiles shall be restor'd again.

XVI.

SIR WILLIAM DAVENANT.

(1606–1668.)

SALMACIDA SPOLIA.

A MASQUE PRESENTED BY THE KING AND QUEEN'S MAJESTIES, AT WHITEHALL ON TUESDAY, JANUARY 21, 1640.

[This was the last of the masques. The Long Parliament met in the following November, and Charles had henceforward more serious matters to occupy his thoughts. But even in the gay composition before us the troubles of the times are not obscurely hinted at, and the murmur of the approaching storm is plainly audible in the midst of all the mirth. Sir William Davenant forms the link between the pre-Restoration and the post-Restoration stage, and under his influence the musical and spectacular attractions of the masque were transferred to the theatre, where, for better or worse, they still reign paramount.]

THE SUBJECT OF THE MASQUE.

DISCORD, a malicious fury, appears in a storm, and by the invocation of malignant spirits, proper o her evil use, having already put most of the world into disorder, endeavours to disturb these parts, envying the blessings and tranquillity we have long enjoyed.

These incantations are expressed by those spirits in an Antimasque: who on a sudden are surprised, and stopt in their motion by a secret power, whose wisdom they tremble at, and depart as foreknowing that Wisdom will change all their malicious hope of these disorders into a sudden calm, which after their departure is prepared by a disperst harmony of music.

This secret Wisdom, in the person of the King attended by his nobles, and under the name of Philogenes or Lover of his people, hath his appearance prepared by a Chorus, representing the beloved people, and is instantly discovered, environed with those nobles in the throne of Honour.

Then the Queen personating the chief heroine, with her martial ladies, is sent down from Heaven by Pallas as a reward of his prudence, for reducing the threat'ning storm into the following calm.[1]

In the border that enclosed the scenes and made a frontispiece to all the work, in a square niche on the right hand stood two figures of women, one of them expressing much majesty in her aspect, apparelled in sky colour, with a crown of gold on her head, and a bridle in her hand, representing Reason: the other, embracing her, was in changeable silk with wings at her shoulders, figured for Intellectual Appetite, who while she embraceth Reason, all the actions of men are rightly governed. Above these, in a second order, were winged children, one riding on a furious lion, which he seems to tame with reins and a bit: another bearing an antique ensign: the third hovering above with a branch of palm in his hand, expressing the victory over the perturbations. In a niche on the other side stood two figures joining hands, one a grave old man in a robe of purple, with a heart of gold in a chain about his neck, figured for Counsel; the other a woman, in a garment of cloth of gold, in her hand a sword with a serpent winding about the blade, representing Resolution, both these being necessary to the good means of arriving to a virtuous end.

Over these and answering to the other side was a round altar raised high, and on it the bird of Pallas, figured for Prudence; on either side were children with wings, one in act of adoration, another holding a book, and a third flying over their heads with a lighted torch in his hand, representing the intellectual light accompanied with Doctrine and Discipline, and alluding to the figures below, as those on the other side.

Above these ran a large frieze, with a cornicement[2]: in the midst whereof was a double compartment rich and full of ornament: on the top of this sate Fame with spreaded wings, in act, sounding a trumpet of gold: joining to the compartment, in various postures lay two figures in their natural colours as big as the life; one holding an anchor representing Safety; the other representing Riches, with a cornucopia; and about her stood antique vases of gold. The rest of this frieze was composed of children, with significant signs to express their several qualities; Forgetfulness of injuries, extinguishing a

---

[1] This is an example of what Bacon calls a *Double Masque*, "one of men, another of ladies", which "addeth state and variety." Essay xxxvii. *Of Masques and Triumphs.*   [2] Cornice.

flaming torch on an armour; Commerce, with ears of corn; Felicity, with a basket of lilies; Affection to the country, holding a grasshopper; Prosperous success, with the rudder of a ship; Innocence, with a branch of fern: all these expressing the several goods, followers of Peace and Concord, and fore-runners of human felicity: so as the work of this front consisting of Picture qualified with moral Philosophy, temper'd delight with profit.

In the midst of the aforesaid compartment in an oval table was written: SALMACIDA SPOLIA.

The ancient adages are these:

> Salmacida Spolia sine sanguine sine sudore, potius quam
> Cadmia victoria, ubi ipsos victores pernicies opprimit.

But, before I proceed in the descriptions of the Scenes, it is not amiss briefly to set down the histories from whence these proverbs took their original.

For the first Melas and Arevanius of Argos and Troezen conducted a common colony to Halicarnassus in Asia, and there drave out the barbarous Carie and Lelegi,[1] who fled up to the mountains; from whence they made many incursions, robbing and cruelly spoiling the Grecian inhabitants, which could by no means be prevented.

On the top of the right horn of the hill which surrounds Halicarnassus, in the form of a theatre, is a famous fountain of most clear water, and exquisite taste called Salmacis. It happened that near to this fountain one of the colony, to make gain by the goodness of the water, set up a tavern, and furnished it with all necessaries, to which the barbarians resorting, enticed by the delicious taste of this water, at first some few, and after many together in troops, of fierce and cruel natures, were reduced of their own accord to the sweetness of the Grecian customs.

The other adage is thus derived.

The city of Thebes, anciently called Cadmia, had war with Adrastus, the Argive King, who raised a great army of Arcadians and Missenians,[2] and fought a battle with them near Ismenia, where the Thebans were overthrown, turned their backs, and fled into their city; the Peloponesians, not accustomed to scale walled towns, assaulting furiously, but without order, were repulst from the walls by the defendants, and many of the Argives slain: at that instant the besieged, making a great sally, and finding the enemy in disorder and confusion, cut them all in pieces, only Adrastus excepted, who was saved by flight: but this victory was gotten with great

---

[1] Cares and Leleges.   [2] Messenians.

damage and slaughter of the Thebans, for few of them returned alive to their city.

The allusion is, that his Majesty out of his mercy and clemency approving the first Proverb, seeks by all means to reduce tempestuous and turbulent natures into a sweet calm of civil concord.

A curtain flying up, a horrid scene appeared of storm and tempest; no glimpse of the sun was seen, as if darkness, confusion and deformity, had possest the world, and driven light to heaven, the trees bending, as forced by a gust of wind, their branches rent from their trunks, and some torn up by the roots: afar off was a dark wrought sea, with rolling billows, breaking against the rocks, with rain, lightning and thunder: in the midst was a globe of earth, which at an instant falling on fire, was turned into a Fury, her hair upright, mixt with snakes, her body lean, wrinkled, and of a swarthy colour, her breasts hung bagging down to her waist, to which with a knot of serpents was girt red bases, and under it tawny skirts down to her feet: in her hand she brandisht a sable torch, and looking askance with hollow envious eyes, came down into the room.

FURY.

Blow winds! until you raise the seas so high,
That waves may hang like leaves in the Sun's eye,
That we, when in vast cataracts they fall,
May think he weeps at Nature's funeral.
Blow winds! and from the troubled womb of earth,
Where you receive your undiscover'd birth,
Break out in wild disorders, till you make
Atlas beneath his shaking load to shake.
How am I griev'd, the world should everywhere
Be vext into a storm, save only here?
Thou over-lucky too much happy isle,
Grow more desirous of this flatt'ring style!
For thy long health can never alter'd be,
But by thy surfeits on Felicity:
And I to stir the humours that increase
In thy full body, over-grown with peace,
Will call those Furies hither, who incense
The guilty, and disorder innocence.

Ascend! ascend! you horrid sullen brood
Of evil spirits, and displace the good!
The great make only wiser, to suspect
Whom they have wrong'd by falsehood, or neglect;
The rich, make full of avarice as pride,
Like graves, or swallowing seas, unsatisfied;
Busy to help the State, when needy grown,
From poor men's fortunes, never from their own.
The poor, ambitious make, apt to obey
The false in hope to rule whom they betray:
And make religion to become their vice,
Nam'd, to disguise ambitious avarice.

The speech ended, three Furies make their entry presented by
M. Charles Murray, M. Seymour, M. Tartarean.

This antimasque being past, the scene changed into a calm, the
sky serene, afar off Zephyrus appeared breathing a gentle gale: in
the landskip were corn fields and pleasant trees, sustaining vines
fraught with grapes, and in some of the furthest parts villages, with
all such things as might express a country in peace, rich, and fruitful.
There came breaking out of the heavens a silver chariot, in which
sate two persons, the one a woman in a watchet garment, her
dressing of silver mixt with bulrushes, representing Concord: somewhat below her sate the good Genius of Great Britain, a young man
in a carnation garment, embroidered all with flowers, an antique
sword hung in a scarf, a garland on his head, and in his hand a
branch of platan[1] mixt with ears of corn: these in their descent sung
together.

I. SONG.

Good Genius of Great Britain, CONCORD.

CONCORD.

Why should I hasten hither, since the good
I bring to men is slowly understood?

---

[1] *Platanus,* the plane tree

GENIUS.

I know it is the people's vice
To lay too mean, too cheap a price
On ev'ry blessing they possess;
Th' enjoying makes them think the less.

CONCORD.

If then, the need of what is good
Doth make it lev'd [1], or understood,
Or 't is by absence better known,
I shall be valued, when I 'm gone.

GENIUS.

Yet stay! O stay! if but to please
The great and wise Philogenes.

CONCORD.

Shall dews not fall, the sun forbear
His course, or I my visits here?
Alike from these defects would cease
The power and hope of all increase.

GENIUS.

Stay then! O stay! if but to ease
The cares of wise Philogenes.

CONCORD.

I will! and much I grieve, that though the best
Of kingly science harbours in his breast,
Yet 't is his fate to rule in adverse times,
When wisdom must awhile give place to crimes.

Being arrived at the earth, and descended from the chariot, they
sing this short dialogue, and then departed several ways to incite

---

[1] Believed.

the beloved people to honest pleasures and recreations, which have ever been peculiar to this nation.

BOTH.

O who but he could thus endure
To live, and govern in a sullen age,
When it is harder far to cure,
The People's folly than resist their rage?

After which there followed these several Entries of Antimasques.

1. ENTRY.

Wolfgangus Vandergoose,[1] Spagrick,[2] Operator to the invisible Lady, styled the Magical sister of the Rosicross, with these receipts following, and many other rare secrets, undertakes in short time to cure the defects of nature, and diseases of the mind:—

1. Confection of hope and fear to entertain Lovers.
2. Essence of dissimulation to enforce love.
3. Julep of fruition to recreate the hot fevers of love.
4. Water of dalliance to warm an old courage.
5. A subtle quintessence drawn from mathematical points and lines, filtered through a melancholy brain, to make eunuchs engender.
6. Pomado of the bark of comeliness, the sweetness of wormwood, with the fat of gravity, to anoint those that have an ill mind.
7. Spirit of Saturn's high capers and Bacchus' whirling vertigo to make one dance well.
8. One drachm of the first matter, as much of the rust of Time's scythe, mixt with the juice of Medea's herbs: this, in an electuary, makes all sorts of old people young.
9. An opiate of the spirit of muskadine[3] taken in good quantity to bedward, to make one forget his creditors.
10. Powder of Menippus' tree, and the rind of hemp to consolate those who have lost their money.
11. Treacle of the gall of serpents, and the liver of doves to initiate a neophite courtier.

[1] We have already had Vangoose, "a rare artist", in *The Masque of Augurs.*
[2] Chemist, a term said to have been invented by Paracelsus.
[3] A rich kind of wine, *vin de muscat.*

12. An easy vomit of the fawning of a spaniel, Gallobelgicus,[1] and the last coranto[2], hot from the press, with the powder of some lean jests, to prepare a disprover's welcome to rich men's tables.

13. A Gargarism[3] of Florio's[4] first-fruits, Diana[5] de monte Major, and the scraping of Spanish Romanzas distilled in balneo, to make a sufficient Linguist without travelling, or scarce knowing himself what he says.

14. A Bath made of a catalogue from the mart, and common places, taken in a Frankfort dryfat[6]; in his diet he must refrain all real knowledge, and only suck in vulgar opinions, using the fricasee of confederacy, will make ignorants in all professions to seem and not to be.

2. ENTRY.

Four old men richly attired, the shapes proper to the persons, presented by ...

- M. Skipwith.
- M. Brough.
- M. Pert.
- M. Ashton.

3. ENTRY.

Three young soldiers in several fashioned habits, but costly, and presented to the life, by ... ...

- M. Hearne.
- M. Slingsby.
- M. Chumley.

4. ENTRY.

A nurse and three children in long coats, with bibs, biggins[7], and muckenders[8].

5. ENTRY.

An ancient Irishman, presented by ... ... M. Jay.

---

[1] A periodical publication in Latin, printed at Cologne 1594–1630, and not remarkable for its veracity.   [2] Courant.   [3] A gargle.

[4] [John] Florio *His first Fruites: which yeelde familiar Speech, merie Proverbs, wittie Sentences, and golden sayings. Also a perfect Induction to the Italian and English tongues. . . . The like heretofore, never by any man published.* 4to, London, 1578.

[5] "Diana", a pastoral romance by George of Montemayor. It was translated from the Spanish by Bartholomew Yong, of the Middle Temple, gentleman. Fol., London, 1598.

[6] A box or packing-case.   [7] Caps.   [8] Handkerchiefs.

6. Entry.

An ancient Scottishman, presented by ... M. Atkins.

7. Entry.

An old-fashioned Englishman, and his mis- { M. Arpe.
tress, presented by ... ... { M. Will. Murray.

These three Antimasques were well and naturally set out.

8. Entry.

Doctor Tartaglia and two pedants of Fran- { M. Rimes.
colin, presented by ... ... { M. Warder.
{ M. Villiers.

9. Entry.

Four Grotesques, or drollities, in the most fantastical shapes that could be devised.

10. Entry.

The invisible lady, magical sister of the Rosicross.

11. Entry.

A shepherd, presented by ... ... M. Charles Murray.

12. Entry.

A farmer and his wife, presented by ... M. Skipwith.

13. Entry.

A country gentleman, his wife, and his { M. Boroughs.
bailiff, presented by ... ... { M. Ashton.
{ M. Pert.

14. Entry.

An amorous courtier, richly apparelled, pre- } M. Seymour.
sented by ... ... }

15. Entry.

Two roaring boys, their suits answering their profession

16. Entry.

Four mad Lovers, and as madly clad.

17. Entry.

A jealous Dutchman, his wife and her Italian
lover, presented by ... ...
$\left\{\begin{array}{l}\text{M. Arpe.}\\ \text{M. Rimes.}\\ \text{M. Tartarean.}\end{array}\right.$

18. Entry.

Three Swiss, one a little Swiss, who played
the wag with them as they slept, presented by ... ...
$\left\{\begin{array}{l}\text{M. Cotterell.}\\ \text{M. Newton.}\\ \text{M. Jeffrey Hudson.[1]}\end{array}\right.$

19. Entry.

Four antique Cavaliers, imitating a manage[2]
and tilting, ...
$\left\{\begin{array}{l}\text{M. Arpe.}\\ \text{M. Jay.}\\ \text{M. Atkins.}\\ \text{M. Tartarean.}\end{array}\right.$

20. Entry.

A Cavaleritro[3] and two Pages.

All which Antimasques were well set out and excellently danced, and the tunes fitted to the persons.

The Antimasques being past, all the Scene was changed into craggy rocks and inaccessible mountains, in the upper parts where any earth could fasten, were some trees, but of strange forms, such as only grow in remote parts of the Alps, and in desolate places; the farthest of these was hollow in the midst, and seemed to be cut through by art, as the Pausilipo[4] near Naples, and so high as the top pierced the clouds, all which represented the difficult way which heroes are to pass ere they come to the throne of Honour.

The Chorus of the beloved people came forth, led by Concord and the good Genius of Great Britain, their habits being various and rich: they go up to the State and sing.

---

[1] Sir Geoffrey Hudson, the famous dwarf, introduced by Scott into *Peveril of the Peak.*

[2] Manège.   [3] Probably *cavallerizzo,* a riding-master.

[4] A mountain between Naples and Puteoli, famous for a subterranean passage nearly half a mile in length, and twenty-two feet in breadth.

II. SONG.

To the Queen Mother.[1]

1. When with instructed eyes we look upon
      Our blessings that descend so fast
   From the fair partner of our Monarch's throne,
      We grieve they are too great to last.

2. But when those growing comforts we survey,
      By whom our hopes are longer liv'd,
   Then gladly we our vows and praises pay
      To her, from whom they are derived.

3. And since, great Queen, she is derived from you,
      We here begin our offerings;
   For those, who sacrific'd to rivers, knew
      Their first rites due unto their springs.

4. The Stream, from whence our blessings flow, you bred;
      You, in whose bosom, even the chief, and best
   Of modern Victors[2] laid his weary head,
      When he rewarded victories with rest;
   Your beauty kept his valour's flame alive;
   Your Tuscan wisdom taught it how to thrive.

Inviting the King's Appearance in the Throne of Honour.
To be printed, not sung.

Why are our joys detain'd by this delay?
   Unless, as in a morning overcast,
We find it long ere we can find out day;
   So, whilst our hopes increase, our time doth waste.

Or are you slow 'cause th' way to Honour's throne,
   In which you travel now, is so uneven,

---

[1] Mary de Medicis, mother of Queen Henrietta Maria.
[2] Henry IV. of France.

Hilly, and craggy, or as much unknown,
    As that uncertain path which leads to Heaven?

O, that philosophers, who, through those mists
    Low nature casts, do upper knowledge spy,
Or those that smile at them (o'er-weening Priests)
    Could, with such sure, such an undoubted eye,

Reach distant Heaven, as you can Honour's throne!
    Then we should shift our flesh t' inhabit there,
Where we are taught, the Heroes [all] are gone;
    Though now content with earth, 'cause you are here.

    The song ended, they return up to the stage, and divide them-
selves on each side: then the further part of the scene disappear'd,
and the King's Majesty and the rest of the Masquers were discovered, sitting in the throne of Honour, his Majesty highest in a
seat of gold, and the rest of the Lords about him. This throne was
adorned with palm trees, between which stood statues of the ancient
heroes; in the under parts on each side lay captives bound in several
postures, lying on trophies of armours, shields, and antique weapons,
all his throne being fained of Goldsmiths' work. The habit of his
Majesty and the Masquers was of watchet, richly embroidered with
silver, long stockings set up of white; their caps silver with scrolls
of gold, and plumes of white feathers.

III. SONG.

To the King, when he appears with his Lords in the
Throne of Honour.

1. Those quar'ling winds, that deafned unto death
    The living, and did wake dead men before,
Seem now to pant small gusts, as out of breath,
    And fly to reconcile themselves on shore.

2. If it be kingly patience to outlast
    Those storms the people's giddy fury raise,
Till like fantastic winds themselves they waste,
    The wisdom of that patience is thy praise.

3. Murmur 's a sickness epidemical;
   'T is catching, and infects weak common ears;
   For through those crooked, narrow alleys, all
   Invaded are, and kill'd by whisperers.

4. This you discern'd, and by your mercy taught
   Would not, like monarchs that severe have bin,
   Invent imperial arts to question thought,
   Nor punish vulgar sickness as a sin.

5. Nor would your valour, when it might subdue,
   Be hinder'd of the pleasure to forgive;
   Th' are worse than overcome, your wisdom knew,
   That needed mercy to have leave to live.

6. Since strength of virtues gain'd you Honour's throne,
   Accept our wonder, and enjoy our praise!
   He 's fit to govern there, and rule alone,
   Whom inward helps, not outward force doth raise.

Whilst the Chorus sung this song, there came softly from the upper part of the heavens, a huge cloud of various colours, but pleasant to the sight, which descending to the midst of the scene open'd, and within it was a transparent brightness of thin exhalations, such as the gods are feigned to descend in: in the most eminent place of which her Majesty sate, representing the chief heroine, environed with her martial ladies; and from over her head were darted lightsome rays that illuminated her seat, and all the ladies about her participated more or less of that light, as they sate near or further off: this brightness with many streaks of thin vapours about it, such as are seen in a fair evening sky, softly descended: and as it came near to the earth, the seat of Honour by little and little vanished, as if it gave way to these heavenly Graces. The Queen's Majesty and her ladies were in Amazonian habits of carnation, embroidered with silver, with plumed helms, baudrickes[1] with antique swords hanging by their sides, all as rich as might be, but the strangeness of the habits was most admired.

---

[1] Baldrics.

IV. SONG.

When the Queen and her Ladies descended.

1. You that so wisely studious are
To measure, and to trace each star,
How swift they travel, and how far;
   Now number your celestial store,
Planets, or lesser lights, and try,
If in the face of all the sky
   You count so many as before.

2. If you would practise how to know
The chief for influence, or show;
Level your perspectives[1] below!
   For in this nether orb they move.
Each here, when lost in 's doubtful art,
May by his eyes advance his heart,
   And through his optic learn to love.

3. But what is she that rules the night,
That kindles ladies with their light,
And gives to them the power of sight?
   All those who can her virtue doubt,
Her mind will in her face advise,
For through the casements of her eyes
   Her soul is ever looking out.

4. And with its beams she doth survey
Our growth in virtue, or decay;
Still lighting us in honour's way.
   All that are good she did inspire:
Lovers are chaste, because they know
It is her will they should be so;
   The valiant take from her their fire.

[1] Telescopes.

When this heavenly seat touched the earth, the King's Majesty took out the Queen, and the lords the ladies, and came down into the room, and danc't their entry, betwixt which and the second dance was this song.

V. SONG.

After the First Dance.

1. Why stand you still, and at these beauties gaze
     As if you were afraid,
     Or they were made
   Much more for wonder than delight?
   Sure those whom first their virtue did amaze,
     Their feature must at last invite.

2. Time never knew the mischiefs of his haste;
     Nor can you force him stay
     To keep off day:
   Make then fit use of triumphs here;
   It were a crime 'gainst pleasant youth, to waste
     This night in overcivil fear.

3. Move then like Time, for Love, as well as he,
     Hath got a kalender,
     Where must appear,
   How evenly you these measures tread;
   And, when they end, we far more griev'd shall be,
     Than for his hours when they are fled.

The second dance ended, and their Majesties being seated under the State, the scene was changed into magnificent buildings composed of several selected pieces of architecture: in the furthest part was a bridge over a river, where many people, coaches, horses, and such like were seen to pass to and fro: beyond this, on the shore were buildings in prospective, which shooting far from the eye showed as the suburbs of a great city.

From the highest part of the heavens came forth a cloud far in the scene, in which were eight persons richly attired representing the spheres; this, joining with two other clouds which appear'd at

that instant full of music, covered all the upper part of the scene,
and, at that instant beyond all these, a heaven opened full of deities,
which celestial prospect with the Chorus below filled all the whole
scene with apparitions and harmony.

VI. SONG.

To the King and Queen, by a Chorus of all.

So musical as to all ears
Doth seem the music of the spheres,
Are you unto each other still;
Tuning your thoughts to either's will.

All that are harsh, all that are rude,
Are by your harmony subdu'd;
Yet so into obedience wrought,
As if not forc'd to it, but taught.

Live still, the pleasure of our sight!
Both our examples and delight,
So long until you find the good success
Of all your virtues, in one happiness.

Till we so kind, so wise, and careful be,
In the behalf of our posterity,
That we may wish your sceptres' ruling here,
Lov'd even by those who should your justice fear,
When we are gone, when to our last remove
We are dispatch'd to sing your praise above.

After this song the spheres passed through the air, and all the
deities ascended, and so concluded this Masque: which was gener·
ally approved of, especially by all strangers that were present, to
be the noblest and most ingenious that hath been done here in that
kind.

The invention, ornament, scenes, and apparitions, with their descriptions, were made by INIGO JONES, Surveyor General of his
Majesty's works.

What was spoken or sung, by WILLIAM D'AVENANT, her Majesty's servant.

The subject was set down by them both.

The music was composed by LEWIS RICHARD, Master of her Majesty's Music.

FINIS.

THE NAMES OF THE MASQUERS.

THE KING'S MAJESTY.	THE QUEEN'S MAJESTY.
DUKE OF LENOX.	DUCHESS OF LENOX.
EARL OF CARLILE.	COUNTESS OF CARNARVON.
EARL OF NEWPORT.	COUNTESS OF NEWPORT.
EARL OF LANERICKE[1].	COUNTESS OF PORTLAND.
LORD RUSSELL.	LADY ANDOVER.
LORD HERBERT.	LADY MARGARET HOWARD.
LORD PAGET.	LADY KELLYMEKIN[2].
LORD FIELDING.	LADY FRANCES HOWARD.
MASTER RUSSELL.	MISTRESS CARY.
MASTER THOMAS HOWARD.	MISTRESS NEVILL.

[1] Lanark.

[2] Kynalmeaky.